STORYTELLING IN BUSINESS

The Authentic and Fluent Organization

Janis Forman

STANFORD BUSINESS BOOKS
An Imprint of Stanford University Press
Stanford, California

04/03/14
LN
$29.95

Stanford University Press
Stanford, California

Special discounts for bulk quantities of Stanford Business Books are available to corporations, professional associations, and other organizations. For details and discount information, contact the special sales department of Stanford University Press. Tel: (650) 736-1782, Fax: (650) 736-1784.

Printed in the United States of America on acid-free, archival-quality paper

Library of Congress Cataloging-in-Publication Data
Forman, Janis, author.
  Storytelling in business : the authentic and fluent organization / Janis Forman.
    pages cm
  Includes bibliographical references and index.
  ISBN 978-0-8047-6871-9 (alk. paper)
  1. Communication in management—Case studies. 2. Business communication—Case studies. I. Title.
  HD30.3.F667 2013
  658.4′5—dc23
                                    2012035315

Typeset by Classic Typography in 10.5/15 Sabon MT Pro

*For Bob Foster and Elwin Svenson—global leaders in
management education and cherished colleagues*

CONTENTS

M Y INTEREST IN STORYTELLING stretches back into the last century to my early childhood when my maternal grandmother, Nana Betty, would tell me stories to coax me to eat. Spoon in hand poised in front of my face, she would tell me about the exploits of a giraffe, her lead protagonist (with an uncanny resemblance to me), who would eagerly stretch its neck up to the top of a tree for a tender morsel at certain moments in the plot, which she would emphasize by pausing; that moment in the story coincided with the moment she would put a spoonful of applesauce into my mouth, transforming me from a finicky eater to an avid listener and participant in the story as I began to catch on to the story's pattern and my role in it. When I was a little older, five or six, she would walk me and my sister, Michele, through the streets of her neighborhood in Manhattan Beach (New York), introducing us as members of "Meet the Press," which she would then point out as the longest-running show on TV (as it still is), and prompting us to tell a story about ourselves to her neighbors sitting on their front stoops, who were apparently eager to hear our latest autobiographical installments.

From the perspective of many decades later, it's clear that this child's play of story listening and story telling was serious business that generated far more than my grandmother could have imagined. After all, we make sense of who we are through the stories we tell about ourselves—and then, in one way or another, live. Over the years, I have told and retold versions of the "Nana" story in multiple forums, both personal and professional. I have also continued my family's storytelling tradition, first by telling my son, Benjamin, when he was a two-year-old, tales of the hardworking garbageman, who, like Benjamin, finished his day with a bubble bath and a bottle, to help my son manage his fear of the loud and unexpected whine of the garbageman's truck, and then by inviting him to lead a family storytelling hour in which he had the authority to set rules about what book should be discussed, by whom, and for how long. Storytelling is an inheritance he has enjoyed from the great-grandmother for whom he was named but whom he never met.

In the many years I've taught organizational storytelling, I continue to recommend that, if nothing else, the professionals I'm working with should read and tell stories to their children or to the children in their lives, even create a "storytelling hour," led by the children, who should be encouraged to tell their own tales, critique the adults', and exchange thoughts about books they're reading. Scholars of literacy recognize the importance of telling stories to children and listening to theirs. This is how storytellers are nurtured.

Early in my career I had a special interest in stories. Though I've spent most of my career teaching business students and consulting with professionals in the workplace, I hold a doctorate in comparative literature, have written a dissertation on autobiographical narrative, and have taught a graduate course in literature on a topic that weaves together students' life stories and those of published writers such as Jean-Jacques Rousseau, Lillian Hellman, Maya Angelou, and Mary McCarthy. I am also a lifelong reader of fiction and history.

Much of my work in organizational storytelling has taken place in the strategic studies programs offered at UCLA Anderson School of Management, where I am the director of the management communication program and advise teams of MBA students (some of whom already hold senior management positions) on strategy projects that require storytelling. In my work with these MBAs, we have tackled projects for organizations that range from high-tech entrepreneurial firms, in our award-winning

Global Access Program, to large multinational corporations like Coca-Cola, Disney, Fox, Hewlett-Packard, Johnson & Johnson, Microsoft, Navistar, Nestlé, Northrop Grumman, Oracle, Sony, and Sun Microsystems. The art of storytelling helps leaders—and aspiring leaders—put together compelling and memorable cases for their recommendations, embedding significant details and data into their stories to substantiate the future they envision for an organization.

This book has been the most social writing adventure of my career. Writing a book can be a very solitary act, but this one is about dialogues, especially with corporate communication professionals, who are often the chief organizational experts in storytelling (though no one holds that title), but also with filmmakers, CEOs of small companies, academic experts in management and communication, MBA students at UCLA Anderson School of Management, and corporate communication students from the University of Lugano's "MSCom" Executive Master of Science in Communications Management program who study strategic management at UCLA Anderson each summer. The Acknowledgments section at the end of the book lists all those whom I've interviewed for the book.

My thanks to all the people involved in the making of the book. At UCLA Anderson, I am very grateful to Professor Alfred E. Osborne Jr., senior associate dean, and to Elaine Hagan, executive director of the Harold and Pauline Price Center for Entrepreneurial Studies, for research and travel support; to head librarian of the UCLA Anderson Rosenfeld Library, Rita Costello, and her assistant Jeannette Boca Monterez for tracking down secondary source material and addressing my research questions; and to John Morris, faculty advisor in the Anderson Global Access Program, Jill Hisey of the Office of Alumni Relations, and Nelson Gayton, executive director of the Center for Management of the Enterprise in Media, Entertainment, and Sports, for putting me in touch with experts in organizational storytelling. I remember and value the many conversations I've had with Nelson exchanging personal stories and reflecting on their impact on our lives and our work.

I am also especially grateful to the senior corporate communication professionals who accepted my request to conduct on-site research at their organizations: Ken Banta of Schering-Plough, Bill Margaritis of FedEx,

Dave Samson of Chevron, Marike Westra of Philips, and Perry Yeatman of Kraft.

Thanks as well to the Arthur W. Page Society for providing a network of corporate communication professionals, which was invaluable to my research. Colleagues who are members of the Management Communication Association, a small group of faculty who lead communication programs at major business schools, also provided me with a much needed forum for discussing parts of the book—at the very beginning stages in the mid-1990s at Dartmouth's Tuck School of Business and more recently at Stanford's Graduate School of Business.

I have been blessed with highly intelligent reviewers who were generous with their time and commented extensively on the manuscript. They include Daphne Jameson (Cornell University), Marty Nord (Vanderbilt University), Kathy Rentz (University of Cincinnati), Barbara Shwom (Northwestern University), and my former colleague and coauthor Jone Rymer. Their questions and comments pushed me to delve more deeply into the topic. Of course, any errors are my responsibility.

When I began putting together a proposal for the book, my colleague Eric Flamholtz introduced me to Margo Beth Fleming, acquisitions editor for organizational studies and economics at Stanford University Press, and told me he thought she'd be an ideal editor for a book that brings together the literary and the managerial. He was so right. Margo's belief in the project and suggestions at every stage have made the book possible.

I am grateful as well to my husband, Don Brabston, for his support (emotional and technical) and patience during those many times when this book took over our home offices and our lives, and to our son, Benjamin Brabston, a young management consultant who continues to challenge and enrich my thinking. Two mathematically gifted men, they understand, in Benjamin's words, "You can't throw around a bunch of numbers and think you'll be convincing." Don suggested that I say at least a word about our two sable-brown Burmese cats, Google and Yahoo: though they do not tell stories, they are the subject of many and a reminder that work should be balanced by at least a little time stretched out in the sun.

Over the last dozen years or so, I have had the great pleasure and honor of working with Bob Foster and Elwin Svenson, the leadership team for

UCLA Anderson's Global Access Program (GAP), our highly ranked entrepreneurial and strategic studies program, and of participating in this inspired educational program since its inception. GAP is the major educational forum in which I have taught MBAs how to put together and deliver memorable cases for their strategic recommendations to outside client organizations—stories that require students to bring together critical thinking and communication capabilities and to embed significant data and analysis in their stories to substantiate the future they envision for their clients. In GAP, I have also been able to revise and sharpen my thinking about data-based organizational storytelling and apply all of this to the continued growth of our students and the companies we are assisting. None of this would have been possible without the standards of excellence and the spirit of openness to new ideas and practical application that Bob and Sven have created. As just one indication of their global impact on education and business, both of them have been awarded a knighthood by the Finnish government for their extraordinary service to business development and US-Finnish relations. This book is dedicated to them.

Manhattan Beach (California)

January 2013

STORYTELLING
IN BUSINESS

I   WHY EXPLORE STORYTELLING IN BUSINESS?

"Meet the Press" and tell them your story.

—NANA BETTY

STORYTELLING CAN BE a personal inheritance, a lifelong and life-sustaining habit of mind, as well as an organizational inheritance, a management tool that helps businesses develop and even thrive. When my maternal grandmother, Nana Betty, encouraged my sister and me as children to tell stories about ourselves to her neighbors—"the press"—whom we encountered on our walks to the beach, she was building our self-confidence in talking to strangers and in finding our place in her small Manhattan Beach (New York) community. Similarly, organizations, like those featured in this book, can encourage storytelling for good purposes, such as making sense of their strategy, communicating it, and developing or strengthening culture and brand. These uses of storytelling generate positive consequences that can have a sustained and significant impact on an organization.

This book is written for business professionals who want to know more about the power of storytelling, how it has functioned successfully in companies, and how, in practical terms, it can help achieve an organization's and a professional's goals.

THE VITALITY OF STORIES

As the "Nana Betty" story illustrates, storytelling may have powerful roots in childhood. Novelist and screenplay writer Larry McMurtry reflects:

> If, for example, you dare to interrupt a five-year-old's thirty-ninth viewing of "The Lion King" in order to find out a basketball score, they will, once they regain control of the remote, immediately rewind the film to the point of interruption, so as not to miss the smallest element of the story. Watching the avidity with which the very young absorb stories . . . leaves one no grounds for pessimism about the survival of narrative itself. The human appetite for it is too strong.[1]

This child's play of "story watching" is closely akin to the serious play of story creation by novelists and nonfiction writers like McMurtry, and filmmakers like the Disney studio, producer of *The Lion King.*

Professional storytellers like McMurtry express our intuitive understanding that people are hardwired for stories. The familiar beginning and ending of fairy tales—"Once upon a time . . . and they lived happily ever after"—act as verbal bookends, marking a child's grasp of how things work (or ought to work), a predictability that can produce emotional reassurance and pleasure with repeated telling of the same story or with repetition of the familiar elements of story applied to a new topic. As the performance of a gifted storyteller, these tales not only compel a child's rapt attention and adamant demand to "play it again" but also create an intimate link between the listener and the teller of the tale, often a trusted parent or teacher. From early childhood on, the best stories, replete with memorable details, make sense of apparently disconnected facts and experiences, arranging them in a sequence that feels inevitable, and take us on a journey led by the teller of the tale, who, having earned our confidence, orchestrates it all.

The livelihood of writers and the fortunes of filmmakers depend on their ability to craft stories, rich in plot and detail, that touch audiences emotionally, from young children to the elders of a society. McMurtry grew up in rural west Texas among storytellers. In *Walter Benjamin at the Dairy Queen*, he reflects on the art of storytelling, weaving into his autobiography an essay on this art by the early–twentieth-century European intellectual Walter Benjamin. McMurtry reminisces about the roots of his writing life in a small town where old men would sit around at the corner store and while away the time by whittling. As they carved wood into rough shapes, an activity that kept their hands busy and their ears alert, they would take turns telling and listening to each other's stories. "Whittling cowboys," McMurtry reflects, are "perfect receptacles for stories."[2] McMurtry's west Texas town was a close-knit community of shared stories, values, and "tribal" memory.[3]

Even though this context for stories has vanished, McMurtry argues, stories have vitality and a sustaining presence: "Watching the avidity with which the young absorb stories . . . leaves one no grounds for pessimism about the survival of narrative itself."[4] And even though we are far removed from the leisurely pace and idyllic setting for the stories he portrays, most of us are nonetheless drawn to them despite—or perhaps because of— the pressured busyness of our organizational and private lives and by our hunger for emotional engagement in our work. As I will argue, it is now time for business to turn to narrative with greater confidence and respect for its capabilities.

WHY TURN TO STORYTELLING IN BUSINESS NOW?

Organizational life is highly pressured. We multitask, we text-message, we surf the Web, we tweet, and we check Facebook in settings, virtual or real, that are galaxies removed from the pastoral idyll of McMurtry's whittling old men: "The decline of whittling," McMurtry explains in an elegiac passage of his autobiography, "has clearly deprived storytellers of many willing listeners—most of the old men who filled the spittle and whittle benches outside the rural courthouses of my youth regaled them-selves as they whittled with story after story."[5]

Unlike McMurtry's rural storytellers, the businesspeople we want to influence are busy, harried, quick to calculate the dollar value of their time, bombarded by multiple messages from a dizzying number of com-munication channels, and likely to respond in haste and in kind to what comes their way. Moreover, as the Millennials who were raised with social network technology increasingly populate the ranks of manage-ment, much of business communication takes the form of instantaneous sound bites. Jim Reilly, former general manager of marketing plans and communications at IBM, acknowledges and laments this shift: "People want to knock things down to a bumper sticker. Everything is shorthand thinking. People need stimulation every twenty minutes. Today, instead of the Emancipation Proclamation, Lincoln would have to say 'Read my lips. No slaves.'"[6] Yet, despite, or because of, all this, a well-chosen, well-crafted story can get through to people.

How do stories reach beyond the pressure and noise to influence people in a sustained and powerful way? According to business communication expert Mary Lang of Comadrona Communications, stories succeed in getting through to people because "humans crave narrative and the use of story builds a narrative for topics that goes deeper and lives longer in a person's psyche than most any other form of communication."[7] (The work of novelists and child psychologists supports her point as well.)

Reflecting on his daily routine as a busy executive, Bob Feldman, former senior corporate communication director at DreamWorks Animation and now principal of the strategic communications firm PulsePoint Group, explains the impact of stories in this way:

When I think about my day . . . I get up, watch the *Today Show*, read the *New York Times*, the *Wall Street Journal*, go to work, listen to the radio, turn on CNN.com. During the day I am hit with thousands of messages. Am I going to take away three or four messages from a CEO about a company? It's a fallacy to think companies have an opportunity to deliver several messages. If they're lucky, I'll have one impression. *So what's that single story a company has to tell that is relevant and memorable?* Take the message and put it into a story for singularity, relevance, and memorability.[8]

Amid the rush and intensity of data from multiple quarters, Feldman suggests (and some economists and historians also agree) that stories have sense-making capability. In the hands of a skilled storyteller who selects from bits of information to create a coherent, succinct message, a story can make a company's case compelling and memorable, especially when those on the receiving end are likely to suffer from what educator and essayist Sven Birkerts calls "attention deficit disorder." This is, according to Birkerts, a contemporary malaise ushered in by the decline in reading

and reflection and characterized by a loss of focus or a "grazing mental-
ity" that is the antithesis of thoughtful assessment.[9]

Having the ability to make sense of things and to influence, stories are
an inevitable expression and tool of leadership. "Stories are unavoidable
if you're going to be a leader," advises Irv Miller, group VP of corporate
communications at Toyota Motor Sales. "Every leader needs a vision,
whether you're a leader of a trash brigade or a big company. You need to
communicate where you're going. A person who's a good communicator
has a grasp of storytelling. If you can't translate your passion, you're hard-
pressed to be a good leader. No one followed a committee into battle."[10]
Some leaders have an easy grasp of storytelling. Betsy McLaughlin, CEO
of Hot Topic, remarks on the capacity of stories in business to reach a diverse audience: "If I have a problem to solve, a big idea to get across, and
I have to reach three people in the room with different backgrounds, I tell
a story. Two weeks later I hear people retell the story."[11]

In the highly contested arena known as organizational life, stories can
help leaders—and aspiring leaders—to emerge from the conflict with a
team of supporters. "Communication is a contact sport," asserts communication consultant Tom Pyden. "You have to do it, look forward to doing
it, and do it as often as you can. Employees then run through walls for
you."[12] At a minimum, stories can be a survival tool for leaders. As Rob
Lively, vice president of corporate government affairs at Schering-Plough,
concludes, "Stories are the pivot point of falling on your face or making
the game-winning shot. Take it seriously. The question is, Are you food
or are you the head of the team?"[13]

More and more, stories are important because people want interaction
and engagement rather than being "broadcast" or lectured to. Especially
with the growing presence of social network technology, employees and
external stakeholders (for example, investors, customers, clients) want to
be heard—and at times have their stories told in their own voices: how I
experienced driving my new BMW; what it's like to work on a Chevron
oil drill platform in the Pacific; the meaning of the Johnson & Johnson
Credo and its emphasis on serving mothers and children as it comes into
play in my work as a salesperson, a researcher, or a senior manager.

In this new environment, businesses themselves need compelling and memorable stories at the enterprise level because people's trust in business is quite low. Bill Margaritis, corporate vice president of global communications and investor relations at FedEx, explains:

In today's world, people are more willing to trust other people than they are large institutions. Authentic stories, well told, remind stakeholders that good companies are the ones that value, celebrate, and empower their people. You've got to deconstruct the cold corporate edifice and focus on the individual building blocks—the people whose stories exemplify a company's culture and values. That's how you gain trust in this increasingly cynical world.[14]

In a business environment where distractions and lack of trust dominate, stories can cut through the busyness to capture attention, engage and influence people, create meaning, exemplify values, and gain trust.

SUPPORT FOR STORYTELLING: A RALLY CRY FROM MULTIPLE QUARTERS

Professionals from a variety of disciplines have long recognized and voiced the importance of storytelling to their field. These include cognitive psychologists, neurologists, physicians, lawyers, city planners, economists, historians, literary critics, filmmakers, and, yes, professional storytellers; each group employs its unique perspectives in working with stories. Locating stories for business on this broader canvas sometimes yields unexpected insights into how stories for nonbusiness purposes are thought of, crafted, and used—and what may be the potential of storytelling for business.

Research by cognitive psychologists and neurologists confirms our intuition about the power of stories; scientific data substantiate the fundamental connection between being human and telling stories.[15] Tracking the cognitive maturity of children from age two to seventeen, child development specialist Arthur Applebee shows how their growth is characterized by the increasingly more sophisticated stories they can understand and tell. The toddler responds to a simple tale, while the older child delights in creating and appreciating more complex stories characterized by multiple voices, characters, dialogue, and plot complications. Exploring a similar set of research questions, psychologist Jerome Bruner reflects on the language development of a precocious child, Emmy, who would express her half-thoughts in emerging stories she'd concoct to make sense of her world to herself as she prepared for bed: "The soliloquies were not just about the routines of the day; she seemed drawn to the unexpected, to things that had surprised her or caught her unprepared. . . . So intent was she on getting her stories right that we came to believe her progress in acquiring language was driven by some sort of narrative energy."[16] In the related field of neurology, researchers using magnetic resonance imaging (MRI) to do brain scans have located our storytelling comprehension in the prefrontal cortex of the brain where our working memory and, in turn, our ability to identify sequence and represent stories are lodged.[17] James McGaugh, research professor in the Center for Neurobiology of Learning and Memory at the University of California at Irvine, who is an expert in brain functioning and memory, has been using MRIs and interview protocols to investigate individuals who have extraordinary powers of memory: "You can ask them what happened in their own lives or what was of significant public interest on a particular date—even years ago—and they'll remember the details, often telling them in a narrative. (We are finding that the organization of their brains is a little different, some regions smaller or larger, than the brains of others.) All of us make sense of our experiences through stories."[18]

Some physician-educators also recognize the benefits of storytelling to the humanistic practice of medicine. Psychiatrist and educator Robert Coles has used "doctor stories," fiction written by famous authors who trained as physicians, for instance, Anton Chekhov and William Carlos Williams, to teach students at Harvard Medical School to go beyond clinical diagnoses by listening fully to patients' stories as a way to connect emotionally with them and to interpret their life circumstances as they struggle with illness. Reflecting on the value ascribed to storytelling by his mentor in psychiatry, Coles notes: "He urged me to be a good listener in the special way a story requires: note the manner of presentation; the development of plot, character; the addition of new dramatic sequences; the emphasis accorded to one figure or another in the recital; and the degree of enthusiasm, of coherence, the narrator gives to his or her account."[19]

Closely akin to the work of Bruner and Coles, graduate programs in the relatively new field known as "narrative medicine" help healthcare practitioners develop their storytelling capabilities. As the program at Columbia University describes, the premise for the study of narrative medicine is that "the care of the sick unfolds in stories. The effective practice of healthcare requires the ability to recognize, absorb, interpret, and act on the stories and plights of others. Medicine practiced with narrative competence is a model for humane and effective medical practice."[20] Rita Charon, a pioneer in the field and both a physician and educator, offers this poignant representative anecdote from her work that captures, in this first interview with a patient, the promise of narrative medicine[21]:

As his new internist, I tell him, I have to learn as much as I can about his health. "Could you tell me whatever you think I should know about your situation?" I ask him. And then I do my best to not say a word, to not write in his medical chart, but to absorb all that the patient emits about himself—about his life, his body, his fears, and his hopes. I listen not only for the content of his narrative but for its form—its temporal course, its images, its associated subplots, its silences, where he chooses to begin in telling of himself, how he sequences symptoms with other life events. After a few minutes, the patient stops talking and begins to weep. I ask him why he cries. He says, "No one has ever let me do this before."[22]

Storytelling can be a catharsis for the patient, and story listening on the part of a physician can open up productive communication with the patient.

In medicine, stories can build a doctor's diagnostic capabilities and responsiveness to patients; in law, stories can help all the players—prosecutors, defense attorneys, litigants, and judges—make arguments. Here the persuasive power of storytelling comes to the fore. Law professor Paul Gewirtz explains: "Both scholars and the public have increasingly been drawn to law as an arena where vivid human stories are played out."[23] These stories, fundamentally persuasive in intent, either reinforce or work against each other in the competitive space of the law court. A defense attorney may craft a story about a pharmaceutical company's honest and thorough efforts to test and retest a drug before release; the prosecutor counters with a story that argues for the company's negligence and abuse.

The "trial process" becomes, then, "a struggle over narrative" in which different versions of the story compete.[24]

Like scholars of narrative and law, those in city planning focus on the persuasive powers of storytelling; for instance, James A. Throgmorton in *Planning as Persuasive Storytelling: The Rhetorical Construction of Chicago's Electric Future*. From his perspective, planners engaged in forecasts and analyses of a city's growth proffer competing stories about the urban future. Readers of these stories, who include the full array of stakeholders (including civic planning commissions, community groups, NGOs, potential partners, and competitors), revise, reject, advance, or embellish these stories to fit their own goals and may pitch their own "counterstories" for the future.

Even the profession of economics, known for its focus on numbers and theory, has found room for stories. Economist D. N. McCloskey argues for seeing economic interpretation in terms of the stories that economists choose to tell and those they leave on the cutting-room floor: "the economist, like a novelist, uses and abuses stories. Once upon a time we were poor, then capitalism flourished, and now as a result we are rich. Some would tell another, anticapitalist story; but any economist tells stories."[25] Economists, she claims, take pleasure in both the "unforeseen consequences" and "trick endings"[26] of stories and need, as a consequence of the ethical dimension of their profession, to discriminate carefully between dishonest "snake-oil" stories and those grounded in data, analysis, and sound theory.[27]

In addition to an interpretive function, stories in economics can shape decisions, as researcher Graham Smart explains in his study of monetary policy at the Bank of Canada (the equivalent to the US Federal Reserve Board). There economists craft sometimes competing macroeconomic stories or "mini" stories about different sectors of the economy, while interpreting patterns in massive amounts of data, and move toward a single overarching narrative, a monetary policy story that is used to make decisions (for instance, about interest or exchange rates) and to explain and defend them to the Canadian public.

Of course, the professionals who place storytelling at the heart of their work are historians, literary critics, filmmakers, and professional storytellers. Historians Richard Marius and Melvin Page underscore the fundamental link between story and history:

Historians try to solve puzzles in the evidence and to tell a story that will give order to the confusion of data we inherit from the past. Historians make connections, assign causes, trace effects, make comparisons, uncover patterns, locate dead ends, and find influences . . . they apply their minds to the sources and their considered judgments to the evidence, writing those stories about the past they intend to be both credible and true.[28, 29]

Those who study how and why history is written consider the purposes for which historians write (for example, to celebrate or critique a nation's past, to provide lessons for the present, to create a reliable and accurate account of events), the scope of histories (for example, everyday life, politics, culture, global history), and the tone of the work (for example, didactic, analytical, impassioned, or some combination of these), all of which are fundamental elements of history as narrative.

Since the 1960s, literary critics have given increasing attention to the theoretical study of narrative, spawning an entire field of research called "narratology." Some of this work provides interesting insights about storytelling in business, in particular about the active engagement of audiences in recreating, and even constructing, stories in their own imaginations as they read or listen to them; on the storyteller and the points of view from which the story is told; and on the choice and sequencing of events in a story drawn from a wealth of possible material. When relevant, narrative theory will find its way into this book, but rest assured that the rather substantial jargon of narrative theory will be kept to a minimum.[30]

Understanding narrative is central to the work of historians and literary critics, but it is the work of filmmakers and their reflections on storytelling that is most familiar and influential today. Interviews with these professionals and published accounts of their work offer valuable insights about many aspects of storytelling: building interest and suspense; working with characters, dialogue, details, and plot; finding the sources and inspiration for stories; and assessing audiences for their films. Indeed, some experts in the field, like screenwriting coach Robert McKee and entertainment executive Peter Guber (who produced such movies as *Batman*, *The Color*

Purple, and *Rain Man*), have drawn explicit links between their work in film and storytelling in business.[31]

And finally, since the late 1970s, a storytelling movement focused on the oral performance of narrative has been active in the United States, sponsored by the National Association for the Preservation and Perpetuation of Storytelling. This organization holds conventions featuring storyteller performers and provides training in the art to children and adults. As the movement has matured, it has increased its efforts to build public awareness of and support for storytelling.

This quick journey across a range of professions and disciplines outside of business reveals a wealth of benefits that stories offer, from making sense of experience to reaching audiences emotionally to wielding explanatory and persuasive powers. Before reading further, you may want to consider whether these benefits are true for business stories as well.

STORYTELLING IN BUSINESS EDUCATION: A RESTRICTED PRESENCE

Though typically finding lukewarm reception in business schools, storytelling has gained a foothold in many of their communication programs. At the Sloan School (MIT), MBA students explore their ethical positions by means of an exercise called "A Tale of Two Stories," which is part of a new curriculum, "Giving Voice to Values." Students share and examine stories about moments when their values conflicted with what they felt pressured to do in the workplace; for instance, circumstances in which they may have been told to inflate billable hours, exaggerate the capabilities of a product, or misrepresent budget information.[32]

At the University of Virginia's Darden School, the required communication course includes a module on narrative that asks students to tell and analyze stories from several angles: about a business, their own or one from a foreign country; about a communication challenge in the workplace; about an example of leadership, their own or someone else's. As James Rubin, the director of the communication program, explains: "The interesting thing tends to be how much of themselves they [the students] reveal and how willing they are to take some emotional risks to connect with the audience, in either a company or a personal narrative."[33] This module sets the stage for discussion of the "narrative logic" in management presentations—beginnings, middles, and ends—and of organizations as storytelling enterprises.[34]

Additional uses for storytelling abound in these courses. At NYU's Stern School of Business, students in a communication elective tell stories about what has most shaped them as businesspeople.[35] At the Mendoza College of Business at the University of Notre Dame, students share stories about an organization in which they've worked, its values and culture.[36] In a public-speaking course at the McDonough School of Business at Georgetown University, they tell, revise, and retell stories to hone their abilities as presenters.[37] Stanford's Graduate School of Business brings in leaders from both the business and entertainment worlds to talk to students about their uses of storytelling and their approaches to it.[38] At the Tuck School (Dartmouth), students in a communication course that uses business cases extensively follow up discussion of the written cases—stories about organizations facing significant challenges—by checking online for updated sequels to the case stories.[39]

Communication courses at several business schools include analysis of speeches by public figures known to be gifted storytellers, people like Steve Jobs of Apple, Jerry Adamic at MCI, Herb Kelleher of Southwest Airlines, General George Patton in his speech to soldiers on the eve of the Normandy invasion, Prime Minister Winston Churchill in his many addresses to the British people during World War II, President Ronald Reagan in his First Inaugural Address, and Jesse Jackson in his campaign address to supporters for his presidential bid in the mid-1980s.

Storytelling also has a place in a few management courses on creativity and on strategy. Wharton offers a course to MBAs on how to develop one's creativity and how to recruit, manage, and develop a creative workforce. For this course, students are invited to use narrative to make sense of "rules" for imaginative thinking or to write an op-ed article on creativity; professionals known for innovation in a variety of fields (for example, medicine, microbiology, computer science, art, and industrial design) are invited to the class to tell their stories about their breakthrough discoveries.[40]

At UCLA Anderson School of Management where I teach, storytelling features prominently in a communication elective and in the capstone

strategy projects in which students think about the business plans and presentations they are crafting for organizations as data-based stories about
an organization's future strategic reality. In the elective course, students
tell a "signature" story, one that defines them as a person, a professional,
and an aspiring leader, and consider the situations in which they'd use the
story (for instance, in a job interview; on Facebook; in presenting to a client, a customer, or, later in their career, to the media).

In the UCLA Anderson Executive Education Programs, participants
who include leaders from around the globe—anyone from a government
official posted in the Guangzhou province of China to a high-tech entrepreneur from New Zealand to the dean of a medical school in California—
are asked to discuss a host of questions about organizational storytelling
to build awareness of this powerful communication tool:

- What story (or stories) will move your organizational initiative
  forward?

- Who are the best storytellers in your organization? What about in
  public life? What makes them effective?

- What stories influence people in your organization? Why do you
  think so? Which ones resonate with outside stakeholders as well?

- Are there stories from the broader culture—your country or
  your region—that capture the attention of members of your
  organization? Do these stories travel well across cultures?

- What are the elements of a powerful story?

Before reading further, you may want to take a moment to respond to
these questions as they apply to your work life.

THE BIAS AGAINST STORYTELLING IN
BUSINESS AND IN BUSINESS EDUCATION

Though storytelling has made inroads in the workplace—and much of
this book covers this territory—it appears to be less valued in business
than in other professions, an unfortunate circumstance attributable to a
number of factors that characterize business education and business life.
First of all, stories seem upon initial inspection to be at odds with data

and theory, both of which dominate business education and are essential to sound decision making.

Second, of those who pursue university degrees in business, very few have devoted time and attention to the humanities, the home base for storytelling, as education has become increasingly specialized. (Humanities majors who pursue advanced degrees in business today are few to be found.) Once business students enter the workforce, they apply, often unknowingly, this antistory bias, with its overreliance on charts, graphs, tables, and PowerPoint presentations crammed with bullet points, which list ideas or information but neglect to find and express the connections among them in story form.

The often unarticulated assumption in the workplace then is that serious business is all about numbers and models, that stories are child's play and as such a stigmatized type of discourse best left behind in adult life or relegated to one's time off from work. As Jim Finn, chief marketing officer at Groovy Corporation, observes: "Businesspeople tend not to appreciate the value of relating a story. They think business is operational only."[41] Yet many senior advisors and CEOs would argue the contrary (as we'll see).

As further evidence of the diminished role of storytelling, note too that even in higher education, storytelling and more generally the humanities have a minor role in the curriculum. This was not always the case. Flash back to the nineteenth century and we find that university students were required to take several years of coursework in the humanities: to engage frequently in analysis of famous speeches and literature, write themes on these subjects, and participate in public oratorical performance like debate, oral reading of prose and poetry, translations, and speeches. These studies were often at the heart of the curriculum. And despite a lack of consensus among educators of the early twentieth century about the function of a humanities curriculum, university students at that time took courses where they focused on writing stories and descriptions, analyzing literary texts, or writing in preparation for being engaged citizens capable of participating in and assessing issues of serious consequence to a democracy.[42]

As earlier examples of storytelling in fields outside of business have shown and as I will argue, neglecting stories and, more generally, the humanities may come at serious cost to business professionals and the organizations they lead. David A.Samson, general manager of public affairs at Chevron, warns that "MBAs can read income statements and balance sheets, and they can use marketing disciplinary concepts, but they get caught up in jargon. They need to know how to explain complex issues in laymen's language. To advance their careers, they need to know how to communicate to people in language people can understand and in stories."[43]

The research and analysis for this book show that the case for stories in business is strong, though it has been relatively muted; by contrast, the case for story in other fields—its emotional, explanatory, and persuasive powers—is strong and more and more assured. Along with the growing uses of storytelling in business, the relative strength of the case for stories *outside* of business should encourage a stronger presence for stories within business.

RESEARCH FOR THE BOOK

My research on storytelling in business required a multipronged approach. As I've described, one approach was to work comparatively, looking at how stories operate in other fields. I also turned to disciplines (for example, literature, rhetoric, management) for theory and examples applicable to the subject.

Perhaps most important, over the course of four years I sought the insights of expert practitioners in organizational storytelling—an established research approach for studies of different types of business discourse—by using a number of questions about storytelling to stimulate open-ended discussion.[44] These expert practitioners are primarily corporate communication executives in the United States and abroad, the professionals responsible for helping to craft and disseminate an organization's stories to multiple stakeholders. In addition to responding to questions about the topic, they provided many examples of effective stories for business. As the interviews progressed, I tailored each to a particular subject for which the interviewee had expertise and experience; for example, on storytelling and social media.

After an initial set of interviews, I conducted on-site research at several corporations selected for excellence in storytelling at the enterprise level. As mentioned before, I focused on the work of corporate communication professionals with an eye to writing cases—or narratives—illustrating best practices in organizational storytelling.[45] Here the interviews focused on the particular roles, responsibilities, and accomplishments of the professionals for that enterprise as well as assessment of company stories, written or online.

To supplement these efforts, I conducted interviews with several other relevant groups: CEOs of small companies, who are in effect their organization's chief communication officer; business communication faculty, the primary instructors of storytelling in business schools; and filmmakers, experts in crafting stories, who are often insightful critics of the place of stories in culture, and, increasingly, resources that organizations turn to to discover and capture their stories. For example, General Electric hired the director of *Seabiscuit*—a 2003 movie about a horse that becomes an unlikely racing champion and inspires his team as well as the nation during the Great Depression—to teach senior executives about storytelling.[46] In total, I interviewed over 140 professionals, who represent approximately fifty organizations.

PURPOSE AND SCOPE OF THE BOOK

The purpose of this book is to help business professionals understand how organizational goals are accomplished through storytelling. I provide a framework for organizational storytelling and four extensive cases of corporate storytelling based on original research, each with important implications and lessons for business practitioners. The four organizations chosen for the cases were singled out for the quality of their stories: they meet criteria for ethical representation and business success. Each case is followed by "lessons learned," that is, commentary on the case that suggests practical application to other workplace settings and circumstances and that addresses how individuals can apply the lessons learned from the case to their own work. The final chapter summarizes the key points of the book and invites readers to develop a significant story of their own.

A WORKING DEFINITION OF *STORY* AND
THE AUTHENTIC AND FLUENT STORY

The working definition of *story* in business derives from what interviewees had to say about story, *from their uses of the term*, along with the examples of stories they told or showed me. It has the following elements:

- The depiction of event(s) that unfold in a sequence with a beginning, middle, and end, requiring choice of what to include and exclude and resulting in a pattern that makes sense of apparently disconnected facts

- A storyteller, either an individual or an organizational voice and point of view, that may not be specifically identified

- A "real-time" audience in the case of an oral presentation or Webcast, or a remote one that's imagined and assessed in the case of a written or online communication

This definition is less restrictive than the many definitions of narrative offered by scholars who study the subject.[47] Though it does not reflect the qualities that make for a compelling story, its three elements are what expert business practitioners of storytelling understand the term to mean and how they use it.[48]

As discussed by my interviewees, stories for business are quite flexible in presentation: they're written, oral, face-to-face, visual, online, or some combination of these formats. Communication expert Andy Gilman notes, "Stories are sometimes a lead grabber, sometimes frame issues, and sometimes are put in later in the Q&A."[49] As social networking capabilities continue to expand, the platforms and presentations of stories are evolving from video clips authored by employees, to blogs and interactive stories on company Web sites, and on and on.

Organizational stories are also quite flexible in scope. They can assume grand proportions or a modest, even an intimate, space. The story writ large may have as its subject strategy, culture, branding, or some combination of these. Some stories are far more circumscribed: for instance, an anecdote woven into a larger story or made to stand on its own; a short online story by a customer or employee about an experience with a firm;

a scenario developed by an engineer or salesperson about how a user can operate a new machine. Cumulatively, these smaller stories can tell a bigger story about a firm.

Things get more interesting when we move beyond the basics of organizational storytelling and consider what makes for *successful* business stories. A successful story can be characterized as both authentic and fluent.

Authenticity is a term that's commonly used in business circles by those who talk about the need for appearances to match reality. Stories must be credible, realistic, and tangible. "Authentic" organizational stories are intended to be truthful—to meet criteria for ethical representation as well as for business success. Think, for example, of the many stories told by employees at Johnson & Johnson about the impact of the "Credo," the company's mission and code of ethics, on their work and their lives. These stories are fact-checked, scrutinized for accuracy in detail (which in no way detracts from their emotional impact). Here's an excerpt from a story told by an employee who works in medical devices and manufacturing about an experience she had at a design and manufacturing show. She had taken aside a speaker whose life had been saved by a stent that was produced by the firm:

I walked up to the man and explained to him that the engineer he was speaking to happened to be one of the leaders of the team that developed the actual stent that was currently in his body. The man went limp, turned pale, grabbed the engineer in a bear hug and said: "If it wasn't for you, I probably would not be here right now." He started sobbing in his arms, then the engineer started crying, and most of us viewing this display of emotion in this large convention hall also got teary eyed.[50]

This and other Johnson & Johnson stories are in sharp contrast to inauthentic stories, which at best "fudge the facts" and at worst land their chief executives in jail. Inauthentic storytelling is perhaps exemplified by the many scenarios from Enron executives about ever-increasing, astronomical profits and global expansion, really flights of fantasy spun at the height of their efforts to fool investors, financial analysts, and others.

The consistent admonition by corporate communication executives is "Don't tell stories that aren't true." Asked what makes stories for business vulnerable, Valerie Di Maria, principal, the 10 company, warns, "Don't embellish for the sake of drama."[51] Gary Grates, principal, WCG Worldwide, emphasizes that "people don't want to hear what your organization wants to do, but what you are. Beware of romanticizing, telling stories about the good old days, which weren't really that great."[52] For Harvey W. Greisman, senior vice president and group executive—worldwide communications, MasterCard Worldwide, "the greatest vulnerability of stories is inconsistency and breaking a promise if the story is about what your company is and how it acts in the world: 'Once a liar, always a liar.'"[53]

To be successful, stories for business need to be fluent as well as authentic. *Fluency* is a term typically used to describe someone's language skills: "She's fluent in French" means she speaks with substantial command of the language, exhibiting an ability to speak conversationally, to craft sentences easily and with accurate grammar and style. As used here to describe storytelling, "fluent" stories represent a catchall description of several of the storyteller's capabilities and the story's qualities: engaging the emotions and intellect of the audience and commanding the elements of a powerfully crafted and presented story—elements such as a place for the novel and unexpected, significant details, compelling language, and a logical sequence in which the story unfolds. These are things business professionals need to know to be fluent storytellers, to master the "language" of stories. In the case of digital storytelling, fluency means working comfortably and flexibly with technology as well.

At first glance, fluency may appear to be at odds with authenticity since fluency requires selection to shape a story and authenticity requires, in simple terms, telling the truth. Looked at more closely, the two actually work in concert: different data, checked for accuracy, can be chosen for a story depending on its purpose, audiences, and the experience and perceptions of the storyteller. When the data are "encased" in stories, only one of various authentic stories results. All stories are necessarily shaped, and they require fluency. Without fluency, we don't have stories but rather a pile of data that's boring and disorganized, or a poorly conceived, poorly crafted, and poorly presented story that falls on deaf ears. At the same time, authentic stories don't distort the facts or otherwise slant the truth. Their goal is ethical representation.

PREVIEW OF THE CHAPTERS

The following chapter presents a framework for thinking systematically about organizational storytelling, giving prominence to the importance of authentic and fluent storytelling. This discussion sets the stage for the central chapters of the book, which offer a number of cases, or stories about organizations that represent "best practices" in organizational storytelling. Each case is based on original research, on-site observations and interviews, and assessment of corporate documents and is followed by a chapter of extended commentary and analysis of the case and implications for other organizational settings and circumstances that call for stories.

Chapter 3 and the commentary of Chapter 4 look at Schering-Plough's strategy as a persuasive story about the future that unfolds in "chapters" crafted and communicated by the CEO and leadership team. Successful stories about strategy, both authentic and fluent, are intended to help stakeholders understand the strategy to envision (and enact) the future. These chapters emphasize the importance of a corporate culture that supports the company's strategic direction; the role of the CEO as the chief corporate storyteller; and the power that stories about strategy can exert in challenging times.

Chapter 5 and the Chapter 6 commentary focus on the complex, mutually enriching relationship between stories and corporate brand at Chevron, how authentic and fluent stories bring a brand to life and give people confidence in it, and how a brand that lives up to its promise can serve as a frame or filter for powerful organizational stories. Such stories also reflect and strengthen corporate culture while showing the strategic differentiation of the firm from its competitors.

Chapters 7 and 8 show how one company, FedEx, brings together technology and craft to tell visual and verbal stories in video clips and blogs that are disseminated across multiple communication channels, including social network media. The company's strong corporate culture and expertise in the craft of storytelling, accompanied by sophistication in communications technology, result in powerful organizational stories. These, in turn, strengthen the culture and build trust in the organization.

Chapters 9 and 10 illustrate how storytelling workshops can educate employees about a company's (Philips's) shift in strategic direction and related changes in branding and culture, and assist professionals in a high-tech or engineering culture in communicating with nonspecialists. The workshops introduce storytelling systematically throughout an organization, helping people develop fluency in the practice through instruction, rehearsal, and review.

Finally, Chapter 11 highlights the key points about storytelling addressed in the book and invites readers to develop a significant story of their own, a model for which is the "Nana Betty" story that opened this chapter.

There are several ways to read this book besides reading the chapters in sequence. After reviewing Chapter 2 on the storytelling framework, if you are most interested in the cases, go on to Chapters 3, 5, 7, and 9, the stories of best practices at Schering-Plough, Chevron, FedEx, and Philips. If you are primarily interested in the lessons learned, based upon the cases, as well as practical application more generally, review the cases quickly and then focus on Chapters 4, 6, 8, 10, and 11.

Although I focus on business cases and their analysis, various journeys outward will continue over the course of the book to include fictional narratives, philosophical and social thought, stories of scientist-essayists, and relevant theory drawn from a variety of disciplines, always as an effort to return to business better prepared for working with stories than had we not ventured out. Explorations of storytelling in business will hold the biggest share of our attention, with cases—which are in effect *stories* constructed from extensive interviews and other primary and secondary research—that represent best practices in storytelling for business. Enjoy the journey.

2   A   F R A M E W O R K   F O R

O R G A N I Z A T I O N A L

S T O R Y T E L L I N G

HOW CAN WE THINK systematically about organizational storytelling? What are its key components and the relationships among
them that apply across the companies that represent best practices? The
research for this book began without a preconceived framework for making sense of organizational storytelling. The framework that emerged is
based on analysis and primary research, including multiple site visits to
best-practice companies, interviews with more than 140 professionals who
have expertise in organizational storytelling, and review of the relevant
company documents and literature in several fields.

Presented here, the framework identifies key components of organizational storytelling that come into play across the best-practice cases of
Schering-Plough, Chevron, FedEx, and Philips, which in turn elaborate
on the framework's components as they apply to a greater or lesser extent
to a particular case.[1] Moving forward, organizations and individuals that
want to build storytelling capabilities can use the framework to guide and
assess their efforts. We turn now to the framework, its key components,
and the relationships among them.

As I introduced in the first chapter, successful organizational storytelling at its foundation should be *authentic*: credible, realistic, tangible, and
intended to be truthful (Exhibit 2.1). It should also be *fluent*: storytelling

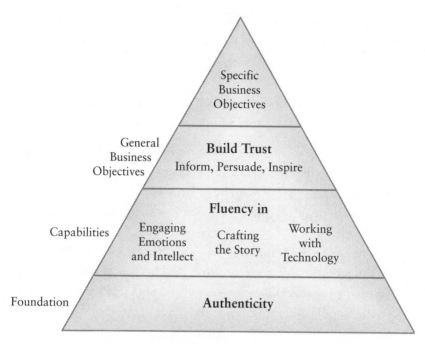

EXHIBIT 2.1.   Framework for Organizational Storytelling

should draw the attention of stakeholders by engaging their *emotions* and their *intellect*; by using the *craft* that makes this form of communication compelling; and in some instances by using *technology*, anything from photographs to state-of-the-art social media. These storytelling capabilities taken as a whole characterize fluent storytelling.

Stories for business have practical purpose. This is, in general, to gain or strengthen the *trust* of the intended audience(s) and, with this achieved, to *inform*, *persuade*, and even *inspire* them. In addition to achieving these *general business objectives*, stories are intended to accomplish *specific business objectives*. These objectives can cover anything from recruiting new members to a firm, to increasing the customer base, to presenting a profile of the senior leadership to the media. In the best-practice cases, these specific business objectives include the quite significant goals of building and strengthening corporate strategy, corporate culture, and corporate branding, the ultimate goal being to build the business, its profits and reputation.

Let's take up each of these components beginning with authenticity, the foundation of organizational storytelling.

AUTHENTICITY IN STORYTELLING FOR BUSINESS

Authenticity is a rule any good communicator should follow. Don't put out a persona or a group of facts you don't have. Don't lie. Everything that is knowable will ultimately be known.

—DICK PARSONS, Chairman of the board, Citigroup, and former Chief Executive Officer, AOL Time Warner

According to the many experts in organizational storytelling interviewed for the book, the dictum "Words must match deeds" is the key ethical criterion by which stories should be judged. Does the story pass the test of being "credible," "realistic," "tangible"—descriptions that come up repeatedly in discussions of organizational storytelling at best-practice firms? If not true now, is the story realistically aspirational? Does it support the organization's strategy, culture, and brand? In addition, stories should not be monolithic expressions of the organization's leadership; rather, they should take into account the voices of significant others, such as employees, customers, and communities.

Words Must Match Deeds

Truth will come to light . . . in the end truth will out.

—SHAKESPEARE, *The Merchant of Venice*

In 2007, the Arthur W. Page Society, a group of senior corporate communication professionals, published a study introducing the importance of "authenticity" as a guiding principle for companies as they respond to the current business environment, which the group characterizes as a "global playing field of unprecedented transparency and radically democratized access to information production, dissemination, and consumption."[2] This environment, they argue, establishes authenticity as a requirement for business success. Authenticity is an ethical concept undergirding the first of two Page Principles that steer this association's work and its understanding of corporate identity: "*Tell the truth*. Let the public know what's happening and provide an accurate picture of the company's character, ideals, and practices." The second principle: "*Prove it with action*. Public perception of an organization is determined 90 percent by what it does and ten percent by what it says."[3]

In such an environment, the corporation that wants to establish a distinctive brand and achieve long-term success must, more than ever before, be grounded in a sure sense of what defines it—why it exists, what it stands for and what differentiates it in a marketplace of customers, investors, and workers.

In a word, *authenticity* will be the coin of the realm for successful corporations and for those who lead them.[4]

In the wake of highly publicized corporate scandals at Enron and World-Com, Bernie Madoff's Ponzi scheme, and the BP oil spill in the Gulf of Mexico—among other crises—there's been a persistent call for honesty in business leaders and for accountability in their actions and those of the organizations they lead.[5]

Regardless of the specific business objective of an organizational story, the teller needs to give scrupulous attention to the accuracy of the story's details. This is especially the case because "story" as a kind of business discourse is often greeted with skepticism: one executive I taught in a storytelling workshop remarked, "By stories, don't you mean fairy tales? Aren't you talking about fantasy?" His comment is fairly routine.

Authentic storytelling about an organization is data-based storytelling. The story's details as well as those in the documents that often serve as a companion piece to the story are "fact-based and fact-checked,"[6] explains Helen Clark, manager of corporate marketing, policy, government, and public affairs at Chevron. Data need to be verified using multiple sources. "There's a need for evidence-based messages," asserts Jeff Hunt, principal and cofounder of PulsePoint Group, "so collect and use the stories of customers and their experience with the company."[7] In a similar vein, documentary story consultant Karen Everett points out that "facts are the ballast—they give stability—and the constraint or burden. You can't create facts or scenes to help you with the storyline. We who deal with real life can't make up scenes."[8] Using reliable data forms the basis for the integrity of organizational stories.

Not only do stories embed facts, but they also work in tandem with other corporate communications, the primary purpose of which is to provide data such as product specs or explanations of policy or technology. A cancer-fighting drug produced by Schering-Plough is featured in a story told by a cancer survivor, and the product's description is also made available to interested parties. A fact sheet on geothermal energy at Chevron is supported by stories that bring the technology down to human scale and make it tangible. A story by a FedEx manager about growing up in Asia, which occurred during a period of unprecedented growth in trade there, is accompanied by data about the company's cargo delivery to these regions. A story about Philips's work in LED-based lighting design for a city center is supplemented by facts about the technology, urban crime, and city festivals that are enhanced by creative lighting.

The big exception to this requirement of fact-checking is authentic autobiographical storytelling for business, what I call a professional's "signature story," for which heartfelt conviction and fidelity to feelings can trump accuracy of detail. This distinction will be discussed in the last chapter of the book.

The Voices of Significant Others

Authentic storytelling should take into account the voices of significant others, such as employees, customers, and communities and give room for their stories. Not just about the organization alone, the story is open to the needs, concerns, knowledge, values, and interests—and even the voices—of others. This requires the storyteller, whether an individual or an organization, to begin the activity by listening.

As a *listening* storyteller,[9] an organization's representatives may invite end users of its products and services to tell their stories; may give a place for these stories in written, online, and oral communications; and may acknowledge the stories of what branding expert Rohit Bhargava calls "accidental spokespeople"—those who are not authorized to speak about the company's brands but nonetheless express their opinions.[10] The CEO of Schering-Plough goes on a listening campaign to learn about employees' concerns about changes in strategy, incorporates their voices in his story of the firm, and knows as a result of his listening how to adjust his story to their needs and concerns. Chevron gives room on its Web site for partners and collaborators to tell their stories about their involvement with the company. FedEx opens up company blogs to interested outside parties to tell their stories about topics like work/life balance or sustainability. Philips invites patients and healthcare experts to storytelling workshops to help their employees understand these outsiders' stories and, in doing so, to improve their own. As one workshop participant noted, "To speak authentically, Philips's employees need a chance to hear the language of people-centric healthcare firsthand and interact with those on the front line."

For stories to be genuine in an organizational setting, companies need to make room in some of them for the multiple personal voices and interpretations of employees, customers, and others who tell stories about their experience of and with the organization.[11] At Schering-Plough, this can mean a researcher linking his passion for medical research to the organizational goals of drug discovery; at Chevron, an employee expressing his unique experience of educating the next generation of scientists, while taking into account the company's norms about "corporate voice"; at FedEx, an employee talking about her personality, in the form of dance and discussion on a video clip available on the company Web site and the employee's Facebook, while linking this digital story to the value the company places on extraordinary effort; at Philips, an employee or customer expressing a personal, emotionally compelling experience with light and connecting this story to the company's brand and business concept.

The balancing act between the personal and the organizational in which the aims of each party, the individual and the organization, are respected can be quite challenging. Some organizations have been successful in achieving the balance by using a combination of instruction and guidelines for storytelling that, on the one hand, encourage an employee's self-expression and individual ownership of a story and, on the other, identify specific topics the organization wants to see communicated; for instance, strategy, culture, or branding.

THE DARK SIDE OF STORYTELLING:
FAKING AUTHENTICITY

To be credible is to be no nonsense. CEOs always need to work to improve their ability to tell the story but they need to work with what's given, the facts, to be well grounded in the business.

—DAVID A. SAMSON, general manager of public affairs, Chevron

Authenticity is foundational to storytelling, but there are many challenges to achieving this goal, and it is important to point them out before considering the other components of the framework for organizational storytelling. One challenge is the overinflated presence of the corporate leader. David A.Samson, who has been a counselor to several CEOs, warns that emphasizing the ego of the CEO, who is the chief organizational storyteller, is quite dangerous, as is straying from the facts. "In this post-Enron period, the days of the Imperial CEO, the CEO who is bigger than the 'corporate personality,' are over."[12] As for straying from the facts, Rob Lively, vice president of corporate government affairs at Schering-Plough, warns that "stories are vulnerable when there are loose threads. When even one thread is pulled loose, the whole thing unravels. Remember the GM CEO who arrived in DC by private jet when he was going to Congress to ask for bailout money."[13]

Even the appearance of falsehood when a story is essentially true can be costly. Betsy McLaughlin, CEO of Hot Topic, tells of an actor friend hired by a company to play the part of an employee in a commercial about the company's corporate giving because the actual employee was not skillful enough to be in the commercial. "The company claims that their employees work at a food bank in their spare time. This is, in fact, true. The problem is that if anyone finds out that an actor and not an employee appears in the commercial, the story will have no credibility."[14]

The story that's too good to be true is yet another problem. Pulitzer Prize-winning historian David M. Kennedy elucidates the persistent wrongheadedness of the facile story in his study of US history from the Great Depression of the 1930s to the end of World War II. The false story in this case is that the stock market crash of October 1929 caused the decade-long depression:

Much mythology surrounds these dramatic events in the autumn of 1929. Perhaps the most imperishable misconception portrays the Crash as the cause of the great Depression that persisted through the decade of the 1930s. The scenario owes its durability, no doubt, to its intuitive plausibility and to its convenient fit with the canons of narrative, which require historical accounts to have recognizable beginnings, middles, and ends and to explain events in terms of identifiable origins, development, and resolution. These conventions are comforting; they render understandable and thus tolerable even the most terrifying human experiences. The storyteller and the shaman sometimes feed the same psychic needs.[15]

Kennedy goes on to explain that careful scholars give no credence to this story; data and analysis yield a more complex, nuanced picture of events. As Kennedy's analysis suggests, the story that "goes down easily," that is fluent but at the cost of authenticity, is sometimes quite a seductive and lazy way out of finding the patterns that the data actually allow for.

Those who engage in the "dark side" of storytelling may tell tales that amuse and engage but lack veracity. Alternatively, they may tell a story which in and of itself is truthful—for instance, about the successful outcome of a patient's use of a newly launched drug by a pharmaceutical firm—but that is not at all representative; in the case of the testimonial about the efficacy of a drug, there may be one hundred stories about the drug's failure to help a patient that outweigh the one positive testimonial that is presented. Telling a story about the exception without honest disclosure is dishonest, as is telling multiple stories, even expressed by multiple stakeholders, to support a desired image while ignoring other stories of equal or greater weight that undermine it.

While apparently truthful, storytellers operating on the dark side may be some combination of out-and-out liars, snake-oil salesmen, and masters in suppressing information, in oversimplifying, or in deflecting attention from the truth by supplying an overload of irrelevant information.[16] Often, they are facile at clouding people's judgment through the use of colorful visuals, a compelling but vacuous tone of voice, an attractive "dress for success" presence, or a story that appeals to the audience's fondest, though unrealistic, hopes and dreams.

Concern about the dark side of storytelling (and of discourse more generally) goes well beyond modern business practices, dating back more than two millennia to Plato, who had his protagonist Socrates call for the banning of poets and rhetoricians from the city-state for fear they would undermine the values of the community. Plato also warned of the drugging effect of their talents—a kind of pharmacological lying—a gift with words detached from the truth and capable of lulling the mind and seducing the listener (though at times the drug had the status of a remedy rather than a poison). This practice was perhaps best exemplified by the mellifluous but empty words of the physically attractive, drunken figure of Alcibiades in the *Symposium*, the dialogue on love.[17] Following Alcibiades is a long procession of spinmeisters infamous for their ability to weave a captivating tale, often admirable for its inventiveness and artistry but intended to deceive: the Ken Lays and Bernie Madoffs of the world and the string of dot-com CEOs who pitched "vaporware"—nonexistent product—at the height of the dot-com bubble of the late twentieth century.

These dark talents for storytelling, when expressed in fiction, drama, or film, have tremendous aesthetic appeal that can provide a window on why their counterparts in business have such allure: Shakespeare's clever rhetorician Richard III; the silver-tongued Satan, leader of the Underworld, in John Milton's *Paradise Lost*; the various representations of the figure Mephistopheles, the devil, of the Faustian legend; the sideshow magician and demagogue Cipolla in Thomas Mann's "Mario and the Magician" (a character associated with the Fascist dictator of the last century Benito Mussolini)[18]; the serpent Kaa in Disney's *The Jungle Book*, who uses his hypnotic stare, soporific tone, and melodic chant of "Trust in me . . . Shut your eyes and trust in me" to ensnare the man-cub Mowgli in his coils. Even a partial sampling of the storytelling capabilities of this rogues' gallery can illuminate the clever tactics used in the dark side of storytelling.

One category that falls within the dark side of storytelling is a virulent and increasingly pervasive celebration of narcissism in business education: the overemphasis upon "charisma" and personal branding based more on conviction alone, in the tradition of the French Romantic writer Jean-Jacques Rousseau,[19] than on accomplishments and values, that is, what young professionals have done and the moral compass that guides their behavior. Communications consultant Mary Lang warns: "In terms of the dangers of storytelling, I would point to the *dangerous myth syndrome* as an outgrowth (sometimes intended, sometimes not) of storytelling in business. This is that [discursive] space that becomes a collection of distorted and destructive fun-house mirrors for both individuals and organizations."[20] This phenomenon, often accompanied by self-delusion rather than intentional falsehood, has quite an old lineage but is also a growing fad that is all too common in the communication coaching of current and future leaders in business. Such stories are characterized by the self-absorption of the storyteller who attempts to dazzle the audience with superficial fluency, the right fashion statement, and souped-up visuals—Narcissus never learned to do research. Why bother with actual accomplishments since everyone's entitled to attention based on surface attractiveness? This drive for recognition, even celebrity, trumps the old-fashioned idea of character—and is at odds with the ethics of authenticity.

Yet another kind of fake authenticity is a product of corporate bullying and hypocrisy. This occurs when companies espouse a rhetoric of authenticity in storytelling but in fact coerce their spokespeople to express the party line in their stories, leaving no room for personal expression. In sum, people are scripted, and the artificiality is apparent. In these instances, organizational storytelling is no more than corporate speak created, owned, and perhaps passionately believed by the higher-ups but inauthentic to others.

FLUENCY IN STORYTELLING FOR BUSINESS

Being authentic is a necessary though not sufficient condition for successful organizational stories. Storytellers need to be fluent as well to cut through the busyness, distractions, and competing demands of work life. Stories then need to engage people's emotions and intellect, live vividly in their memory and imagination, and move them to respond in ways the storyteller intends. To be fluent, an organization's spokespeople need competence in the craft of storytelling and, in some cases, in the use of communications technology. As we'll see in later chapters, best-practice companies may provide workshops, guidelines, and expert help to assist employees in developing these capabilities.

Engage the Emotions and Intellect

The overwhelming consensus among the storytelling experts interviewed for this book is that organizational stories are successful when they engage people's emotions as well as their intellect, when they touch their hearts as well as their minds. Perry Yeatman, senior vice president of corporate and legal affairs at Kraft Foods, may have expressed this claim best: "A great story is one that the listener can relate to, uses language that makes sense, brings in emotion, makes it visual, takes us on a journey, brings together intellect and emotion."[21] Similarly, educator Anne Grinols talks about the need to have stories "to reconnect with the audience (or cause them to reconnect to me); to bring their imaginations into play as they react to or put themselves into the story; to focus authenticity (real-world-ness) rather than a kind of textbook dryness in a situation."[22] For instructor and actor Roger Manix, the appeal of stories to the emotions and intellect signals a fundamental change in how business is conducted:

I believe the direction we are moving in socially is away from an ego-based hierarchy to more of a heart-centered culture. And that profound paradigm shift will bleed over into all of our business affairs. We'll need to develop a trusting relationship with our audience, clients, consumers. How we cultivate this shift is through the power of storytelling, which cuts right through to the hearts of others. It's the stories that "stick."[23]

As shown earlier in many examples of storytelling *outside* of business, the ability of stories to engage the hearts and minds of people is at the core of storytelling across all fields—though it's perhaps most apparent in narrative medicine, literature, psychology, and film. Moreover, if people are hardwired for stories, as both novelists and neurologists argue, then stories are powerful ways to reach their core humanity.

How do stories appeal to both the emotions and the intellect? Reflecting for a moment on our own experience with stories (business or otherwise) provides a preliminary answer to this question. If we think about listening to or reading stories, we're likely to identify several mental processes that come into play. When a story begins, we may experience a kind of psychological sea change as we shift attention to the universe depicted in the story, its setting, characters, and conflicts, exercising what the poet Coleridge called a "willing suspension of disbelief" as we become immersed in the story world and picture it in our imagination. If we're listening to a story, we're likely to be caught up in the voice and presence of the storyteller and the emotional mood created through the performance. Moreover, while alert and present to the speaker and to the story world constructed, we may notice that the constructed story world evokes concrete images and triggers emotionally rich memories, episodes in our own life that resemble or differ from the constructed story world. In sum, our hearts and minds are fully engaged.

Craft the Story

General rules in art are useful chiefly as a lamp in a mine, or a hand-rail down a black stairway; they are necessary for the sake of the guidance they give, but it is a mistake, once they are formulated, to be too much in awe of them.

—EDITH WHARTON, *The Writing of Fiction*

Although there are no rigid formulas, the craft of storytelling (I use *craft* as both a noun and a verb) involves making good choices about a variety of story elements. Many books have been devoted to this broad subject, and it's of course implicit in every successful film, short story, and novel.[24] Here let's consider what experts in storytelling for business—including filmmakers asked to reflect on this subject—have singled out as important to the craft of storytelling in business and what may also be inferred from their comments. There is substantial overlap among these elements, but for the sake of clarity let's take up each separately.

The Right Purpose, Audience, Moment, Storyteller, and Characters   Good selection of these story elements comes from careful response to these questions:

- What purpose do you want to achieve in story form?
- With whom?
- Why now?
- Who should tell the story?
- Who should be included in the story?

When purpose, audience, and timing come together dramatically, stories may be a matter of exigency. A company like Schering-Plough, at a certain moment in its history, *needed* to tell a series of turnaround stories to all its stakeholders to get the company back on track, and those had to be carried initially by the CEO, the chief storyteller about strategy. The right purpose may be to convey news that is important to the organization as a whole and to all of its stakeholders, though the importance of the news may not be apparent to all stakeholders unless explicit connections are made to their needs and interests in the story. As we'll see in the best-practice cases, some companies provide their spokespeople with formal workshops, coaching, and supplementary material to show them how to assess stakeholders' needs and link them to a central organizational purpose, such as strengthening corporate strategy, culture, or brand.

"Why now?" or the timing of the story, is so important that the ancient Greeks, early practitioners of storytelling, had a term for it: *kairos*, or the "opportune moment" (to be distinguished from *chronos*, or what we'd call clock time today). Kairos may be a matter of choosing the opportune moment—for instance, an annual meeting of senior leaders as the time and place to deliver a story about strategy—or it may be a matter of creating the circumstances in which people are ready to hear the story, such as scheduling a corporate event to celebrate a company's past and to convey in story form the CEO's vision for the future. According to Jim Finn, chief marketing officer at Groovy Corporation, politicians are often very good at timing stories. "They're absolute weather vanes. It's a gift. FDR used storytelling by radio to great effect during an economic crisis of massive proportions."[25] Roosevelt created what he called "fireside chats," informal radio addresses to the American public conducted in a tone of familiarity and comfort one would use in talking neighbor to neighbor, to quell people's fears during the Great Depression. In his discussion of politicians' talent for timing stories, Finn concludes that business leaders would do well to study politicians' knack for identifying and capitalizing on the opportune moment for stories.

The right storyteller may be the CEO if the purpose of the story is to carry the "grand story" about strategy, culture, or brand but is increasingly an employee, customer, or "unauthorized spokesperson." As important as the selection of the storyteller is voice: a sense of the human being behind the story and a dimension of story constructed by the storyteller's language, choice of details, and pacing, among other things. Does the storyteller sound like a self-absorbed egotist? (too much "I" in the story?). A guy with a zany sense of humor? A patient and thoughtful expert capable of explaining her expertise without being condescending? That's voice.

As discussed earlier, voice in organizational stories should represent a balance between the organizational and the personal—a negotiation as it were—and its creation benefits from the kind of formal instruction or guidelines offered at the best-practice companies.

According to Tom Martin, reflecting on his work as head of corporate communication at ITT, a high-tech engineering and manufacturing firm, a story built around the right characters

gives a company a personality by highlighting the engineer [in the case of ITT]. ITT is best known for its engineering talent. Customers would say, "I don't know about ITT but I know about Joe, Sven, and the reliability of services." ITT worked with an ad agency and came up with "Engineering for Life" as the cornerstone of our brand, in logos and in advertising. When launched back in 1998, we used engineers as heroes of our campaign—real people, not actors. During the opening bell of Wall Street, engineers were on the dais. The CEO at the time was an engineering grad from MIT. Engineers were also paired with the CEO on satellite media tours and featured on the Web site and in the ITT annual report. The stories are about real people. This is a robust effort. Selling water pumps is impersonal, so don't tell a story about water pumps but about water shortage.[26]

Especially for technical products and services that are not easily understandable, stories about people enjoying the benefits of the technology humanize a company and what it sells.

Novelty and the Unexpected   Without exception the filmmakers interviewed for this book singled out novelty and the unexpected as essential elements of successful storytelling. The comments of Fred Rubin, Emmy-nominated television writer and producer and faculty member at the UCLA School of Theater, Film, and Television, are representative of this consensus:

Good stories take the world we've all seen and turn it on its head. They don't use stereotypes. A character who was a lead on *Family Matters* named Steven Urkel is a black nerd. In one episode he has to go against bad guys on an inner-city playground. That's the initial premise of the story. I said, "Let's have him go against three girls instead of three boys. It would be so much more interesting and so much more fun to write."[27]

Arguably the world's experts in visual storytelling, filmmakers know that stories must surprise and delight to bring viewers to the screen and keep them wondering, What's next? Why? How will this get resolved? Who wins? Who loses? Novelty, as a technique, can mean an incongruous juxtaposition of unlikely qualities or the subversion of a stereotype—a rap singer and dancer in a FedEx digital story who also happens to be a senior vice president. It may also be found in significant details, compelling language, and visuals.

Significant Details, Compelling Language, and Visuals   Screenplay writer and UCLA film professor Neil Landau talks passionately about the importance of detail—down to the choice of a single word—to the craft of storytelling:

I go through ten to twenty drafts of a screenplay. Little details of behavior are important. Nuance is important to really get to know character. [In a student's screenplay] the kid's dad is self-important and tells him, "Careful, you'll get water on my Bruno Maglis." In a later draft, the kid picks up the shoes and sees they're a knockoff. That's the detail.

I like to use the metaphor of a golf game. You hit the ball and try to get it on the green. Each draft gets you closer to the hole. All the detailed work: it's craftsmanship. Each word counts.[28]

Details that evoke the five senses are especially important. In consulting with corporate clients on storytelling, Jeff Hunt of PulsePoint uses a novel illustration to underscore the importance of this appeal, in this case to the visual imagination: "Imagine that my mother is blind. If she's listening to your story on NPR, you don't want to be routine and monotonous: I did this and she did that. Imagine, instead, a canvas. Do you want to fill it with black-and-white stick figures or use every color on the palette so that she can really see?"[29] "Human details"—specific people, their actions, concrete images, and appeals to the five senses—are then the rich fabric of stories for business that distinguish them from the largely abstract language of corporate mission and vision statements and from the lifeless concrete language of product specs.

Communication expert Nancy Duarte, who writes and consults about corporate presentations, emphasizes the visual appeal of slides, their color, and design in talks that take the form of stories. She argues that "stories are how people understand and relate to the world, and they naturally associate those stories with appropriate imagery."[30] Edward R. Tufte, a pioneer in the study of the visual display of quantitative information,[31] repeatedly points out the importance of visuals to telling a story. Jim Finn at Groovy Corporation keeps a Tufte chart on his wall at work showing Napoleon's march into Russia and subsequent retreat. He sums up the power of a visual to tell a story:

The whole story of Napoleon's march into Russia and his retreat in the early nineteenth century can be shown as a visual with the march plotted against time and temperature. The lines on the plot get thinner and thinner as the retreat is plotted. Hundreds of thousands of troops dwindle down to hundreds of people. A hundred years later the story literally repeats itself with the Nazis' ill-fated march and retreat over similar territory. Tufte was an advisor to the *New York Times*, and their graphical presentations are brilliant.[32]

As we'll see in all the best-practice cases, visuals have a prominent place in organizational storytelling, be they photos of "wellness" around the world in the Philips case or video clips of employees serving the public at FedEx. Visuals fortify the emotional appeal of stories.

Narrative Logic   Stories need to have a narrative logic, or what novelist and literary critic David Lodge reminds us is the "classic notion of narrative unity. It [the story] has a beginning, a middle, and an end as defined by Aristotle: a beginning requires nothing to precede it, an end is what requires nothing to follow it, and a middle needs something both before and after it."[33]

For the storyteller, this means the need to choose the starting and end point or goal of the journey and, just as important, what communication executive Sharon Young calls the story's "pulse points," "the moments to be emphasized that show the story's heart [as well as] the connections from one pulse point to the next."[34] Consider, for example, the "pulse points" in a personal story I told to inspire a group of PepsiCo's corporate communication professionals at their annual retreat, held at the Marriott Hotel at the foot of the Brooklyn Bridge. I wanted them to take risks, to cross bridges between their current work and their aspirations by first considering whether they have had a mentor who might have encouraged them in their professional and personal lives. The story, as I told it to the PepsiCo group, is in Exhibit 2.2.

My "Nana Betty" story consisted of a sequence of pulse points: a brief reference to my grandmother's immigrant story against the backdrop of the Statue of Liberty, the "Meet the Press" episodes, my grandfather's questions about his company's ad, and the interpretative move—linking my childhood experiences to the adult's ability to take risks and cross bridges—and the request to the group to consider how this story might relate to their own experience. Of course, the timing and setting for the story are important here—and serendipitous, since in 2009, the date of my talk, it had been exactly one hundred years since my grandmother had arrived on these shores not far from the Brooklyn Bridge, located right outside the hotel's doors. The bridge is a majestic architectural structure, celebrated in poetry and historical accounts and photos, that connects the borough of Brooklyn to the commercial life of lower Manhattan. Yet at least as important as the timing and setting are the pulse points, their sequencing, and the end point of the narrative: triggering people's memories of a mentor, a relative or boss, in their own lives, and the support this relationship may have given them to dare to take risks in their careers. I wanted them to take comfort and strength from that relationship and use it as a launchpad for professional growth.

Versions of Stories   Storytelling in business requires versatility, the talent to adjust the story's pulse points, details, and language to the varied purposes of a story and the needs and interests of a given audience. Angela A. Buonocore, senior vice president and chief communications officer at Xylem Inc., emphasizes this "secret of the best communicators,"[35] quoting lines from the poem "If" by Rudyard Kipling as an eloquent expression of this capability: "If you can walk with crowds and keep your virtue / Or walk with kings—nor lose the common touch."

Versatility can mean creating different versions of stories; for instance, one for a high-powered business discussion, replete with technical details,

Exactly one hundred years ago, my maternal grandmother, Betty Heller, whom we called "Nana Betty," sailed in steerage past the Statue of Liberty, which you can easily see today if you look due west between the low-rise buildings near the Marriott toward the Hudson River. Nana was a very beautiful blue-eyed girl of nine with chestnut-brown hair, an immigrant who did not speak a word of English. (She later perfected her English by reading the novels of Charles Dickens, so her accent and vocabulary were occasionally nineteenth-century British—and a cause of more than a few laughs in those of us who noticed the incongruity between her twentieth-century dress and demeanor, on the one hand, and her dated vocabulary, on the other.)

Nana Betty gave me an early immersion into media relations every time she would introduce me and my sister, Michele, as little children, to her neighbors, who sat on their stoops as we walked to the beach. She would invite us to "Meet the Press," to tell a story about ourselves to this attentive group of strangers who occasionally asked questions about our latest exploits. When we returned to her apartment in Manhattan Beach (Brooklyn, New York), my grandfather Al would show me the latest ad in the *New York Times* for his employment agency on Madison Avenue, Heller Sales Personnel, and ask for my opinion: "Is the size of the letters in 'Heller' large enough? Does the name stand out?"

Unbeknownst to my grandparents, these early practice sessions in communication became my inspiration later in life for crossing the Brooklyn Bridge that linked their home in Manhattan Beach (and my personal playground and sanctuary of sorts) and Manhattan, which became, literally and metaphorically, a representation of my public life.

Who or what has inspired you to cross the Brooklyn Bridge—which I see is the logos on our PepsiCo T-shirts, the theme of this conference ("Crossing the Bridge"), and literally the bridge that many of us walked across yesterday afternoon to enjoy the sun, the vista, and the mix of people who traveled alongside us?

EXHIBIT 2.2.   My "Nana Betty" Story

and another for a more general audience that strips away the specialized language. In the "Nana Betty" story, I have shaped and deployed different versions for different purposes and audiences. In the Preface to this book, I used a version of the story to show the roots of my interest in storytelling, its generative power in my family and professional life, and its potential impact on the lives of my readers. My intention is to invite readers to consider the powerful influence of this type of communication, one that has depth and reach. At the beginning of the first chapter I used a shorter version to underscore how storytelling can be a personal as well as an organizational inheritance: I have identified at the outset a basic claim about storytelling. Here, in the second chapter, I show how a longer version of my "Nana Betty" story (which also includes my grandfather) allowed me to connect emotionally to the corporate communication professionals in my PepsiCo audience, who were themselves quite familiar with media relations and advertising and were open to an inspirational tale. I will return full circle to refer to "Nana Betty" in the last chapter to illustrate an example of a "signature story," a personal story about a significant experience, relationship, accomplishment, or failure that can provide self-understanding to the storyteller and serve many business purposes in the teller's professional life.

Since organizational storytelling takes into account audience, it begins with listening to and assessing the needs, concerns, knowledge, values, and interests of the intended audience and then adjusts each version of the story to fit the purpose and audience.[36] So important is this receptivity to the audience that the CEO of a major consulting firm I know requires his consultants to leave company literature behind in the office and walk into a meeting with a potential client with just a blank yellow pad to jot down the client's concerns; only with these in mind, the CEO asserts, should the consultant begin to weave the story about how the company's solutions can address the client's problems.

Versatility in storytelling may mean expanding or collapsing the length of a story, adjusting the language, emphasizing some details, and leaving others on the cutting-room floor.[37] The craft is akin to the talent of a jazz musician who can play variations of a melodic theme in different keys, at different tempos, with changes in volume and other dynamics, but retain that recognizable melody and awareness of the audience's reactions. Tena Clark, CEO of DMI Music & Media Solutions, herself a songwriter and producer, exhibits this talent for versatility in her story about the company's past, and her own:

When I talk about the company, the story I tell depends upon the part of the country I'm visiting. If I'm talking to African Americans at Best Buy, I talk about what led me to all the successes with huge iconic black artists like Aretha Franklin, Dionne Warwick, and Patti LaBelle. I was a writer and producer for them. If I'm in the South, I bring in my Southern background. I was raised on a farm there. If I'm speaking to Hispanics, I tell them that I don't speak Spanish, that I'm from Mississippi and barely speak English, but that I hear Spanish 24/7 because I'm married to a Costa Rican.[38]

Use Technology

The craft of storytelling reaches way back to the roots of storytelling in ancient times; by contrast, the *technology* used to create or transmit stories is much more recent. It refers to anything from photography, a nineteenth-century invention, to today's state-of-the-art social media, communication platforms that allow people to create, spread, and strengthen relationships and build communities through conversations among users about common interests and concerns.[39, 40]

According to the Page study on authenticity, social media offers businesses "new avenues to develop deeper and more extensive relationships—relationships that can unlock new kinds of value for the enterprise through collaboration across complex business ecosystems."[41] The study describes this phenomenon as a digital network revolution that

is driving a shift in the way that people interact with each other and with companies and institutions. It changes how dialogue occurs, how perceptions are shaped and how relationships are forged. We all must deal with a dramatic increase in the overall volume of communication; marked changes in the content, tone and purpose of those communications; an exponential increase in the speed of those communications; and entirely new, low-cost tools and capabilities to search, structure and make sense of all this information and interaction.[42, 43]

Along with these opportunities afforded by technology come substantial threats. Critics of business, both the honest and the disreputable, have new capabilities to inflict damage on an organization's reputation thanks to changes in technology that allow for intense scrutiny and rapid, widespread communication. Communications expert Tom Martin notes the importance of this threat in this way: "The Web has changed things completely. A company can tell a story to the world but so can its adversaries who can have a voice shouting at the same level. A disgruntled employee or an NGO has the same size megaphone as a company."[44]

The most dynamically changing component of the storytelling framework, technology affects organizational stories in several ways. First, the availability of "low-cost tools and capabilities" that are simple to use means that organizations have increasingly less control of stories created and told about them. Anyone with a cheap camcorder can create stories about a firm and draw significant traffic. The technology then gives new power to individuals who can support or undermine a company's reputation through stories and other communications on blogs or other social media outlets. Moreover, the power of individuals to influence their peers has grown. People increasingly value word of mouth in assessing the authenticity of a company and its claims: "The vast majority of eyeballs and ears really don't care what you're trying to say. They are going online and searching for what interests them, forming networks with people of similar interests, and ignoring the mass communications that corporations throw at them,"[45] explains Katie Delahaye Paine, CEO of KDPaine & Partners, a public relations and social media research firm. According to the Center for Media Research, studies demonstrate that people believe recommendations from those they know more than from any other source.[46]

Second, the "broadcast" approach to corporate communications—"one-way, top-down" corporate messaging—has given way more and more to the recognition that stakeholder audiences are neither captive nor passive. Companies must focus on active engagement with all sorts of people within and outside of the organization, listening and monitoring their stories and encouraging supporters to craft and distribute them. As an example, Ford has an online site called "Ford Story" (www.fordstory.com), a platform in which Ford offers stories about its cars and, more importantly, invites people to read, write, and share their favorite personal stories involving a Ford car and to move these stories out to their Facebook account.

Third, digital stories, when compelling, "go viral": they are retold and reframed by others online and in person. Of course, the retelling of stories, digitally or not, demonstrates their vitality, incremental development, and staying power. The new technology just makes it easier to spread stories. A digital story may elicit a response, even another story or a revision of the posted one, and be linked to stories or information and opinion on other sites. It may first appear on a company Web site or blog as a user-generated video and migrate to personal sites like YouTube and Facebook—or to whatever new platform emerges to extend the reach of social networking. For example, GE's "Thomas Edison Workbench" is a very active blog with stories about research which in turn may be posted to the GE Eco-innovation page and commented on in other venues such as the Huffington Post. The migration of a story from one channel to another and from one storyteller to another builds its strength and influence in the process and can make the original authorship less important. In fact, companies like GE encourage this "loss" of sole authorship in service of their corporate goals.

Finally, evidence from multiple sources shows that the technology for digital storytelling may be able to affect the craft of storytelling; for example, the whole notion of authorship and "ownership" of a story, as the discussion of viral stories suggests. On the horizon are new technologies and applications that will stimulate innovation in storytelling. Consider, for example, two applications currently in development: the first is the use of lifelike avatars capable of telling a company's stories onscreen when a potential customer walks into a store or asks a question online; the second consists of advanced special effects—color, design, and sound—to enhance the visual and auditory impact of stories. Technological innovations, often produced initially for the entertainment sector, are likely to migrate to storytelling for businesses in other industry sectors. We will need to stay tuned. As digital media expert Carolyn Handler Miller reflects, "When creating a work for a brand new medium, it is extremely difficult to see its potential. People in this position must go through a steep learning curve to discover its unique properties and determine how they can be used for narrative purposes."[47] In sum, this component of the storytelling framework needs to be updated continually as may also be the case for the related component, the craft of storytelling, when influenced by technological innovation.[48]

GENERAL BUSINESS OBJECTIVES: BUILD TRUST, INFORM, PERSUADE, INSPIRE

Unlike most personal stories, film, and literature, organizational stories have business objectives. These include building trust in the organization, an objective that depends on the story's authenticity and fluency. Once trust is won, a company's stories are on the way to achieving the general objectives of informing, persuading, and even inspiring, or some combination of these objectives.

Build Trust

Trust is a new line of business.

—RICHARD EDELMAN, CEO, Edelman

Speaking before a group of corporate communication professionals at ITT, Richard Edelman, CEO of Edelman, explained: "It's a stakeholder world, not a shareholder world. People want a high quality product, transparency, and a company they can trust."[49] This means, he went on to elaborate, that companies need to encourage public engagement of all stakeholder groups, listen to stories being told about them from multiple quarters, and provide new content, new stories. While the authority of the traditional media is shrinking, every company, he continued, becomes a kind of media company—regardless of the industry sector it works in—in that employees' stories are important, and new, interesting video content about the firm should be made public: "An employee who is innovative should be viral in a moment. Get employees to talk." The "Edelman Trust Barometer," a worldwide survey on trust in institutions conducted annually since 2000,[50] has shown that trusted companies enjoy tangible benefits, such as increased sales of products or services and positive word of mouth, at the same time that distrusted companies have suffered losses.[51]

Inform, Persuade, Inspire

With trust gained, organizations have a good chance of achieving their other general business objectives, to inform, persuade, and inspire. Regardless of a specific business objective, anything from advancing an agenda for cultural change to informing others about what the company stands for, stories for business can be informative, persuasive, inspirational, or some combination of these. (These general categories often overlap: a story that is primarily informative can make a persuasive case for an organization as well.)

Stories intended primarily to inform may explain technical subjects that can be dry or inaccessible to anyone but an expert. Gary Sheffer, executive director of corporate communications and public affairs at General Electric, reflects, "Stories bring bigger technical concepts down to the human level and engage and mobilize people. The language of business is so jargony and technical that people stop listening."[52] Tom Martin, formerly a senior communications executive at ITT, underscores how storytelling can bring a technical concept to life by featuring the actions of the hero-inventors: "In hearing about a fifty-year submarine mission, people don't want to read about inanimate objects but about the engineers who figured out the challenge of conducting the mission. Stories connect the things we do to the people we are. They're much better than a catalogue of widgets."[53]

Of course, even if the primary purpose of a business story is to inform, it is never far from efforts to persuade (as noted in the use of stories by lawyers, economists, and city planners in Chapter 1). Ron Culp, partner at Ketchum, a public relations firm, singles out the way that stories can teach without preaching and how this attribute leads listeners by example to act as the storyteller would like:

In an indirect way, stories can get someone to understand why we are doing something. A story can soften a prescription. I can conceal how strongly I feel about an action one of my clients or staffers wants to take by telling a story with a moral. I don't say, "Don't do it. It's stupid. Are you out of your mind?" Instead, I tell a story.[54]

Like Aesop's fables, which deliver moral instruction, Culp's cautionary tales teach obliquely and ultimately persuade by inviting his listeners to imagine the story, take it into their minds and hearts, and draw the necessary conclusions for themselves. Listeners participate, even "own" the story, rather than being lectured to by an authority.

Stories, then, help business leaders put across a point while avoiding heavy-handed didacticism. Betsy McLaughlin of Hot Topic recognizes and uses this capability in her storytelling: "Stories can be a better alternative to pitching your point of view directly. People will listen through to the end of the story and judge later."[55] Such stories do, however, derive much of their power from the gravitas of the storyteller: a storyteller lacking authority based on some combination of expertise, experience, track record, and formal position, or presenting a sloppily conceived or delivered story, doesn't have a chance of changing the attitudes and behavior of an audience.[56]

Using stories to teach and persuade may be a tool to manage *across* to clients or *down* to subordinates (or to one's children in Culp's case) but may also be used to teach and persuade *up*. At GE, senior leaders in charge of potential new products—what are known as "Imagination Breakthroughs"—are required to make their case by standing up in front of CEO Jeff Immelt and telling a story that explains the features of the product and argues for its likely success against the competition. The presenter is restricted to using one slide, preferably a picture of the product.[57]

Sometimes entertainment may need to have a primary place in a story intended for persuasive purposes if there is any hope of achieving the business objective. Case in point: when senior corporate communication expert Perry Yeatman worked in Russia for a PR agency in the mid-1990s, she turned to storytelling to help 180 million Russians understand the country's transformation to a market economy and the implications of the change to their daily lives and to inspire them to change:

Some people working on this project wanted to explain "shareholder" and "share rights," but those unfamiliar with a capitalist system would just not understand this. Instead, we developed a soap opera along the lines of *Dynasty* and *Dallas*, which were popular then. In the soap opera, we told the story of a Russian family living in a market economy. Dad loses his job and then gets a new job. The kids and parents learn they have risks to take, but they also have options. They can travel. They have choice of employment. The stories in this soap opera portrayed what it's like to live in a market economy and portrayed values. Before, if someone lost a job, this was a social stigma. In the soap opera, they'd find a new job and have a life with more options.[58]

In this example—ultimately the most ambitious and broadest kind of business story because it sets out to illustrate the benefits of a free market economy and moves tens of millions of people to change—the story worked where abstract technical definitions would have been met with indifference at best and more likely with fear of the unknown.

SPECIFIC BUSINESS OBJECTIVES: CORPORATE STRATEGY, CULTURE, BRANDING

In addition to achieving general business objectives—to build trust, inform, persuade, inspire—stories have specific practical business objectives. These run the gamut from selling a product by showing how a customer benefited from it to recounting the early days of a company in order to instill pride and purpose in employees. In the best-practice cases, the specific business objectives include building or strengthening corporate strategy, corporate culture, and corporate branding. These important organizational concerns are often interrelated as well. For example, a change in strategy may require changes in culture and corporate branding to reflect the strategic shift. For the sake of clarity, let's take up each dimension separately, beginning in each case with a working definition that will be useful in subsequent discussion.

Corporate Strategy

Strategy expert Richard Rumelt, professor at UCLA Anderson School of Management, defines the term *strategy* as "a set of objectives, policies, and plans that, taken together, define the scope of the enterprise and its approach to survival and success. Alternatively, we could say that the particular policies, plans, and objectives of a business express its strategy for coping with a complex competitive environment."[59, 60]

Strategy guides the near- and longer-term future trajectory of an organization. Mapping this trajectory may be considered, as in the case of Schering-Plough, a "story in chapters." Each chapter defines and illustrates a stage of development, makes a case or argument for it (akin to the argument a lawyer might make about a trial's outcome or a policy maker might make about a city's future), guides the actions to complete the stage successfully, and motivates, even inspires, employees to take steps to achieve the company's strategic goals. The CEO and his leadership team use this story about the future to influence the hearts and minds of employees and to put the company on a successful path.

Although strategy is not typically framed as a "story in chapters," organizational stories often have an important role in illustrating and supporting strategy and strategic change. For example, Chevron uses stories to illustrate and support its "human energy" business, the company's strategic solutions to increased global demand for energy. Philips encourages employees to craft and express stories about how the company's technology can improve people's lives, a change in strategic direction from an earlier focus on technology per se and a way to differentiate the company from the competition by emphasizing customer and end user benefits. Entrepreneurial firms or units in larger organizations may also use stories about strategy, in written plans and presentations intended to convince investors and other significant stakeholders to support organizational growth, as a "story about the future." These communications emphasize the attractiveness of market opportunities and the firm's or unit's value proposition for particular customer segments.[61]

Corporate Culture

All organizations are tribes of one sort or another, and story binds tribes, particularly in matters of culture.

—MARY LANG, Comadrona Communications

Ancient kingdoms used everything from fables, which are short tales with a moral, to epics—long stories begun in the midst of the action and covering a vast panorama of places, heroes, and grand events—to express and celebrate the core values of the kingdom.[62] The "whittling cowboys" of McMurtry's west Texas town built a culture, a sense of community, around storytelling. Today organizational stories can build, express, strengthen, and even celebrate an organization's corporate culture, defined by management experts Eric G. Flamholtz and Yvonne Randle as a set of shared values, beliefs and norms that govern the way people are expected to behave on a day-to-day basis. *Values* are what the organization believes to be important with respect to product quality, customer service, treatment of people, and so on. *Beliefs* are assumptions that people in the corporation hold about themselves as individuals and about the firm as an entity. *Norms* are the unwritten rules that guide day-to-day interactions and behavior, including language, dress, and humor.[63]

As explained by management expert Edgar H. Schein of MIT's Sloan School of Management, corporate culture is the "shared tacit assumptions of a group that have been learned through coping with external tasks and dealing with internal relationships."[64] Established corporate cultures, Schein argues, can be characterized in three ways: as deep, or fundamental to "how to do things, how to think about things, and how to feel" as a member of that culture[65]; as broad, or applicable to what motivates most aspects of workplace behavior, prescribing what is rewarded and what is disapproved of; and as stable, or giving meaning and predictability to behavior.[66] In building his case for the importance of culture, Schein emphasizes that "culture is not just about people and how we manage them. It is not just about teamwork or reward systems. Cultural assumptions develop over time regarding the core fabric of the organization and its basic mission and strategy."[67]

Across the four best-practice cases presented in later chapters, stories are linked to culture in a variety of ways. At Schering-Plough where story is primarily a way of envisioning future strategy and bringing it to life, strong "leader behaviors," such as teamwork, listening, and shared accountability, are expressed in story form. Stories about the leader behaviors also help to introduce new employees from acquired firms to Schering-Plough's culture and, ultimately, to ease the transition of Schering-Plough talent into Merck. Those stories that were repeated, especially ones about the CEO, his values and behavior, had substantial impact. Speaking more generally about the capacity of stories to bring new members into a culture during mergers or acquisitions, Bill Ellet, an instructor in management communication at Harvard Business School, notes: "Storytelling can be critical to on-the-job training. When people tell stories about their organization, they convey information that the audience might not gain in any other way. The stories also have emotional content that can shape how the listeners feel about the organization."[68] Ellet also implies that with repetition, these culture stories take on greater strength.

At Chevron, stories strengthen the culture and communicate the company's values to important stakeholders. "Human energy" stories are not only about the company's corporate brand but also about its central vision and core values: a focus on people, partnerships, and performance and on the importance of ingenuity, high performance, and diversity, among other things. At FedEx, telling stories about employees committed to extraordinary effort and excellence in customer service creates a more unified culture around heroic stories, reaffirms the culture, and inspires similar behavior in others. At Philips, storytelling is itself a significant cultural norm and practice that is built and extended through the widespread network of formal storytelling workshops and supporting activities. The stories themselves embody cultural values and serve to perpetuate and underscore "employee behavior" for carrying out the new strategic focus on how technology and innovation can help improve people's lives.

Though not central to our four best-practice cases, stories at some organizations can convey fundamental *values* by invoking significant historical moments in the life of the company, such as its founding or the development of a breakthrough technology. For instance, at Kraft stories are collected and told about its founder's humble beginnings and the early and subsequent generations' creative scientific work that resulted in iconic brands like Jell-O and Cheez Whiz. At 3M, the story about the invention of Post-it Notes is told and retold to emphasize the company's culture of innovation, which gives room for trial and error with sometimes serendipitous rewards—new inventions—resulting from the freedom to make mistakes. The Post-it Note was one such mistake.

Corporate Branding

According to marketing expert Wally Olins, "brands are devices we use to differentiate between otherwise indistinguishable competitors."[69] For marketing expert Nicholas Ind, "A promise is implicit in a brand. From the combination of corporate messages and experience we believe that we will receive a certain experience from a brand. . . . Whether the promise of performance is delivered or not defines my evolving relationship with the brand."[70] Brands should be true to expectations and aspirational.[71] Distinguishing between product and corporate brands, Paul Argenti of Dartmouth's Tuck School and I have explained that a corporate brand generates many associations and impressions that employees, customers, investors, government, and other stakeholders link to an organization, and helps to create the overall image of an organization in people's minds.[72]

Companies use their corporate brand to influence stakeholders in a variety of ways:

- To promote product attributes that may favorably position a company's products and services relative to the competition's.[73]

- To invite emotional connection, bringing the company closer to people by becoming a familiar presence in their lives.[74]

- To build trusting relationships and, for employees, to instill and reinforce values.[75]

- To demonstrate the behavior of a company's employees, the brand ambassadors. To be effective, a corporate brand must be aligned with an organization's culture, which in turn needs to be understood, appreciated, and acted upon by employees.[76]

- To create an impression that a company is clear and consistent in what it does, communicating a sense of stability. According to marketing expert Olins, "[brands] give us the reassurance that what we have today is the same as we had yesterday and the same as we will have tomorrow."[77, 78]

- To complement and reinforce a company's strategic vision. The brand relies on senior management's involvement in shaping the company's identity and its strategy going forward.[79]

- To raise stock price. Though difficult to measure, positive brand equity occurs, according to marketing expert Kevin Keller, "when a relevant constituent responds more favorably to a corporate ad campaign, a corporate-branded product or service, a corporate-issued PR release, . . . than if the same offering were to be attributed to an unknown or fictitious company."[80, 81]

Although brands can be conveyed in many ways (for instance, through logos, sponsorship of events, PR releases, packaging and design), the focus here is the role of stories in building, supporting, and conveying a corporate brand. Stories can show that the corporate brand is authentic—credible, realistic, and tangible—by anchoring it in specific actions and people who fulfill the brand's promise or have enjoyed the benefits promised by the brand. This is illustrated in the Chevron case and the multitude of stories told about "human energy," its corporate tagline and key branding platform that, like most, is packed with meaning expressed concretely in stories. At the same time, a corporate brand serves as a frame for stories, showing the common themes about the company that unite apparently very different stories. At FedEx, stories strengthen the brand by illustrating its emotional elements like "customer-focused" and "likely to buy." At Philips, stories have a central place in communicating the corporate brand of "sense and simplicity" as well as the sectors' brands, all of which are aligned with the company's strategic focus on end users' needs and aspirations. In sum, stories can take the promise of the brand and make it authentic. Conversely, stories about "broken" or "false" promises told, for instance, by an unhappy customer, employee, or investor may demonstrate that a brand is inauthentic.

The framework for organizational storytelling identifies the key components of storytelling and the relationships among them. The best-practice cases and commentary in the chapters that follow will animate the framework, giving it concrete expression and showing that it can't be mechanically applied. Instead, the primary research data collected for each case guide and constrain how the story of each company can be told and what conclusions, or lessons, can be drawn from that story.

3   STORIES ABOUT STRATEGY: SCHERING-PLOUGH

CEOs who know about storytelling and strategy will bring people along. Storytelling allows you to connect with people and allows them to participate in the story as characters. They will be brought along through the journey. This is not a formula. The CEO must get this in his core.

—TOM SABATINO, executive vice president
and general counsel, Schering-Plough

ASKED ABOUT THE ADVICE he would give to executives and MBA students about storytelling, Tom Sabatino emphasized the need to understand a story as it is linked to strategy, or the next-stage development of a firm, whether one is the head of a company or the manager of a small business unit. Imagining and depicting an organization's future in story form is a powerful function for stories.

The Schering-Plough case illustrates several components of the storytelling framework. Above all, the case demonstrates how stories can help a company achieve the specific business objective of articulating and getting buy-in for its strategy. They help executives convince stakeholders to "picture this future for the organization, find it compelling and achievable, and support its enactment."[1] Rather than the stuff of legend, "story" in this context involves both a vision and a substantiated argument for a particular trajectory proposed for an organization.

As with all the best-practice cases, successful stories at Schering-Plough are authentic and fluent. "Realistic," "tangible," and "credible" have specific meanings at Schering-Plough:

- *Realistic*: The CEO and the management team forge powerful links between the proposed strategic reality and the actions that the company is taking. The story about strategy matches the facts, the actions taken. Words match deeds.

- *Tangible and credible*: With the support of an effective corporate culture, the story is brought to life for employees, who grow to understand how their daily activities play a role in moving the story forward.

Because the story is about next-stage development for the firm, the chief storyteller is necessarily the CEO, who presents and orchestrates authentic stories from the top.

Fluency brings to mind the talents of the CEO as the company's chief storyteller, his ability to persuade and inspire, and similar qualities in his leadership team, as well as the "cohesiveness" of the parts of the story. More specifically, fluent stories are

- *Persuasive and even inspirational*: A story about strategy makes a case for a particular vision of the company depicted in the story, and motivates people to rally behind change.[2]

- *Cohesive*: The story has a flow, a "connectedness" or "narrative logic," such that the beginning leads to the middle and it in turn leads to the end, with the sequencing of action steps or "chapters" having a greater probability of success than would those in alternative stories about the organization.[3]

Let's turn now to the Schering-Plough case, its stories about the future under the leadership of CEO Fred Hassan.[4, 5] A global healthcare company of over fifty thousand people, Schering-Plough conducts research and manufactures and markets drugs in three segments: prescription drugs, animal health, and over-the-counter consumer healthcare products (like Claritin allergy pills, Coppertone sun-care lotions, and Dr. Scholl's foot-care products).[6] Hassan, who had previously been CEO of two other major pharmaceutical companies, joined Schering-Plough as its CEO and chairman in April 2003.

FRED HASSAN'S EARLY DAYS AS CEO OF SCHERING-PLOUGH: COMPANY CHALLENGES

As Fred Hassan began his tenure, he faced a host of challenges that pre-dated his arrival. The Federal Drug Administration (FDA) had imposed a consent decree that required the company to fix both quality and compliance problems in manufacturing drugs in its New Jersey and Puerto Rico plants, remedies that would result in considerable costs. In blunt terms, the company was told to upgrade the plants or to shut down. Schering-Plough needed to execute a multitude of complex corrective actions, such as facility and laboratory upgrades and equipment qualification studies that had to be validated by outside inspectors. Moreover, remediation had to be performed without disrupting manufacturing operations at the troubled plants. Performing both activities, remediation and drug manufacturing, proved to be quite difficult for the plants in question. These challenges, along with other legal ones, eventually required the company to pay nearly one and one half billion dollars in fines or settlements.[7] Among the legal challenges, the company was involved in litigation in Boston and Philadelphia regarding its sales and marketing practices. (These issues were eventually resolved by large payments and the company's agreement to implement compliance training programs.)[8] Not surprisingly, morale was low, as was the company's stock price.

On his third day at the company, Hassan gave a presentation to the company's shareholders at its annual general meeting in which he outlined what his head of corporate strategic affairs, Ken Banta, called a "six- to eight-year journey of transformation from being in severe stress to high performance."[9] In other gatherings, Hassan acknowledged the challenges he had inherited, characterizing Schering-Plough as "a wounded company in prolonged decline . . . but one that can be turned around."[10] Among other things, its stock price had plummeted and key drugs like Claritin and Nasonex had suffered steep declines in market share from July 2002 to July 2003. (The allergy drug Claritin lost its patent protection in 2002 and was thereafter sold over the counter in competition with cheaper generic drugs.) Despite these sizeable challenges, Hassan believed that Schering-Plough had several significant bright and promising dimensions: a global reach of nearly twelve thousand sales representatives, solid R & D with several drugs in early-stage development, leadership in allergy and cancer-care medications, and good first steps in building a senior management team to address the challenges. The company, he added, needed to take a single-stepping-stone approach, "handling one challenge and progress step at a time—like focusing on the next mile of a journey. In this way people can focus on execution of something achievable; however they also see it as a step toward a destination that is clear and compelling."[11]

With his assessment of the company as a backdrop, Hassan, still early in his tenure, articulated his "Action Agenda," or story about the company's future, in five "chapters": *stabilize, repair, turn around, build the base*, and *break out*. And he proposed his case for how Schering-Plough could realize these results. In particular, he highlighted his confidence in the team of senior managers he was assembling and their ability to lead the change agenda. Some of them had followed him from other pharmaceutical companies, but others were brought in from other companies or from within Schering-Plough. The managers either knew from earlier shared experiences or learned about the "need for story and its staying power" and the importance of "culture as the driver of change."[12]

On his fourth day at the company, Hassan announced the story in chapters to employees in a town-hall meeting, which was video broadcast, taped, and rebroadcast. Following the town-hall announcement, Hassan took an extensive road trip to key sites.

THE CHAPTERS OF SCHERING-PLOUGH'S STRATEGY

Called an "Action Agenda," the story about the future was introduced at the first board meeting and then told and retold many times. The story was recounted as a sequence of five chapters:

Stabilize

This chapter began immediately and focused on identifying the company's new "leader behaviors" (described later) and strategic direction. "Stabilize" overlapped with "repair," which centered on the immediate steps the company needed to take to remedy a number of damaging situations.[13] Viewed together, these two chapters ran from April 21, 2003, to the fall of 2005.[14]

Repair

Hassan launched this chapter with a "200-Day Action Checklist" at his November 24, 2003, presentation to various audiences. Publicizing wins built self-confidence among Schering-Plough employees about their role in the story. "Stabilize and repair" involved a range of external and internal activities. Externally, the company needed to respond to the compliance and quality issues raised in the FDA consent decree and to settle legal cases in Boston and Philadelphia. As a result of addressing these problems, the company took its first steps in establishing good relations with the FDA and government stakeholder groups. Internally, the company needed to conduct systematic cost cutting and cost control and reinvest savings in the R & D pipeline for new products; create a system for managing product development; and rebuild customer relations. The human resources needs were substantial as well: the company had to install a new senior leadership team, align and motivate frontline managers, rebuild the sales team, and continue to attract new talent while reenergizing the existing talent.[15] (See Exhibit 3.1, excerpts from Hassan's earnings conference call of April 2004, which identifies key points in the "stabilize and repair" efforts.)

For this stage, building trust with external stakeholders like the FDA and customers was high on the list; at least as important was motivating a demoralized workforce. As one senior manager reflected on these early days: "Fred was dealing with people who were shell-shocked. The company had been flying high with Claritin, but it had lost the patent protection for the drug in late 2002. Fred came in, and he needed to capture the hearts and minds of people."[16]

So let me begin with my observations. As we had predicted last year, our first quarter results reflect the very difficult challenges that we had anticipated and will continue to face throughout '04. . . .

We will continue to take essential actions designed to transform this company into a high-performance competitor. We have continued to invest in the sales force to prepare for the launch of Vytorin which is planned for the second half of this year. We also continue to invest in R & D to help build the company's long-term future. . . .

As we anticipated, the major change actions required in the organization, the impact and the cost of implementing the FDA consent decree, the investment needed to support the key brands, and the very tough competitive situation with many of our major products have been important factors affecting the company's performance. . . .

Overall, *we're pleased to report that we are making solid progress and continue on track with our five-stage action agenda. We have been working on the stabilization and the repair phases, and this work will continue through the bridge year of '04 and, we continue to anticipate, the beginning of the turnaround phase starting in '05.* (emphasis mine)

EXHIBIT 3.1.   Excerpts from CEO Fred Hassan's
Earnings Conference Call of April 2004

SOURCE: "Q1 2004 Schering-Plough Earnings Conference Call," Final.
April 22, 2004. Courtesy of CCBN and FDCH e-Media ©2004

Turn Around

This chapter encompassed the period from late October 2005 to the fall of 2006.[17] Completed in just a year, it was characterized by several actions that yielded solid results.[18] After completing the steps required under the consent decree (which was later dissolved), the company began to regain the FDA's trust. In conjunction with this achievement, Hassan announced: "This is an important milestone for Schering-Plough as we continue to put the issues of the past behind us and make further progress in our Action Agenda. Schering-Plough colleagues have worked hard to establish continuous quality improvement and compliance as part of our culture.

In turn, we have been working diligently to earn the trust of stakeholders. Ensuring quality in our products and systems underpins everything we do."[19] In addition, the right salespeople were hired; the company enjoyed double-digit sales and earnings growth; a new major cholesterol treatment was launched; and the R & D pipeline was advancing. At the same time, the company expanded into other areas of treatment with Remicade (for rheumatoid arthritis and other indications) and into new markets in China, India, Turkey, and Eastern and Central Europe. As an important indication of fundamental internal change, the culture of the organization began to crystallize. This change had taken several years but was now happening as a result of systematic efforts on the part of Hassan and senior management to tell the company's story and to link it to a set of values articulated in a CORE document, which included Schering-Plough's "leader behaviors" (detailed in Exhibit 3.3).

Build the Base

As the phrase "build the base" suggests, this chapter of the story, which began in the fall of 2006, refers to building positive cash flow, launching the later-stage pipeline of drugs, developing an enhanced pipeline, creating a strong general presence, and continuing to gain entry into new markets.[20] Perhaps most central to this chapter was the agreement to purchase Organon BioSciences (OBS) on March 12, 2007, and its subsequent integration into Schering-Plough. This $16 billion purchase was the largest, by far, in Schering-Plough's history. OBS's two operating units, Organon and Intervet, enabled Schering-Plough to expand its presence in pharmaceuticals through a new focus on animal health (Intervet) and women's health and the treatment of the central nervous system (Organon), and through the acquisition of several new drugs in late-stage development. Taken together, these acquisitions added 20,000 people to the 35,000 employed at the company.

The company leadership's telling and retelling of the story, in particular the chapter on building the base, helped to make the integration of OBS a success in the face of significant obstacles. Among these were the initial circumstances for the acquisition. OBS had put together an IPO, and the day before they were supposed to go public, Schering-Plough made an offer to buy the company. OBS never went public. In fact, the people at OBS found out they were sold to Schering-Plough on the day they thought they would go public. The sudden change in direction and the resulting disappointment among the OBS people made integration with Schering-Plough an even greater challenge than it might otherwise have been.[21]

Hassan led the integration effort, holding town-hall meetings in the Netherlands on the day the company announced plans to acquire OBS, and he led with a story about the powerful strategic, scientific, and financial fit between the two companies.[22] He reminded his audiences that integrations often fail because companies get distracted during the period of adjustment, and sales growth may decline because customer relationships tend to be neglected in this climate of uncertainty and rapid change. In addition, the acquiring companies, as he explained, "lose their humility. They get arrogant and assume a takeover mindset. That mindset does not build trust among the new colleagues who will be joining the company."[23] Aware of these failings suffered by other companies, Hassan promised to focus on sales growth and the R & D pipeline, to welcome new colleagues, to motivate talent on the combined team, to achieve synergies, and perhaps most important, to earn people's trust.[24]

Group vice president Alex Kelly, who was involved in these communications, concluded that these town-hall meetings "raised the volume" at the same time that Hassan was open to answering tough questions from his audiences.[25] Another senior leader who participated in the integration effort, Brent Saunders, senior vice president and president of consumer healthcare, provided this summary of the process:

This deal [buying Organon BioSciences] was a deal about strategy. We created a story about why we did the deal that made sense, a story about the science and the pipeline and bringing larger scale to Schering-Plough. Buying Organon and Intervet was part of "build the base." The Organon and Intervet people were angry and disappointed. They wanted to be an independent company. We had to work double time to tell them our story, to establish credibility.

There is power in storytelling to build faith and credibility. We could show how Organon fit strategically into the Action Agenda. We could show this was an actionable and real story, and by doing so we built faith. Stories can build faith. People at Organon were initially skeptical, and the skepticism lasted for some time. We had to work especially hard with the scientists of Organon who were naturally concerned whether their work would be appreciated. We used "high touch" processes to break down the skepticism. There were lots of town-hall meetings. I made forty-seven trips to the Netherlands in fourteen months. I went to all the major locations. Fred and other senior managers, including Tom Koestler, head of R & D, did this kind of travel too. We all told the same story over and over. This sounds simple, but the executive team told the story many, many times, one on one or in group meetings—to one person or to hundreds. It was critical to do this—to show conviction in the journey and the story, to show how 1 [Schering-Plough] and 1 [Organon and Intervet] equals 3.[26]

Four teams of senior global communication managers worked together on this integration effort: a team from Schering-Plough, one from Organon in the Netherlands, one from Intervet, and one from the Organon US communications group.[27]

Organon BioSciences had to make the transition from being an organization in which, according to one senior manager at Organon, "the CEO thought culture was not a high-priority issue,"[28] to one in which the CEO placed great value in culture. The organization needed to go from being an environment of strong subcultures, such as the close and long-term working relationships among scientists on research teams, to one in which the culture of the organization as a whole was most important.[29]

The Dutch, led by Helma Van Leeuwe, were particularly helpful in providing a cultural perspective from outside the United States, preventing potential problems in miscommunication due to differences in language. (For instance, Hassan's reference to a "bulging" pipeline of numerous products and his use of the terms "leadership edge" or "leadership engine" did not readily translate into Dutch or into other languages.)[30] The progress of all the teams, plotted on a Gannt chart (a bar chart that shows a project schedule), provided evidence of the movement toward integration. As Saunders reflected:

Senior managers carried the Action Agenda story. There were 35,000 people at Schering-Plough and 20,000 at OBS. As the teams [of communication professionals] interacted, everyone was saying the same thing. I'd go around the world and look at offices in Thailand or Egypt or France or Russia, and all of them would have the same posters showing the same story. Some posters were in different languages. I'd get e-mails from people in Korea thanking us for accomplishing the story. The story soaked all the way through.[31]

(See Exhibit 3.2 for Hassan's summary statement about the success of the OBS acquisition and integration.)

At the time of this writing, Schering-Plough had achieved early financial success with its OBS purchase, and is still working on "building the base," especially its strong late-stage pipeline.

Break Out: The Chapter That Won't Be Written

This was to be the final chapter of the story, but it won't be written—at least not in the form in which it was originally articulated. Instead, in March 2009, Schering-Plough entered into an agreement with Merck to combine the two companies. Merck had begun to approach Schering-Plough in December 2008, and in the end the premium was too large to be rejected.

ADAPTATION OF THE STORY: INTEGRATION WITH MERCK

The anticipated integration with Merck will mean, in Hassan's words, that "Schering-Plough's story as a stand-alone company will come to a close. There's an end to the chapters."[32] Nonetheless, during this important transitional period, the storytelling capabilities of the firm have come to the fore to support the continued efforts to bolster morale, retain and motivate the company's substantial talent, and build the base in preparation for the integration.

With this big change in course, how has the company continued its storytelling efforts to "build the base"? First of all, Hassan is a strong presence in town halls, in one-on-one dialogues, and in written communications. According to Alex Kelly, group vice president of global communications and investor relations, Hassan doesn't shy away from telling the story about why the integration will occur: "He increasingly became aware in the new competitive environment that the company needed to be bigger to mitigate the risks associated with clinical trials for new drugs and to compete in the current economic climate of Big Pharma, and he recognized the power of the combined R & D capabilities of the firms."[33]

Hassan has appointments to see dozens of people, in large town-hall meetings and in small groups. Aware that cost cutting is typically the

At Schering-Plough we are proud of what we do and of what we have accomplished in the past five years.

Our company begins with science. We seek to discover and make available new and innovative medicines for the patients and physicians who need them—and for the veterinarians, farmers, and others who care for animals.

We have made great progress since 2003 when we launched our Action Agenda. This has been our road map for building a company that can meet our goal to deliver high performance for the long term.

Today, our company is pursuing a broad array of exciting growth opportunities.

The strength and diversity we built under the early years of the Action Agenda enabled us last year to acquire Organon BioSciences N.V. (OBS) of the Netherlands, beginning an important and exciting chapter in our company's transformation. With the Organon franchises, we become a world-class leader in women's health and fertility treatments. With Intervet, the animal health unit of OBS, we become one of the largest animal health organizations in the world. And the expertise and broad project base we had built in our R&D organization has been supplemented by important pipeline projects from the Organon portfolio.

Our new combined company can now do more for the patients, doctors, customers and other stakeholders who depend on us. Meanwhile, we stay resolutely committed to a culture of integrity, to doing what is right for the patients, and to driving high performance for the long term. Our vision remains constant. To earn trust, every day.

One important reason we are confident about this company's future is our people. The colleagues who drive Schering-Plough are the reason for our progress to date. And they will be the reason for our success in the future.

> Sincerely,
> Fred Hassan
> Chairman and Chief Executive Officer

EXHIBIT 3.2.   "A Message from Chairman and CEO Fred Hassan"

SOURCE: http://www.schering-plough.com/company/message.aspx.
Courtesy of Schering-Plough Corporation ©2009

only major focus during most mergers, he instead wants to focus on what the company has accomplished and can continue to do well during the transition. To underscore achievement, he tells stories about the people of Schering-Plough who are the heroes—the scientists who make discoveries that save people's lives; the role of innovation as a generator of the company's strategic difference; and the work of sales and marketing. He emphasizes the importance of company values—getting responsible results within the regulatory environment, being innovative in R & D and in sales and marketing—and how these values have allowed the company to succeed. He talks about the pride that derives from success as a business and as an enterprise for promoting the health and well-being of people. As Vas Nair, vice president and chief learning officer, explains: "Fred wants people to be resilient, to deal with the unexpected, to have passion, courage, and tenacity."[34]

Along with Hassan's involvement, the work of the strategic communications group supports his efforts to keep everyone engaged in building the base and moving through the transition. Global communications executive Van Leeuwe and her team have developed an online magazine called *Splash*. Kelly and Banta led the development of a series of ten videos in which stories are told about employees' core capabilities, accomplishments, and values. These are intended to build employee engagement and acknowledge the company's important work and legacy while creating a repository of memorable moments. In some video clips, Schering-Plough scientists talk about major projects, such as work on a blood-clot treatment for cardiovascular disease, and the teamwork involved in creating new products, as well as what they can mean to patients. These stories emphasize the human side of medical breakthroughs and the capabilities and dedication of the teams working on these efforts. In other video clips, patients themselves talk about life-saving treatment. In one case, a man in his midthirties with a wife and two young children talks about the fear he felt in learning that he had brain cancer and about the difficulty of undergoing surgery for removal of a "lemon-sized" tumor. His neighbor, the patient's good friend and an employee in the finance group at Schering-Plough, then talks about pitching in to mow his friend's lawn during the months the man underwent treatment, and about the pride he felt that his company had created a drug that was helping his friend recover. Employees receive an e-mail alert whenever a new video is rolled out and can access it via a link or on the intranet.[35] The online channel also allows employees to ask and receive responses to their questions about integration.

Although Schering-Plough may not *on its own* move to "break out," executive vice president and general counsel Tom Sabatino thinks of the Merck integration as a "morphing" of the Schering-Plough story, an "alternative ending of a movie," as it were: "Merck comes along and will allow us to 'break out' in a meaningful way. When we complete this integration, we will be able to sustain the momentum and keep the best of the great things we have built, such as the late-stage pipeline of drugs. Through the strengths of the combined companies we can significantly break out."[36]

THE CORE DOCUMENT OF LEADER BEHAVIORS
AND THE COMPANY'S STORY

To ensure that the Schering-Plough story in chapters would be understood and enacted, Hassan introduced a "playbook" for action. Six or seven months after his arrival in 2003, he announced Schering-Plough's six "leader behaviors" in the "CORE" document distributed to the global employee population (Exhibit 3.3). (Hassan had developed and used similar leader behaviors in the successful execution of earlier turnarounds.)

The six leader behaviors were shared accountability and transparency, cross-functional teamwork and collaboration, listening and learning, benchmarking and continuously improving, coaching and developing others, and business integrity. These identified both a set of values and norms of behavior that employees were expected to adhere to and that the company as a whole was expected to follow in advancing through the chapters of the Schering-Plough story. In fact, and as evidence of the strength of the values, they were linked to the story chapters as early as the first leader behavior workshop. For instance, consider a key question that participants were asked to respond to at the workshop: "I understand the importance of the Schering-Plough Leader Behaviors and how they will *fuel our turnaround*."[37] As one manager reflected on the introduction of the leader behaviors in this period of great uncertainty, "The company

Our Leader Behaviors

Our six Leader Behaviors:

- Through **shared accountability and transparency,** we act as owners of our company—taking a broad perspective that considers the long-term implications of our actions and decisions. Shared accountability means that all units and individuals engaged in a project or process take responsibility jointly for getting the job done. We avoid finger-pointing or casting blame when setbacks occur. We exhibit peripheral vision and work with a high level of emotional intelligence. We assure that work is completed and does not fall through the cracks. We take accountability—even when we have to rely on others in our global matrix environment. Transparency means that relevant information is shared freely. In this way, the organization can make the best decisions.

- **Cross-functional teamwork and collaboration** are special strengths required to deliver high performance in our complex, global business. No individual alone has all the expertise or all the answers. On complex issues, multiple inputs, sometimes accompanied by open debate, are usually better than unilateral decisions. We should be proactive in reaching out and working with colleagues—regardless of where they may be on the organization chart. We must accept full ownership of our personal responsibilities, but also work together as an integrated team. We should avoid being held back by hierarchy or departmental and geographical boundaries. We should see success as the job completed—with excellence.

- Active **listening and learning** enable us to encourage and receive constructive feedback, openly share ideas, gain insights and continuously advance our knowledge and skills. We must display the humility to ensure that the winning idea is expressed, heard and acted on. We must listen and learn from our stakeholders, our competitors and each other.

- **Benchmarking and continuously improving** drive us to become the best at what we do. Again, a sense of humility makes this possible. We need to constantly measure ourselves

EXHIBIT 3.3.   "Our Leader Behaviors"

SOURCE: Courtesy of Schering-Plough Corporation

was in trouble then, and Fred was passionate about the six leader behaviors from a people and a cultural perspective."[38]

Hassan himself became the chief spokesperson and exemplary model for these values, using many opportunities in his global communications, both formal presentations and informal discussions, to introduce

every colleague can be a leader

against the strongest competitors and high-performing companies in other industries, assess ourselves candidly and make positive changes. Even after reaching the competitive benchmark, we must keep improving and thus create our own benchmark for competitors to follow. We must ask our stakeholders what they need and expect—and then we need to find ways to exceed those expectations.

• By **coaching and developing others,** we energize one another and build the capabilities needed now and in the future to create a competitive advantage for our company. Coaching can come from any direction—not just the direct supervisor. We must encourage each other to achieve the highest level of professional excellence, and foster an environment that values diversity and rewards growth and achievement.

• **Business integrity** is "doing the right thing." It begins with following the letter and the spirit of the law, and the letter and the spirit of company policies and procedures. Business

integrity also means following our own moral compass to do what is right, even when the rules are not clear, and to ask for counsel and advice when there is any doubt.

How will we know when we are successfully modeling the Schering-Plough Leader Behaviors?

Here are some indicators:

• We feel a real passion for our Mission and our business.

• We demonstrate a clear commitment to constantly learn and understand our business, including areas outside our direct responsibility.

• We are demonstrably committed to the success of our colleagues.

• We are committed to personal success—but not at the expense of other Schering-Plough colleagues.

EXHIBIT 3.3.   Continued

the values and to show their relationship to how the company was moving forward with its strategic story. For example, as Hassan traveled to Spain, he would post letters online about "building the base," saying, in reference to the leader behaviors, "I was pleased to see strong elements of cross-functional teamwork."[39]

Hassan also created a new position, a vice president and chief learning officer. One of the initial responsibilities of the position was to build and manage a thorough and formal approach for introducing the behaviors globally and to ensure that they would be understood, internalized, and acted upon.[40] Vas Nair, who was hired for this new position, ran training, leadership, and development programs for all levels of management worldwide and became responsible for global implementation of the behaviors. (By late March 2004 the behaviors had been translated into German, Italian, Spanish, French, and Japanese.)[41]

As Nair reflected on the early days and later rollout, she noted why the values took hold in powerful ways: "Fred would consistently reiterate their importance in his communications. We also didn't call the behaviors 'leadership behaviors' but, rather, 'leader behaviors,' to underscore that they were not just for the leadership. They were for everyone."[42]

Nair also singled out the importance of line management as well as senior leadership to global acceptance of the leader behaviors. The training and responsibility for implementing the behaviors fell to both groups. For example, once the performance and evaluation process was launched for identifying and measuring "leader behaviors," managers were asked to establish their own development plans to include the behaviors, to receive training in the process, to model the behaviors for others, to coach their team on how to achieve the actions that underpinned the behaviors, and to evaluate the performance of their subordinates.

Each employee was required to put together an individual development plan for using the leader behaviors at work. For instance, for the leader behavior of "listening and learning," employees were asked to do the following: Identify two or more people who can give you a frank assessment of your listening behavior in specific situations; use open-ended questions, those that require more than a "yes" or "no" response; improve nonverbal communication (for example, gestures, eye contact); refrain from multitasking while listening to others; pause before speaking so as not to interrupt someone in midsentence; develop an understanding of cross-cultural communications; and create a learning group at work to continue professional development.[43] For "shared accountability and transparency," employees were asked at a workshop to consider a recent situation in which they had made a decision that either cost or saved the company money, and to extrapolate from this experience lessons for prudent financial decision making.[44] A variety of training opportunities, such as online resources and mentors, were also provided for those who sought to improve or were told they were deficient in one or another behavior. In sum, the CORE document was tied to performance evaluation and pay, and the leader behaviors were reinforced day to day.

Let's look more specifically at how the behaviors came into play in employees' daily activities and in the evaluation of their work. Take the example of Vice President Susan Wolf, who was responsible for governance and social responsibility, and her use of the CORE document in working with her direct reports. Wolf would first meet with each of her managers to help them set individual objectives for developing this skill set. Then she would coach them and observe how they were progressing. Following this, she would conduct performance appraisals of the managers to see how they measured up to each of the six leader behaviors. For instance, in evaluating an employee's ability to "listen and learn," she would want to see whether an employee who had received a complaint from a shareholder who was unhappy with the plastic packaging for Dr. Scholl's had investigated the complaint: Had the employee spoken to the packaging people? What, if anything, was done? Had the employee gotten back to the person complaining? If Wolf was evaluating another employee, in this case a lawyer, on "cross-functional teamwork," she would want to see whether he had productively shared his expertise in document control (managing the comments on and multiple iterations of a legal document) with the other members of the legal team.

Senior management agree about the importance of the leader behaviors. For Executive Vice President Tom Sabatino, they "marked a cultural transformation and a huge accomplishment for the organization."[45] A firm sense of values, a culture of integrity, permeated the firm, and the old bureaucratic silos gave way to a flatter organization in which the CEO was accessible and employees at all levels were moving forward in efforts to listen and learn through more frequent and more focused discussion. Frontline managers and country managers, in particular, felt valued, and expectations for *their* leadership of *their* people were raised. Those who could not embrace the values left the firm; those who embraced them enjoyed being good performers and felt emboldened.[46] For Rick Bowles, senior vice president of global quality operations, "leader behaviors were at the heart of the transformation begun in '03 after a near-death experience, and they were not so much a code of conduct as they were a set of aspirational covenants that created unity within the greater Schering-Plough community."[47]

As the Schering-Plough case illustrates, one use of stories in business is to help stakeholders understand the strategy of a company so that they can envision (and enact) the company's future. Successful stories about strategy are championed by the leadership but rely on a strong and functional corporate culture to make the strategy real and operational to employees, and to gain their support.

4   SCHERING-PLOUGH:
LESSONS LEARNED

A SUCCESSFUL STORY ABOUT A COMPANY'S strategic direction focuses the attention and energies of the full enterprise, requires the coordinated efforts of the leadership, and brings into play formal systems (for example, culture management programs, performance appraisals, reward systems) to bring the story to life. Formulating the story is not even half the job; implementation requires huge sustained effort.

At the beginning of the Schering-Plough case, we noted several qualities that characterize successful stories about strategy. Such stories need to be credible, realistic, and tangible—hallmarks of authentic storytelling. They also need to be persuasive, even inspirational, and cohesive, a challenging aspect of the craft of storytelling and a characteristic of fluent stories. Finally, stories about a company's overarching strategy should be orchestrated from the top. This is a very tall order indeed.

This chapter analyzes the Schering-Plough story, focusing on how the company exhibited these qualities. It may suggest how to think about strategic storytelling in your own circumstances when you are called upon—or decide—to formulate and help implement a story about your organization's or your business unit's future.

BUILD A CORPORATE CULTURE THAT
SUPPORTS THE COMPANY'S STORY

Stories about a company's strategic intent require a culture, a set of agreed-upon values and norms of behavior, that mobilizes individual employees and guides their judgment and behavior as they bring the story to life. In fact, a well-formulated story *in the absence of a culture that supports it* has little chance of being implemented.

Experts in organizational development Eric Flamholtz and Yvonne Randle underscore the central role of a corporate culture—one which employees understand and believe in—in sustaining organizational change, especially in companies with more than $100 million in revenues. According to their research, a culture management plan needs to be part of a strategic management plan for a company of this size. They also warn of the likely detrimental consequences when disparities exist between a company's real culture and its nominal or stated one. Companies must walk the talk.[1]

Too often, corporate statements about culture are no more than a hollow rhetoric, a list of platitudes stapled on the walls of headquarters and left to fade and die of inattention, promoting cynicism in their wake. Instead, statements about culture need to be "baked into" the organization through training, example (especially from those at the top), performance evaluations, reward systems, metrics—and, of course, stories. At Schering-Plough, the leader values were defined, linked to the unfolding strategic story, taught, and evaluated. Employees were assessed and rewarded for performance in aligning their actions to the leader behaviors. And these were ongoing, iterative processes. "The Action Agenda [the story] is the journey," remarked Vice President Tom Sabatino, "but the CORE document [the "leader behaviors"] showed us how to operate as a company as we got there."[2]

The CORE document was a set of values that was brought in at the beginning of Hassan's tenure. It helped make the story tangible and credible, key characteristics of authentic storytelling. Ken Banta, Head of Corporate Affairs, reflected on the importance of the CORE: "The cultural element embodied in the CORE document made the content of the story meaningful. Early on there was a sense that there was a huge and unsolvable set of problems—going from survival to stability and then beyond. We needed to break the problems down into smaller pieces that were manageable."[3]

USE THE STORY AS A TOUCHSTONE TO GUIDE
AND TRACK STRATEGIC DECISIONS

An organization's leadership needs to consistently and repeatedly refer to the parts or "chapters" of the story as the company moves forward, showing how the story guides decision making and tracks decisions against the story. If stories of the future are to be authentic, then words must be accompanied by deeds.

In describing the important link between words and deeds, Banta noted that "there was coherence in the story in the sense that an action taken was linked to the stage or chapter of the story to which it belonged. Every two or three weeks the CEO would send a letter to all employees, and he would constantly link actions taken to where the company was in the bigger journey."[4] Thus, when the company completed the turnaround, Hassan took a road trip, making presentations that showed where the company was in terms of the Action Agenda, and connecting metrics to the turnaround. Measurement—numbers—confirmed the completion of the chapter.

In addition to making these connections for employees, Hassan would link the actions taken to the story in his communications with the financial community and the media. After all, a story about strategy has important external as well as internal audiences. Note his discussion in a conference call to investors in the first quarter of 2004: "We are making solid progress and continue on track with our five stage action agenda. We have been working on the stabilization and the repair phases and this work will continue through the bridge year of '04 and we continue to anticipate the beginning of the turn-around phase starting in '05."[5] The overarching story is then given substance through discussion of specific achievements. Similarly, in a 2005 report of financial results, Hassan announced that the turnaround phase was about to begin and followed this with a discussion of concrete achievements in sales of pharmaceuticals, partnerships, and an enlarged pipeline of new drugs.[6]

A story about the future can provide the criteria against which to make strategic decisions and to make sense of them. As Vice President Wolf reflected: "Using storytelling and strategy helped us see what assets are dear and where the flaws are, what's important and what's not critical. So, for 'build the base,' we added two new therapeutic areas, women's health and central nervous system drugs, and continued with the strong pipeline."[7]

Stories embedded with relevant numbers and their interpretation are authentic. As we discussed in Chapter 2, numbers are not at odds with story; rather, as Banta explained, they can demonstrate the truthfulness of a company's stories: "Data provided proof points about where we were in the story. We looked at quarterly results, and we also had International Health Survey Research monitor the organization's health. The first surveys in 2003 indicated that there was demoralization and lack of focus, but newer surveys revealed that there was a transformation in the health of the organization. People felt they could speak out freely."[8]

As long as the storyline is not overwhelmed by numbers, stories embedded with numbers can retain their inspirational quality, an important business objective of stories about strategy. There is a fine balance between the two. According to Sabatino,

The chapters of the story are more tangible than numbers alone. People can feel the phase; people are living at that point in the narrative. The story encourages people, gets them excited, because "we all have done that. We've all gotten through the plains and are at the Rockies headed for California." Stories are important plans for a company. Sometimes companies are too short-term focused on the quarterly results. Fred said early on, "Here's the plan for the next several years. Here's a company we can be proud of for many years from now."[9]

Other instances of the link between story and strategic action, between word and deed, abound. For example, the purchase of Organon BioSciences was communicated to employees as part of "building the base," as was the report of a new use for the drug Remicade.[10] Even setbacks, like the Vytorin problem (during the "build the base" chapter) were discussed in the larger context of the story: Yes, there were problems with Vytorin, a combination of Schering-Plough's Zetia and Merck's Zocor, when results of a research study put in question the drug's effectiveness in treating heart disease relative to Zocor alone or to a cheaper generic drug; but the company was still continuing with the story of "building the base" by, for example, investing in R & D and integrating with Organon and Intervet.

Authenticity in storytelling also means the avoidance of hype, and often leaders must exercise considerable restraint not to "get ahead of the facts." Although a CEO might be tempted to label a $1.6 billion acquisition like Organon BioSciences as an indication of the "breakout" stage, Hassan did not (breakout would have required a whole set of blockbuster advances and metrics to substantiate the move to the new chapter). As one employee noted, the CEO "would remind us where we were in the chapters. 'We're on track or we're in phase three.'"[11] If a story gets ahead of the facts, the overinflated claims about a particular decision (such as the purchase of another company) can undermine trust in the story—and the storyteller. Stick to the facts, interpret them judiciously, and reap the benefits in the long run.

Without the necessary links between the story expressed and the actions taken, stories about the future can be grandiose schemes far removed from reality. This is inauthentic storytelling to the extreme. Think, for instance, about the Enron debacle, one among several major scandals in the last decade or so. Here was a story about the company's future, unfolded in Jeffrey Skilling and Kenneth Lay's last letter to shareholders (among other communications) that piles up a dizzying enumeration of hyperbolic claims about the company's past success and future prospects. Summarizing the track record of the company, Lay brags that "Enron hardly resembles the company we were in the early days. During our 15-year history, we have stretched ourselves beyond our own expectations. We have metamorphosed from an asset-based pipeline and power generating company to a marketing and logistics company whose biggest assets are its well-established business approach and innovative people."[12] His story for the future is even more exaggerated. Here are excerpts from the same letter:

Enron has built unique and strong businesses that have tremendous opportunities for growth. These businesses . . . can be significantly expanded within their very large existing markets and extended to new markets with enormous growth potential. At a minimum, we see our market opportunities company-wide tripling over the next five years. . . . [13]

No other provider has the skill, experience, depth and versatility to offer both energy commodity and price risk management services, as well as energy asset management and capital solutions. . . . [14]

Our performance and capabilities cannot be compared to a traditional energy peer group. Our results put us in the top tier of the world's corporations. We have a proven business concept that is eminently scalable in our existing businesses and adaptable enough to extend to new markets.[15]

Of course, the fundamental problem with this story about the future is that it is in fact a shared delusional fantasy that relies for its flimsy and precarious foundation on group think and a culture of deceit and on disregard for anything resembling ethical practices. The lack of substantive, data-based analysis is breathtaking.

Were the detachment from reality of a story about an organization's future not a serious matter but rather an occasion for comedy, one would be reminded of the farcical antics of the fictional leader Picrochole in Rabelais' classic French novel *Gargantua*.[16] This narcissistic, arrogant, and greedy prince, who rules in an obscure corner of France, aspires to a position of universal monarch. To realize his goals, he accedes joyfully to his fawning advisors' story about the future, namely a tale of rapid, easy conquest of the world's extant kingdoms, beginning with neighboring regions and moving vertiginously on to the far reaches of the known world: Tunisia, Algeria, the Barbary Coast, Majorca, Minorca, Sardinia, Corsica, Languedoc, Provence, Rome, Naples, Sicily, Rhodes, Jerusalem, and on and on. In his manic enthusiasm for the story, he takes over the verbal construction of this megalomaniacal vision and piles up many more territories in the catalogue of proposed conquests. His is yet another grandiose story about the future spiraling into the ether and setting the stage for the downfall of its creators—a story that is comical in its pure excess but not so far removed from the corporate cases of delusional storytelling we have seen and their serious consequences for all parties involved.

BE FLUENT: TELL A COHESIVE
STORY ABOUT THE FUTURE

The five chapters of the Schering-Plough story had an inherent "connected-ness" or "narrative logic" as we understand these terms. The sequencing of the chapters makes good sense: the company needed first and second to stabilize and repair, third to turn around, fourth to build the base, and fifth to break out. Each new chapter depended on the ones that preceded it, and the sequencing of chapters was logical.

Given the substantial challenges that Hassan faced when he took the reins, one might have expected the firm to go careening from one remedial short-term action to another, reacting defensively and haphazardly to improve things in a scattershot fashion. These actions would most likely have been complemented by story fragments, by bits and pieces: here an announcement and there a PowerPoint presentation featuring chunks of unrelated pieces of information.[17] In other words, there would have been no story, just fragments and sound bites. In fact, the Schering-Plough story had a strong narrative logic: the sequencing of the chapters represented the logical stages of organizational development, and the CEO referred frequently to the chapters as they related to specific actions the company was undertaking.

ORCHESTRATE THE STORY FROM THE TOP
WITH AUTHENTICITY AND FLUENCY

People want to feel touched. They want the CEO to walk the talk.

—KEN BANTA, Head of Corporate Strategic Affairs

There is a wealth of literature about the role of the CEO as chief strategist for the organization, some of which invokes the origins of the term *strategy* in the Greek word for *generalship*. From this perspective, strategy is about winning and accomplishment and about the CEO leading the way—the CEO who sets overarching goals in a climate of risk and uncertainty, understands a dynamic and competitive business environment, recognizes the oftentimes ephemeral nature of external opportunities, penetrates the confusion of competing policy frameworks, mobilizes organizational capabilities, and in the end, may achieve the desired objectives.

To this list of capabilities one must add the need for the CEO to be the organization's chief storyteller about strategy. He or she needs to assume "narrative authority," that is, take the discursive space as the major champion of new strategic realities for the firm as a whole. Even in instances when several leaders in an organization proffer competing stories about strategy, which may be negotiated through dialogue and debate, the resolution—the story that's agreed upon—needs to be spearheaded by the CEO. By leading this effort, a CEO can set direction, boost morale, and instill employees' confidence in the organization and its leadership.

In many cases, the CEO is the subject of stories as well as the chief storyteller, and the best of these go viral. For example, when Hassan held a meeting of the salespeople early in his tenure, he told them that he didn't want them to do anything that was unethical just to make a sale. In effect, losing business was okay. When he made this announcement, the salespeople stood up and applauded. This story about the CEO was then repeated throughout the organization, becoming part of the company folklore and serving as an example of the CORE principle of integrity.

In identifying his choice of CEOs with powerful storytelling skills— Herb Kelleher of Southwest Airlines and Jerry Adamic of MCI—communication professor James O'Rourke IV of Notre Dame's Mendoza School of Business explains:

Both were brilliant at conveying the sense of corporate culture, confidence, and continuity they wanted. Their stories were always true, but they were intended to be repeated. Hence they became embellished and morphed in many ways. It is through repetition that Kelleher and Adamic achieved their greatest success because their stories went viral and spread through the fabric of the system. They ultimately became part of the lore of the company.[19]

Leaders like Hassan shape the larger strategic story for their organization. They put into words and pictures the current story of the firm—its history, products, and services, its accomplishments in business and as corporate citizens—as well as their vision for the firm's future direction and why and how they think it is achievable. From this perspective, the "story about the organization's future" is really a kind of argument, a case for the direction and scope of the company's growth based on analysis, data, and the capabilities of its leadership.[20]

A CEO's story can also refer to "ministories," based on the business or taken from other sources, or brief personal anecdotes that get at the heart of a company's strategy and culture. For example, in presentations to employees, CEO Sergio Marchionne of Fiat would tell a story about the White Rabbit from *Alice in Wonderland* and a story about Napoleon. The literary example and the history lesson serve as provocative ways to stimulate the redirection of the company's strategy and to rebuild the culture. Each story conveyed an important strategic point. The White Rabbit, that frenetic hare who runs in circles, is always late, and never seems to get anywhere, represented the CEO's assessment of how work was often done at the company. The story about Napoleon highlighted the emperor's unorthodox way of conducting battle, an approach that undermined the enemy's tactics. Marchionne used the stories to signal the need for disruptive change in strategy and culture.[21]

To illustrate the strategic differentiation of his firm, the CEO of a real estate investment firm I've worked for likes to begin his presentations to investors by telling a brief anecdote about how he would discuss the "Waldo" books with his young son at bedtime. ("Waldo" books are big, multicolored picture books that invite children to hunt for the figure of Waldo in a crowd—in a football stadium, at a train station, or in a big city.) Holding up a copy of the picture book in front of the investors, he explains how he realized during one of these bedtime-story sessions that his company reminded him of successful "Waldo hunters" who are good at finding Waldo hidden in a crowd. In other words, his company's strategic differentiation from the competition is its ability to seek out "Waldos"— undervalued and undeveloped commercial properties, such as hotels or office buildings—to purchase these Waldos, develop them, and sell them at a substantial profit to the company and its investors.[22]

The rest of the investor presentations, his and his staff's, consists primarily of financial analysis of current properties as the basis for projections about future earnings. (The presentation slides serve as written documentation or "stand-alone takeaways" for the investors.) Were we to ask investors what they remembered from the presentations, we would likely hear them say that it was the Waldo story: a story about the company's strategy presented by its senior leader; a gestalt of what differentiates the company from the competition; and an example of self-disclosure on the part of the CEO in his effort to connect emotionally and personally with investors, to show his human side as well as his strategic acumen.[23]

For the chief storyteller about strategy at Schering-Plough, what communication style was effective and what might work elsewhere? Openness is essential. Banta, who works closely with Hassan on his speeches, says that the CEO "wants to communicate with people that they've been listened to. He wants to connect with them emotionally and give them a sense of ownership, a sense of where we've been, where we are, and where we're going."[24] Another member of Hassan's senior team describes Hassan as "genuine," as "having a sense of humility," as "the opposite of the imperious CEO."[25] Yet another observes that "he is incredibly engaging, but not a polished speaker or a movie actor. The delivery of his speech is not perfect, but it's genuine, and he articulates where we're going."[26]

In reflecting on Hassan's communication style with external stakeholders, Rob Lively, vice president of corporate government affairs, observed that "Fred has a disarming openness. There's no pretention, no ego, a sense of humility. This is a man you feel you can trust and bond with and want to help. In a lunch with Max Baucus [senator from Montana], we were told that Baucus had just one hour. He ended up giving Fred two and a half hours. Fred builds confidence and trust."[27]

Hassan's business intelligence comes through clearly as well. As an onlooker to Hassan's conversation with Jon Corazine, then United States senator from New Jersey and former co-CEO and chairman of Goldman Sachs, Lively immediately noticed the "high speed of transmission, the high speed of exchange of answers between the two. These are the big brains of business discussing things. Corazine's face lit up when he sensed he was talking to someone at his level."[28] In speaking to other members of Congress who are not as versed in business, Hassan talks more in terms of overarching goals, people, and processes, weaving a story about the company in the context of the overall societal good it can contribute: "Fred is passionate about where the drugs end up," concluded Lively. "He wants to help someone with cancer, to help a child. He draws out things he sees at trips to the labs, for example, and describes them."[29]

In reflecting on his accomplishments as a CEO and chief storyteller, Hassan's leadership team underscored three qualities: his ability, as is the case of every skillful storyteller, to engage hearts and minds; the sense of direction he provides; and the positive spirit and confidence he instills:

Fred came and fixed things, and he tried to capture people's hearts and minds. He provided a sense of direction for the company, where the company could go. With his vision he engaged colleagues every day. He was open and transparent about what was happening in CEO messaging and in town halls. Telling people what was going well and what was not going well was refreshing to people. That approach built trust. As we moved through the Action Agenda, people felt, "I got it," and we saw this positive reaction in employee surveys.[30]

Fred put out the Action Agenda, and it took the Schering-Plough people ten months for them to believe in it. We did employee surveys and we scored off the charts in high morale and faith in management. The primary cause for this was the story, the Action Agenda. It brought everyone together.[31]

When we started, people were demoralized and had no sense of direction. There was no road map. With the story, people had a sense of the future, but there needed to be a lot of follow-through. Initially there was lots of skepticism, but what was new was that there was a story. The story gave people realistic hope who had felt there was no future. They could see the story unfolding and that it was more than just a turnaround. Fred did not say that the turnaround was the ultimate goal. The turnaround was a step going forward. It was not just about cuts and the bottom line. With all of this there grew new energy, constant transformation. We were not reaching for a steady state, but for new thinking and new capabilities.[32]

RECOGNIZE STORYTELLING AS AN ANCHOR, A STRATEGIC ASSET, AND A LEGACY

As we saw earlier, the announced integration of Schering-Plough with Merck brought, in Hassan's words, "an end to the story with chapters," which fell during the "build the base" chapter. Nonetheless, the company's storytelling capabilities take on a key role in this important period of transition as an anchor in rough waters, a strategic asset, and a legacy.

Why "rough waters"? According to human resource management experts Lea Peterson and Stella Voules, mergers and acquisitions are often fraught with significant challenges, which may threaten the stability of ongoing business operations, undermine confidence in the senior team, and diminish the chances for a company to retain talent.[33] Various leaders at Schering-Plough have expressed concerns:

Our story is coming to an end, and this is tough on people. It's tough for them to understand because the Action Agenda was so powerful.[34]

It's generally hard to keep people together during an integration; usually there's a letdown. People are distracted, and we need to find ways to keep it together.[35]

There are stresses and strains. People on our side have been through adversity and then upward movement, and now there is Merck. We understand that we need to be bigger and tougher in getting to market. Still there is a sense of loss.[36]

Here is a company that has made great strides in a few short years and is now asked to take on another big challenge: integration with Merck. Here is a company with a powerful story and an effective culture—one that had "turned around" and is "building the base"—and now is asked to make an abrupt change: integration with Merck.

Senior management at Schering-Plough appear to have the experience and expertise to address these challenges, and the storytelling capabilities of the leadership and the organization as a whole have a prominent role in this regard. As Banta summarized: "There have been various shocks to the system—the Organon integration was tough. People were asking, 'Will I have a job?' And there were shocks with the cholesterol franchise. These things are destabilizing, but in many parts of the company the culture did hold. The integration into Merck is another significant shock. But taking this into consideration—the various shocks—the approach of using stories pays off."[37]

Authentic and inspirational stories centered on the achievements and values of employees and the company as a whole can serve as both a strategic asset and a legacy as the company moves through the process of integration. The stabilizing and unifying influence of storytelling in this time of change plays out in two ways:

- In the CEO's voicing the reasons for the integration and in his decision to communicate directly—online, in town halls, one-on-one—across the organization. This is especially important because oftentimes employees other than senior leadership are insufficiently informed and prepared for change. When communication with employees is limited, only a small group of insiders connect to the change while others are left behind.

- In the "cascading" efforts of senior and line managers to speak repeatedly and continue the dialogue with direct reports in meetings, focus groups, and one-on-ones about the change and its impact on individual employees' futures

The key message or story about integration that is presented is threefold: it will allow for a more robust business due to the increased size and capabilities of the combined organization in times of increased competition; in preparing for the integration, Schering-Plough will continue to go forward with building the base; and the company's talent will be acknowledged and rewarded in the process.

Although the clarity of the CEO's story about integration with Merck and his accessibility are essential to anchoring the firm as it travels through the rough waters of integration, clarity alone is insufficient. Story needs to inspire and instill pride—to foreground the company's legacy and, as one member of the senior team describes it, to show that we "embrace our original ideals."[38] Through stories of company heroes, scientists, and others in the online employee magazine *Splash*, employees are reminded of the pride they can take in what they have accomplished in the earlier chapters of the story; encouraged to stay the course and go with their strengths to Merck; asked to reflect on the lives they have saved or significantly improved through the drugs provided to the marketplace; and urged to continue with their mission of helping people. The Schering-Plough story is coming to an end. Nonetheless, the storytelling capabilities of its talent have a good chance of crossing over as a strategic asset to Merck and as one of the company's legacies to its employees.

APPLY LESSONS LEARNED FROM THE SCHERING-
PLOUGH CASE TO YOUR WORK

You may not have the authority or responsibility to set the strategic agenda for an entire organization, as was the case for Schering-Plough's CEO, but you may very well want to turn to storytelling on a smaller scale to support your initiatives at work.[39] Gaining acceptance and support for them often poses daunting challenges as you bring them forward in the busy and oftentimes politicized arenas of organizational life. In a sense you are saying to the people you want to influence, "Picture this future for the organization, find it compelling and achievable and support its enactment."[40] To do so requires trust and imagination on the part of those you want to influence and considerable persuasive capability on your own.

As we have seen, stories can get a hearing above the roar of competing communications because they can engage people's hearts as well as their minds, tapping into some of their earliest experiences with discourse that makes sense of their world and its possibilities as the story is narrated by a trusted guide. In the most powerful stories about the future, people can imagine themselves as characters in the story, which represents an improved state of things.

If your general business objectives are to persuade—and even inspire—as is the case for stories that support your initiatives, your efforts to get people to embrace them can come up against substantial challenges. If broad and ambitious, an initiative can disrupt people's view of how things should or can be in the organization; compete with counterstories, different views of the future proffered by others; and face the power of organizational inertia, which is often underestimated (Why don't we just continue to do things as we always have?).

In my work as a communication consultant, I have helped many hundreds of professionals address these challenges. Exhibit 4.1 provides a checklist that identifies questions relevant to these challenges along with commentary about the questions. Consider the checklist and commentary when you are planning and deploying a story that supports your strategic initiatives. The questions are based on both the Schering-Plough case and my work with business professionals.

- *Identify the people whose support is essential to your success*: Whose support do you need? Whose support can you afford to lose with little or no cost to your initiative? Focus on the former.

- *Determine what will motivate people to resist or support your initiative*: Do you know what may influence them to resist your story of the future, such as bad experience with trying to implement a similar agenda, different interests than your own, or low morale? What biases or competing agendas—if any—may make people resistant to supporting your efforts? Do you have sufficient knowledge of what will motivate people to go along with your initiative? Can you appeal to them through shared values and the likelihood of positive outcomes that you can embed in your vision of the future in story form? Can you include their concerns, interests, values, and even their language in your story about the future? If inertia motivates them *not* to act, can you show the negative consequences of doing nothing and how your story about the future addresses compelling problems and provides solutions that are, in the words of one of my colleagues, a "pill" to alleviate the pain, and not merely a "vitamin" to make a good or benign situation a little better?

- *Consider whether you'll need different versions of the story for different stakeholder groups*: If your story of the future requires that different action steps be taken by different groups or individuals, can you provide a realistic, tangible picture of how they are participants in the story and tailor it to address their needs and the actions you want them to take? If, on the one hand, branch managers will be required to work with greater independence and risk to their bottom line, how do you address this in the story? If, on the other, those in research and development will have greater access to investment funds, what emphasis would you then give to that element of the story? A story about a new vaccination for pigs

EXHIBIT 4.1. Checklist for Using Stories
to Support Your Strategic Initiatives

and salmon needs to focus on the biochemistry for the scientific community, but on commercial possibilities for investors. Can you adjust the length, point of view, details, and language of the story to increase the likelihood of a positive response from different stakeholders? In other words, what modifications can you make in your story to respond to their circumstances and expectations?

- *Identify the "pulse points" of your story*: How should you begin your story; what moments should be emphasized in the middle; and what should be the end point given the objective you're trying to accomplish?

- *Assess whether the company's culture and reporting structure will help or hinder your initiative*: Will elements of the organization's culture and the informal and formal reporting structures interfere or assist with your ability to influence others? For instance, is yours a culture of open collaboration and debate, or are new visions squashed unless they are authored by those with formal authority or with informal sources of power that you don't enjoy? Are reporting lines rigid, or can you cut across these divisions with impunity?

On the basis of your understanding of the people you want to influence, consider a communication strategy for shaping and deploying your story:

- *Decide whether the story is sufficiently broad or ambitious in scope to warrant story chapters*: As in the Schering-Plough case, does it make sense to segment your story into chapters and require completion of one chapter before moving on to the next?

- *Figure out what compromises you are willing to make in the goals and scope of the story about the future*: What aspects of the initiative are you willing to open to negotiation? On what aspects are you inflexible? Since your story may be deployed in a highly dynamic and contested arena in which multiple parties are vying

EXHIBIT 4.1.   Continued

for air time and resources, how do you persuade people to support your initiative in these circumstances? Can you, for example, include some elements of *their* story about the future in the one you're proposing? What insights and concerns of those you must influence can you incorporate in your initiative?

- *Monitor your key stakeholders' responses to your story*: What can you learn about people's attitudes about you and your initiative as you begin sharing the story with others? What information or persuasive appeals might convince them to go along with your initiative? What can you learn from the critiques of trusted colleagues and from formal or informal surveys about how your story is received? For example, are you overly ambitious or too modest in your goals? Is your story a touchstone that guides decisions; that is, a set of criteria by which to judge what actions should be taken?

- *Develop supporting material to accompany your story*: Since data and analysis are powerful companion pieces to a story and can also be embedded in it, what can you provide to support and supplement your story? For instance, do you have relevant financial models, macroeconomic data, best-practice cases from similar organizations, or prior analyses of the challenges you're facing?

- *Decide who should champion your initiative*: Do you enjoy sufficient credibility to be the major advocate for your initiative; that is, do you have the requisite experience, expertise, track record, and relationships within and outside the organization? Would it be preferable to step aside or take a subordinate role and have others champion the story? Since stories generate their staying power through being retold by multiple storytellers, who can you enlist and how?

- *Determine the sequence in which to seek people's support*: Would it make sense to begin with your strongest supporters, who are ideally those who would be frank with you about your likelihood of

EXHIBIT 4.1.   Continued

success—and what you might do to improve your story? Should you tell your story about the future first to peers, subordinates, those at a higher level of the organization, or other stakeholders?

- *Choose the right moments and the best settings*: When will the people you want to influence be most receptive to your story and most likely to go along with the vision of the future you're depicting in story form? Should you tell the story at a regularly scheduled organizational event, such as a monthly meeting? When are the worst times to introduce your story (for instance, during the busiest time of a work cycle)?

- *Orchestrate your communication of the story*: What is the best mix of communication channels for telling your story? Face to face? Informal or formal presentations? E-mail? Formal written reports? Speaking allows you to accomplish several things: learn immediately from the nonverbal responses (for instance, facial expression, body language), questions, and comments of your listeners whether your message is understood and well received; adjust what you have planned to say in response to your audience's questions, comments, and nonverbal responses; establish a personal rapport with your listeners; take advantage of the positive impression you can make on people by the way you look and speak; and clarify and reinforce written messages. Writing (e-mail or formal written communications) allows you to create a permanent record of your message; to be certain that the details of your message are communicated; to provide readers with a reference; and to clarify and reinforce messages delivered orally. Sometimes your organization's cultural norms about channel choice dictate your decision about whether to speak or to write. (The discussion of channel choice is based on Janis Forman with Kathleen A. Kelly, *The Random House Guide to Business Writing* [New York: McGraw-Hill, 1990], 589.)

EXHIBIT 4.1.   Continued

In the opening of the Schering-Plough case, Tom Sabatino, executive vice president and general counsel, told us that "CEOs who know about storytelling and strategy will bring people along. Storytelling allows you to connect with people and allows them to participate in the story as characters. They will be brought along through the journey."[41] This is true not only for CEOs but for leaders of small firms and of business units in large ones who know about storytelling and strategy. Even if you work for a small firm or manage a business unit for a large one (and have little or no access to experts from a corporate communication function or a PR agency), thinking about your organization's or your unit's future in story form adds a powerful dimension to your efforts to shape the direction that your organization or unit will take.

As we have seen in the Schering-Plough chapters, stories, even stories about strategy—a business function that is often thought of as primarily analytical and metrics-based—can touch the hearts and minds of people while promoting organizational agendas in a compelling way. Stories can give a human face to an organization, boosting morale and imbuing confidence in its leadership. They can create a human link between the teller of the tale and the audience, and in doing so, the whole "tribe," the organization or the business unit, can go forward on the same journey. Even if the journey of that business comes to an end, its storytelling capabilities can live on as a legacy—an inheritance—from which its former employees can benefit.

5   STORIES AND
      THE CORPORATE
      BRAND: CHEVRON

COMMENTING ON HER COMPANY's branding platform, Helen
Clark, manager of corporate marketing at Chevron, underscored
how "Human Energy" creates a huge set of associations in people's minds
and how stories bring the brand to life, distinguishing the company from
the competition through an emphasis on people:

"Human Energy" is not just a slogan or tagline. It's an expression of what we
do every day and why we do it. It is grounded in a core belief in the potential of
people, their ingenuity, and the importance of partnership. Human Energy is
about people working together to keep the world moving forward. Why stories?
Because we are a people company and choose to show this. We want people to
experience us from this perspective, and humans tell great stories. They don't
just relate facts.[1]

Anyone opening Chevron's external Web site in 2010 would have seen
Human Energy stories featured at the top of the home page. These included stories about producing energy, using it efficiently, and working with
communities. Despite their diversity in content, each extended people's
understanding of Human Energy.

As the storytelling framework identifies, authentic and fluent storytelling, such as Chevron's, can build trust in an organization, a general

business objective, and can strengthen the brand, a specific business objective. In the case of Chevron, stories can support the trustworthiness of the corporate brand and, by extension, the company. Stories about a brand that are credible, realistic, tangible, and intended to be truthful give people confidence in the brand, and well-crafted stories engage and hold people's attention.

The Chevron case focuses on the complex, mutually enriching relationship between authentic, fluent stories and corporate brand. The case illustrates how such stories make the corporate brand concrete and credible; how they rely on accurate data while appealing to the heart; how they may evoke the values of the broader culture, appealing to what is admired in the human spirit; and how much is lost if stories are absent or play a minor role in a brand campaign.[2] The case also shows how a brand that lives up to its promise can serve as a frame or filter for choosing and giving meaning to organizational stories.

From one vantage point, a brand tagline frames corporate stories, serving as an umbrella that includes under it stories and specific brand attributes and behaviors that the stories illustrate. Whether the tagline is Chevron's "Human Energy" or GE's "Imagination at Work" or Dow's "Human Element" or Philips's "Sense and Simplicity," it assigns meaning (or meanings) to a story just as a moral assigns meaning to that very old story type, the fable. From another vantage point, stories bring a brand to life. Then, too, since the brand is the expectation or promise of performance,[3] stories, their concrete agents and actions, show that a company is trustworthy—has "lived the brand," has delivered on expectations, has "walked the talk."

Although brands can be conveyed in many ways (for example, through logos, sponsorship of events, PR releases, packaging and design), our focus here is on stories and the corporate brand, using the best-practice case of Chevron and the roles that stories play in its corporate brand platform, "Human Energy."[4] A global energy company of over sixty thousand people, Chevron has oil and gas operations, including the discovery, drilling, and production of crude oil and natural gas as well as the refining and marketing of natural gas and other petroleum products.[5] We begin by describing the challenges out of which "Human Energy" emerged.

O'REILLY AND THE NEW ENERGY EQUATION

In June 2004, David J. O'Reilly, CEO of Chevron Corporation (then called ChevronTexaco), gave a speech to the US Chamber of Commerce, a forum made up of close to 250 business and civic leaders. In his talk, O'Reilly emphasized that global energy challenges were exerting accelerated pressure on world economic activity and underscored the urgency of these challenges: "How we manage them [energy issues] will play a role in national security, the economic health of our nation, and the overall quality of our lives. . . . It [energy] is quite literally the lifeblood of our economies."[6] Summarizing this set of problems in a language outsiders to the energy industry would understand, O'Reilly called these challenges a "New Energy Equation": *Increased* global demand for energy accompanied by *increased* difficulty in meeting this demand as sources of energy dry up and geopolitical complexity accelerates.

As the CEO developed his argument, he referred to the growing accumulation of statistical evidence that supported the seriousness of the challenges. Growth in global energy demand would expand by 40 percent over a thirty-year period. Car ownership in China would increase by thirty million in five years. Demand for cleaner-burning natural gas would rise by 25 percent for the next fifteen years in the United States. US refineries were running at near full capacity. At the same time, this crescendo of worldwide demand would come up against inadequate supply and barriers to increasing it. As O'Reilly explained, "Another new complexity in the energy equation is this: It is becoming more challenging—and more expensive—to develop new production sources today. In many places, the easy discoveries are behind us." Besides the technological challenges of extracting oil from deep waters or other remote areas, geopolitical ones would emerge where deposits were located in politically unstable parts of the globe.

To address this host of problems, this "New Energy Equation," O'Reilly stressed the need to value resources and use them wisely. An engineer by training and a businessman, he encouraged the corporate leaders he addressed to take specific, practical steps: bring "less-desirable" energy sources, like nuclear and coal fuels, back into the mix; invest in alternative energy sources or "renewables"; tap into energy resources of the outer continental shelf of the United States, Alaska, and the Rockies as well as other parts of the world; increase refinery capacity; and create uniform gasoline standards across the United States so that energy could be moved more easily from state to state. In a broader appeal that reached beyond this forum to the public, O'Reilly called for greater efforts to conserve energy, offering his own company, headquartered in California—a state widely recognized for leadership in environmental awareness—as an example of how to do this: Chevron had achieved a 20 percent reduction in energy use in the twelve years preceding the talk.

In his final remarks, the CEO called on specific stakeholder groups to take responsibility:

I ask the *business community* to lead the strategic debate to ensure that America continues to have affordable and reliable supplies of energy.

I ask *government officials* to support access to new resources, to help manage the risk of international investments, and to rationalize regulations that prevent the safe, efficient development of energy supplies.

I ask *local communities* to embrace new ventures . . . which can promote the economy, add new jobs and ultimately improve the quality of life for everyone.

I ask *environmentalists* to ensure we protect the earth we live on, but to recognize that environmental progress is more important than perfection.

Finally, I ask each of you to leave the room making a promise—a promise to act as if your future depended on it. Because, it surely does.[7]

In the following year, O'Reilly invoked and extended the implications of his New Energy Equation in a speech before the Cambridge Energy Research Associates, a research group that provides advice to global energy companies and other interested stakeholders.[8] Yet again, he signaled the urgency of energy problems and sounded the alarm for action:

I believe we are entering another phase that is being shaped by globalization in production and trade, economic growth and surging demand, and declining oil production in the OECD [Organisation for Economic Co-operation and Development] countries.

These factors are making us more energy interdependent than we have ever been. They have created what is, in effect, a new energy equation.

The most visible element of this new equation is that relative to demand, oil is no longer in plentiful supply. The time when we could count on cheap oil and even cheaper natural gas is clearly ending.[9]

Going beyond his earlier talk to the US Chamber of Commerce, O'Reilly called for a national energy policy to address the problems of the New Energy Equation. To make that policy work, he called for broad-based public dialogue: "I believe a constructive national discussion of energy policy would bring about a much better understanding of energy issues among key stakeholders, including the American public."[10] To be productive, such discussion required a public informed about energy issues; O'Reilly assigned this educational task to his own organization and to peer groups:

Educating key stakeholders and the American public and getting the United States to think strategically about energy is an ambitious objective. And while making U.S. energy policy is the job of government, it can't be done by government alone.

There is a role for all stakeholders. And we in this room today have a critical role. That role is education.

You see, we understand the vital strategic importance of energy. We all understand that energy is a fundamental component of economic growth and national security. In fact, it is a fundamental component of the quality of life.

I think the American people need to be educated to get to the same set of understandings—and it will be a challenge.

Americans must begin to think about energy in the same way they would think about national security, or education, or healthcare—as an essential enabler of our quality of life. And to do that, we have to get our message out.[11]

O'Reilly assured his audience that fostering energy literacy would be an assignment that an engineering, "can-do" group of leaders could take on successfully.

Immediately following the election of Barack Obama as president of the United States in late 2008, O'Reilly appealed to him directly in an open letter asking that he respond to energy challenges by carrying out two broad recommendations:

- Urge Congress, business, and consumers to conserve energy and use it efficiently
- Create a strategic plan to broaden and diversify all domestic US energy sources

These steps, O'Reilly argued, would address the challenges of increased demand for energy, promote US leadership in this arena, reduce our reliance on foreign oil, create new jobs, and place at the forefront what he called "human capacity building," that is, "advancing human development across the globe, particularly basic human needs, education and training, and support for small and medium-size businesses."[12]

The CEO's formal addresses represented a call to global leaders in government and business for collaborative problem solving to address energy challenges. Closer to home, David A. Samson, Chevron's general manager of public affairs, worked with his team to help present these challenges to the company's multiple stakeholder groups and to formulate responses to the challenges.

Through research with these groups, the company learned that people didn't expect energy companies to have all the solutions to energy problems but did want companies to be engaged in addressing them. In response to people's expectations, Chevron launched the "Real Issues" campaign in 2005, which focused on dual engagement, the company's and its stakeholders'. Chevron began to reach out to people through multiple channels, such as the Web, town-hall meetings, and discussions with key influencers (for instance, government and policy leaders in the United States and across the globe, nongovernmental organizations, lobbying groups, academics who write about energy, financial analysts, and journalists who cover the business). A 2008 Forrester report gave the company high marks for addressing public concern about the company's environmental policies.

FROM THE NEW ENERGY EQUATION TO HUMAN ENERGY
Asked to discuss the genesis of "Human Energy," Russ Yarrow, general manager of corporate affairs, explained that "'Human Energy' is a kind of logical story extension of the New Energy Equation. We migrated from the New Energy Equation, or the articulation of the problems, to Human

Energy, which provides solutions. 'Human Energy' arose as the solution to the problems articulated as the 'New Energy Equation' by Chevron's CEO."[13] The CEO had identified the major worldwide energy challenges and expressed his desire for the company to be part of the solution, and for people to learn more about the issues, engage in informed discussion, and ultimately, act.[14]

But how specifically did "Human Energy" emerge as a way to name and frame these solutions? The answer depended upon the research and analysis conducted by Chevron's corporate affairs department to reassess what the company represented to key stakeholders. In 2004, the department led an exercise with the company's senior management to determine what the company stood for, what would contribute to its future success, and how the brand might be further developed. Over several months, members of the department talked to executives on the strategic planning committee, including the company's chair and vice chair, heads of operating businesses, and the chief financial officer. At the same time, the department looked outward, performing benchmarking to assess the company's position vis-à-vis the competition, using focus groups and conducting surveys with "energy influencers." The research was also extended to the general public, consumers of oil and gas; in total, about five hundred people were interviewed.[15]

According to the research, what differentiated Chevron from the rest of the industry was *people*. Whether the research tapped into the opinions of internal or external audiences, employees or journalists who write about energy, the company appeared to stand for collaboration, being open, honest, and friendly. This is what corporate marketing manager Helen Clark calls "'people attributes,' providing energy for human progress, for people to do things, providing employment."[16] This profile stood in sharp contrast to those of key competitors: BP, which was then associated primarily with the environmental impact of oil and gas; Exxon, which stood for technology leadership; and Shell, which represented sustainability operations in local communities, and innovation.[17] This assessment helped the corporate affairs department come up with the tagline "Human Energy."

The generative power of "Human Energy" to stimulate the selection of stories became evident from the start. In fact, there was an overabundance of appropriate ideas for development in story form. According to Clark and her colleague Robert Raines, who were responsible for this effort, stories were selected in areas where Chevron had strength relative to the competition, for instance, in renewable and geothermal energy and in energy efficiency. If a good story was put together in another part of the world, the company would use it across the enterprise and across channels to broaden the audience. Topics were rejected that were too difficult to produce or excluded the human element, for instance, the description of a technical process without the human agents involved.[18]

Today, the evolution of stories is partially experimental but also relies on Web analytics to monitor a story's popularity and on interviews with Web users. New stories develop, some originating with employees, such as a geologist's story about deepwater exploration, a piece produced on an inexpensive flip camera, placed on YouTube, and then picked up by *Newsweek* for a story called "Journey to the Center of the Earth."[19]

HUMAN ENERGY STORIES

Like those of us who have a signature story—a personal story about a significant experience, relationship, accomplishment, or failure that provides insights into the storyteller and can serve many business purposes in the teller's professional life —brands may have a signature or overarching brand story that offers the brand proposition in brief. The Chevron brand story appeared in the corporate TV spot "Untapped Energy," a 2.5-minute commercial that launched the "Human Energy" campaign nationally during *60 Minutes* in the fall of 2007.[20] The commercial illustrated how Human Energy provides the solution to the New Energy Equation. The ad opens with the debate about energy demand and the environment, identified as "the story of our time" because the need for energy affects everyone, not just oil companies. It then moves from challenges to solution: Chevron's response to the energy demand is "Human Energy" in the form of the persistence, focus, and "can-do" attitude of the many Chevron employees and partners. These are people who drill for oil while respecting the environment, conserve energy, and find alternative sources of energy. They are "not corporate titans" but "men and women of vision, part-time poets and coaches," and they are "trying to find cleaner ways to provide energy for the world." Human Energy is the teamwork, ingenuity, and hard work needed to address the demand for energy, and is the value or selling proposition that distinguishes Chevron from the competition. Additional print ads and stories followed this commercial.[21]

HOW CHEVRON WORKS WITH STORIES ON THE WEB

Human Energy stories are prominent on the Chevron Web site. Let's see how the company works with stories and then turn to how stories on the Web work in concert with other communications on and off the Web.

Chevron's decisions about how to work with stories on the Web began with understanding the profiles of the Web users: who they are and what they seek to learn about Chevron from the Web site. Survey research revealed several broad types of users: those looking for a job, those with questions about credit cards for gasoline, investors, media, academics seeking information on energy policy and about the industry, and the general public interested in what Chevron is doing. For those with specific, narrowly focused questions—for instance, what jobs are available in accounting in the San Ramon headquarters—the Web site offers quick links to answer these questions; however, for those with a broader interest in the company (including job seekers, who often want to know what the company stands for in order to determine whether there's a good fit between their own values and the company's), the Web site features stories about Human Energy.

Story Themes, Stories Featured

Exploring all the stories on the Web site reveals that Chevron sees story format as elastic. Under the umbrella of "Human Energy Stories,"[22] there are audiovisual film clips of about two to four minutes featuring a variety of people speaking on camera, such as an employee who has worked in his community's food bank; visuals that show a step-by-step technical process complete with animation and narrated by someone who has expertise in the process; descriptions and explanations of technical processes without sound, just visuals with textual explanations; and a fifteen-minute interview with the CEO on climate change.

The stories, twenty-four in total in January 2010, appear under the general category of "Human Energy" with the following explanation: "Finding newer, smarter, cleaner ways to power the world begins with this one energy source we have in abundant supply: the power of Human Energy." Each story is placed in two or more categories: "All" (a category which expands or contracts as stories are added or deleted), "Editor's Picks" (which, drawn from the other categories, fluctuates depending on the number of "hits" that a particular story receives), "Producing Energy" (six stories), "Applying Technology" (nine stories), "Using Energy Efficiently" (four stories), "Investing in Emerging Energy" (four stories), "Protecting the Environment" (seven stories), and "Working in the Community" (seven stories). At first glance, only the last theme—"Working in the Community"—appears to necessarily involve human agents and actions, including some kind of partnership between Chevron and outside stakeholders; however, on closer inspection, it becomes apparent that the stories under each category focus on one or more aspects of Human Energy, anything from employees' efforts to give back to their communities by teaching middle school girls about science, to team efforts by engineers and managers to search for new sources of energy while respecting the environment.

In the stories about "Producing Energy," those directly involved in the activity are featured as both narrators and actors in the events.[23] For a story on investing in liquefied natural gas and natural gas in the remote nature preserve of Barrow Island off the coast of Australia, a Chevron employee involved in the project explains the dual pursuit of economic activity and protection of the environment, and the prime minister of Australia talks about job creation. For a story on producing oil in the Gulf of Mexico, Chevron engineering manager Gordon Rorrison describes how an enormous platform for deepwater exploration is built, a story that makes ample use of visuals showing the huge structures that are put in place, piece by piece, the platform itself weighing over 40,000 tons. The enormity of the platform's floating hull and its twenty-four-day journey from Norway, where it was constructed, to the Gulf of Mexico suggests a kind of romantic journey and an awe-inspiring human technical achievement. With similar effect, the building of the giant Agbami vessel, a floating oil-production unit in Nigeria, is told by the lead Chevron employee, who emphasizes job creation that resulted from the project. Another story, the deepwater project in Angola, is told by installation manager Walt Curtis, who describes the huge machinery involved, including dual-crane lifts featured prominently in the clip. The story on innovation is told first by Trond Unneland, head of the Chevron group that invests in entrepreneurial ventures, and is then picked up by John Woollard, president of BrightSource Energy, a start-up that received Chevron investment; this segment is accompanied by stunning visuals that show his firm's work. Even the discussion of how liquefied natural gas is transported, which describes a technical process using supporting visuals and text (no audio), pulls in the human element at the end: step 6 shows the lights of buildings going on in a city; step 7, a woman cooking with natural gas while her family, the ultimate beneficiaries of the process, looks on.

Many of the stories categorized under "Applying Technology" also appear under "Producing Energy," in particular the stories about liquefied natural gas and how it works, the deepwater project in Angola, oil production in the Gulf of Mexico, and the building of the giant Agbami vessel. (The duplication suggests that if people are producing energy, they are applying technology to do so, and the use of two categories seems justified in that the Web user may find one or the other category to be a compelling "hook" that encourages exploration of the multiple stories.) "Producing Energy" also includes the story of Chevron's expansion into Kazakhstan and the community partnership that was forged, told by a company employee and native of the region.The category also features a story consisting of successive diagrams with text that explain the step-by-step process of deepwater drilling.

In stories about "Using Energy Efficiently," Dane Zehrung, a Chevron sustainability advisor, walks around Chevron's headquarters in northern California, showing how the facilities have been improved for energy efficiency. For another story—"Visit Our 'Green' Building"—an architect explains how a building's construction met high standards for managing environmental impact and how it became the first gold-certified LEED building in the state of Louisiana. In the same section, a college spokesperson and a Chevron representative tell the story of the solar panels Chevron installed at a local community college and their benefits. For a story on saving energy by using vanpools to drive to work, a corporate recruiter for Chevron who drives a van speaks enthusiastically about the comradery that comes from traveling together to work.

The stories about "Investing in Emerging Energy" include Chevron's support of entrepreneurial firms in that space, its use of solar energy, its production of geothermal energy, and its dual focus on producing energy in out-of-the-way places like Indonesia and on protecting the forests. All these stories appear elsewhere but, when reviewed as a cluster of related stories, point to the company's varied approaches to energy investment as well.

Taken as a whole, the stories about "Protecting the Environment" portray Chevron as an ecologically aware corporate citizen. Some of these stories appear in other categories we have seen above: the creation of the LEED-certified building in Louisiana; the solar energy panels in the local community college; the production of the renewable resource of geothermal energy in Indonesia; and the production of natural gas on Barrow Island without damage to the environment. Other stories are included here as well:

- A story that features an ecologist talking about his study of an endangered turtle species
- A long piece on producing geothermal energy, farming, and protecting the forest in the Gunung Halimun Salak National Park in Indonesia

The latter story introduces multiple spokespeople: a Chevron employee who works in the park and is Indonesian, a farmer, and the park director. Each is named and appears on screen to narrate the relevant part of the larger story in which he participates: the Chevron employee about partnerships between the company and NGOs; the farmer about the program partnership and the opportunity it affords him to learn new methods of farming, something described as an example of "*gotong royong*," an Indonesian expression meaning "working with others"; and the park director who emphasizes his trust in the company and his loyalty to his home, which he sees improved by partnerships with Chevron.

"Working in the Community" puts Chevron's role as a socially responsible corporate citizen to the fore, again with an emphasis on partnerships: with local schools in California to foster young girls' interest in engineering by introducing them to women engineers at Chevron and their work; with remote schools in Angola, Venezuela, Nigeria, and South Africa where children talk about their daily lives and aspirations, and teachers speak about the impact television has had on education; in various parts of the world where Chevron sponsors AIDS and HIV awareness among employees and others; with food banks where Chevron employees volunteer; and with local businesses that promote diversity in the workforce.

The most elaborate story representing working in the community, "Caring for South Africans with AIDS," exemplifies the visual and auditory power of organizational storytelling on the Web.[24] The story concerns the South African-based Dunoon Community Home-based Care Center (HBCC), an organization set up to meet the needs of home-bound AIDS patients in the Cape Town area. The video begins by taking the viewer slowly past the dirt road and huts of the community, a domestic scene with kids playing and adults going about their daily routines, like washing clothes and talking to neighbors. The scene is shown against the sound track of people humming a traditional South African chant and the voice of Ms. Thandiswa Priscilla Stokwe, a local community leader beautifully dressed in a charcoal-grey and bright yellow-patterned outfit with an elaborate headdress of matching colors and pattern. She speaks emphatically and with authority to underscore the urgency of the problem: half of the 100,000 people in the community suffer from HIV or AIDS and "750 people are dying every day." The scene shifts, first to Haymish Paulse, an employee of the Chevron Cape Town refinery, who talks about how local community leaders approached Chevron for help with the AIDS epidemic, and then to a horseshoe-shaped table in a community center around which about twenty Chevron reps and community leaders are seated as Paulse tells the founding story of HBCC, that is, how Chevron worked with local community leaders and with "Heavenly Promise" (the South African government's department of social development) to establish the organization. The chairperson of "Heavenly Promise," Enid Sithole, then appears on screen, dressed in a dramatic outfit with a black-and-white geometric pattern and a beaded and woven multicolored headdress, and carries the story forward by talking about the support Chevron provided, as the camera moves to a kitchen facility where workers are making soup. Sithole comments on Chevron's huge contributions to the effort, food production capabilities as well as training in project management skills. We then catch a glimpse of a group of women, all dressed in white, seated around a rectangular table and reviewing information about project management while chanting a native song. A new narrator appears, community leader Andile Peter, who explains how the community has taken ownership of the center, how women have assumed leadership roles with pride, and how they have reached out to those in need by delivering food to the homes of HIV victims. Not quite halfway through the story, Lindelwa Mdovu introduces herself. She's a young and energetic home-care giver and is passionate about her work. As she talks about the needs of her patients, she walks purposefully with a fellow worker through the dirt streets and past the huts while commenting on the importance of her training and her job of preparing and delivering meals to homebound AIDS patients. Ntombekaya Gloria Gqobo, another community leader, explains the role of the caregivers in providing meals for those who are homebound and sick.

Now at the midpoint of the story, we meet Bulelewe Njingala, an AIDS patient, who talks about the soup she receives. The food is what stands between her and starvation. Lindelwa has carried the soup to Bulelewe, and—at the emotional heart of the story—Lindelwa expresses what her patient may be unable to voice: "After you came, when I saw you I get better. I get power, I get energy." She summarizes the moral of this story: "They get energy from us." Here is Human Energy at its most basic: food and the necessary partnership that is behind the efforts to deliver this form of Human Energy. It is the partnership of community and company; of government, community, and company; of caregiver (who sees 150 patients each week) and patient. The camera then focuses on the community center and on the voice and presence of Chevron senior manager Wayne Klahs, vice president of global marketing for Africa, Europe, and Pakistan, who explains that the company has given $30 million to the Global Fund to fight AIDS, Tuberculosis, and Malaria. As part of that commitment, the company contributed $5 million to fight AIDS in the Western Cape. Shifting back to Sithole, the story ends with the community leader expressing hope for the future, the same rhythmic choral music heard at the beginning of the story now filling its last moments.

In addition to this prominent story and the multiple stories for particular themes, Chevron uses different versions of a story on the same theme in adjusting to the interests of different audiences. Take, for instance, vanpools. In the video, an employee talks about her enjoyment in driving a vanpool. The internal news article tells about incentives to start a vanpool and how in some locations like Houston, the company provides subsidies for mass transportation. It also gives the data that underscore the success of these efforts; for instance, "Since the launch of the program [incentives to take mass transit or share rides], the number of our 41,000 downtown-Houston employees who drive to work alone has plummeted from 70 percent to nearly 30 percent."[25] Deborah McNaughton, manager of internal communications, explains: "There is a broader story about vanpooling on the intranet. In the story, we wrote about the benefits for participants in San Ramon and Houston."[26]

Stories On the Web Site in Concert with Other Communications
Human Energy stories work alongside and complement other communications on the company Web site to convey that Chevron is about people, partnership, and performance—the core corporate values—-and about making the world a better place.[27] Corporate social responsibility issues are front and center, and the visual images in the stories often involve people in nature. In fact, almost all the pictures on the site have breathtaking landscapes with plants, animals, and people, who are a big part of the visual imagery.

Besides the Human Energy stories on the Web site, each of the other sections of the Web site is devoted to a broad topic, such as global issues, and a number of subtopics such as energy efficiency or emerging energy. In some instances, these topics include explanation and elaboration (for example, a CEO letter to then president-elect Obama on global energy policy) of topics raised in the Human Energy stories. Relevant facts and explanation dominate these sections (for example, discussion of various kinds of energy sources).

Some sections of the Web site invite dialogue with the user, such as the "I Will" campaign for energy conservation and efficiency, which offers simple lessons for conserving energy like biking to work. There is also www.willyoujoinus.com, an interactive Web site for exchanging ideas about energy literacy and promoting energy conservation. Like the Human Energy stories, the other content on the Chevron Web site can be refreshed daily, has a consistently inviting tone, and is easy to access by topic. This "nonstory" content reinforces and elaborates on the Human Energy stories and extends discussion, but it lacks the human agents and actions that are central to storytelling.

In communication channels beyond the company Web site, Human Energy—whether or not in story form—holds a central place in everything from the announcement of the "Human Energy" launch by the CEO in his letter to shareholders in the 2007 annual report, to TV spots on Human Energy. Even guidelines for visuals emphasize the need to link them to Human Energy: "When choosing or shooting photography, strive to make conceptual and visual connections to Human Energy themes of people and progress."[28]

The company also invites the media to collect stories firsthand. For instance, external relations advisor Mickey Driver has conducted twenty-five offshore media visits since 2006 with the primary aim of "humanizing" the company, for, as Driver emphasizes, "behind the company are the people." Driver has taken reporters on "follow the barrel" media tours to Chevron's deepwater drilling platforms in the Gulf of Mexico, where the oil is produced, to the pipeline storage facilities offshore, to the refineries, then to tanker trucks that deliver the gas, and finally to the stations where the gas is sold. The reporters blog about the journey along the way. After a one-hour helicopter ride into the Gulf of Mexico to one of Chevron's platforms for interviews with employees, ABC's *World News Tonight* reporter David Muir remarked that he was awestruck by the journey and the size of the new facility, a $3 billion-plus platform sitting in 4,300 feet of water.[29] For an ABC *Good Morning America* (GMA) live broadcast,

Driver arranged for transport of 6,000 pounds of broadcast equipment and more than a dozen GMA staffers for a two-night stay on the *Petronius*, the tallest freestanding platform tower in the world.[30] During NBC reporter Janet Shamlian's piece from the Gulf platform—the first major TV network broadcast from such a site—she asked Driver to say what he'd like her audience to know. Driver's response: "The platform is the other end of your gasoline hose,"[31] a pithy summary that links an engineering accomplishment difficult to comprehend to an everyday activity that's taken for granted. The "follow the barrel" stories give this fact human dimension while dramatizing the enormous distance in space and proportion between offshore drilling operations and pumping gas at the local station.

Cutting across all of Chevron's communications is an engagement strategy with policy makers and the public that harks back to CEO O'Reilly's direct call for everyone to be part of an energy solution; to the "Will You Join Us" Web site asking people to consume less energy; and to ads that advocate conserving energy by carpooling, using less electricity, or recycling.

AUTHENTIC VOICE IN STORIES: COMPANY NORMS AND INDIVIDUAL EXPRESSION

Many people tell Chevron stories, each from a unique perspective and in a distinctive voice. Yet, despite the multiplicity of voices, there is a consistency in voice across the speakers. This is partially due to the company's explicit guidelines for voice—a set of key attributes linked to Human Energy but broad enough to allow for personal expression—instructions that facilitate the necessary balancing act between personal and organizational expression I've identified as a hallmark of authentic storytelling (see Exhibit 5.1 for the list of attributes).

Joerden Legon, editor of Chevron.com and author of the "Chevron Web Voice Brief," instructs people who are to appear on the Web. The overarching purpose of the brief is "to help people tell the stories about Chevron so that the people going to the Web site can meet the people of Chevron."[32]

In Legon's extended discussion of voice, employees who tell stories are asked to create a "tone of voice that is human, accessible and friendly,

Chevron.com
Key Voice Attributes

- ❖ **Human**: Warm and friendly, without being too familiar; recognizing the stakes for real people in all that we do.

- ❖ **Accessible:** Understandable to a general audience, while being precise and technical where warranted; in general, adapting each section to its intended audience.

- ❖ **Direct**: Interesting to read, while not adding extraneous or distracting content; expressing facts, intentions, plans and activities without excessive embellishment.

- ❖ **Savvy**: Reflective of the fact that we are a major global business competitor that plays hard but fair; finely attuned to perceiving and addressing business opportunities.

- ❖ **Optimistic:** Positive about the possibilities of the future, without being unbelievable or sugar-coating real challenges.

- ❖ **Grounded**: Deeply rooted in the facts; accurately describing the world as it is, while being clear about where we intend to go.

EXHIBIT 5.1.   Chevron.com Key Voice Attributes
SOURCE: Chevron Corporation

while at the same time direct, focused, and indicative of business savvy."
(This guideline prompted the company to strip technical jargon out of earlier communications; for instance, references to "upstream" [a technical
term referring to activities ranging from oil exploration to transportation
to the pipeline] and "downstream" [the refining and selling of oil]). The
Voice Brief also identifies "key tensions" or "points of balance," such as
"Be proud of what you do, but in a 'quietly heroic' way; at the same time,
don't be afraid to talk about the great work we do—after all, the whole
point is to tell our story." Captured in these guidelines is the focus on presenting the engaging and forward-looking exemplary Chevron employee.

Linking these goals for voice with the tone and choice of story, Legon's
brief also provides a checklist for evaluating a story or other Web-based
communication:

Does the tone and subject-matter of the content:

Convey the spirit of "Human Energy"?

Reflect the values and attributes of the brand?

Highlight the positive role that Chevron plays?

Create a real bridge and bond between the company and its audiences?

Look to the future?

Create an informative and engaging experience? i.e., steer away from
verbiage that is: dry, too cold and technical, stilted?

Maximize opportunities for interaction?

Make for a site that you'd like to visit yourself?

And, ultimately, does the content sound like it's coming from a real person,
someone who has an engaging voice and who doesn't use standard, monotone,
corporate-speak?[33]

If voice is the sense of the human being behind the words, then guidelines for the Chevron voice in stories attempt to close the gap between the
speaker and listener by suggesting the use of an informal but respectful
tone that displays the positive attributes of a people-focused engineering
culture—one that's direct and fact based—while creating a human connection to the audience. At the same time, the guidelines are sufficiently
general to allow Chevron storytellers to retain their unique perspectives
and distinctive voices.

HUMAN ENERGY AND "THE CHEVRON WAY":
BRAND PLATFORM AND COMPANY VISION AND CULTURE

"The Chevron Way" is the company's articulation of its vision and values. The short brochure on the company's values "explains who we are, what we do, what we believe and what we plan to accomplish." The vision of the company is "to be *the* global energy company most admired for its people, partnerships and performance." "The Chevron Way" and many elements of this vision statement bring to the fore qualities associated with Human Energy:

Our vision means we:

- Safely provide energy products vital to sustainable economic progress and *human development* throughout the world
- Are *people and an organization with superior capabilities and commitment*
- Are the *partner of choice*
- *Earn the admiration of all our stakeholders—investors, customers, host governments, local communities and our employees—not only for the goals we achieve but how we achieve them*
- Deliver world-class performance.[34]

"The Chevron Way" focuses on people—employees, investors, customers, partners, governments, communities—and on the key values the company holds in working with people: integrity, trust, diversity, ingenuity, partnership, protection of people and the environment, and high performance. According to Russ Yarrow, general manager of corporate affairs for Chevron, "It's not a bunch of slogans but a way to do business."[35] So central is "The Chevron Way" that it is discussed at orientation for every new employee, including those who join the company during a merger or acquisition, and is often referred to by senior leadership.

Chevron stories, reviewed for this best-practice case in early 2010, have grown in number and variety since that date. The company uses its online capability to stimulate dialogue between the organization and its stakeholders. Its company Web site includes an invitation to those accessing it to submit their own "Chevron stories" online about their experiences with the company. As I've noted, the technology component of storytelling is quite dynamic and is likely to stimulate greater and more varied uses of organizational storytelling at Chevron and at other organizations.

At the heart of the Chevron case is the complex, mutually enriching relationship between authentic and fluent stories, on the one hand, and corporate brand, on the other. Such stories help to make the brand trustworthy. A brand that fulfills its promise stimulates the choice and development of stories and acts as an umbrella under which to include stories having diverse content but a single message, which, in this case, is that they illustrate Human Energy.

6 CHEVRON: LESSONS LEARNED

THE COMPLEX AND MUTUALLY ENRICHING relationship between brand and stories begins with finding a realistic and credible brand. As communications consultant Christine Miller points out, "This task can take months of research, analysis, and testing, and discovering the unique selling proposition of a brand is ultimately what makes the company different and meaningful to its audiences."[1]

Once the brand tagline is formulated, it can serve as a frame or filter for stories. In turn, authentic stories—those that are realistic and credible—can make the brand concrete and enhance its credibility. As with all the best-practice cases, stories also require fluency. They need to appeal to the heart as well as to the mind, an aspect of which may be their appeal to shared values of the broader culture. By extension, the discussion presented here also suggests how to judge and even strengthen the combined branding and storytelling efforts for your own organization.

USE A REALISTIC AND CREDIBLE BRAND
TAGLINE TO FRAME STORIES

Rather than a flight of rhetorical fancy, a brand tagline like "Human Energy" needs to be anchored in reality. As we have seen at Chevron, "Human Energy" is securely located in the "New Energy Equation," which is central to the CEO's vision for the company and his policy statements, to the polled perceptions of the company's major stakeholders, and to Chevron's core values. The concept and term "Human Energy" emerged as the solution to the New Energy Equation, the set of energy challenges that Chevron's CEO David J. O'Reilly repeatedly articulated in speeches. It is articulated today by John S. Watson, the CEO since January 2010: How do we meet the increased global demand for energy and the increased difficulty in meeting it while remaining socially responsible global citizens respectful of the environment?[2]

A brand tagline should also speak to a company's core values, which in the case of Chevron are its focus on people, partnerships, and performance. As one executive notes, "Human Energy stories are narratives that illustrate core values, such as a focus on economic progress and human development, on people with superior capabilities and commitment, on partnerships, and on stakeholder needs."[3] Another executive comments: "'Human Energy' fits our culture. The company started as a California company, more than 130 years ago, and although it has become one of the largest independent energy companies in the world, it has maintained its friendly, pioneering spirit, a 'little engine that could' which grew larger but acts like a smaller company with a family-friendly atmosphere."[4] As yet another executive remarks, "'Human Energy' communicates our value proposition that we are good at partnering."[5]

A brand tagline should be a memorable, succinct shorthand for what a company stands for—or aspires to become. Chevron executive Russ Yarrow explains, "It is both an affirmation of who we are and an aspirational call for who we want to be."[6] "Human Energy" has "sticking power" in our minds. At a basic semantic level, "Human Energy" seems eminently appropriate, even predictable: an "energy" company might well feature that term in its tagline. Yet, at the same time, placing "human" before "energy" creates a novel juxtaposition of two ordinary words that piques interest—What's human about energy?—and shows that the company focuses on the business of energy but looks beyond that to a broader set of energy issues. What is meant by *Human* Energy"? As David A. Samson, general manager of public affairs, states:

We see what we do in very particular terms—human terms. First, we make the most of all our human potential. Working tirelessly together, both inside and outside the company, brings out the best in all of us, accomplishing important challenges and doing things the right way.

And, secondly, but no less importantly, we produce energy to power life on this planet and to make sure that people can get where they're going—in every sense of the term. The energy we produce serves the best interests of people everywhere and the planet we all inhabit.

Human Energy is always about *people* and *partnerships* for addressing the challenges, and the stories illustrate this in one way or another, illustrating what distinguishes the company from the competition.[7]

Brand taglines can also serve as *frames* for stories. Language expert Kenneth Burke points out how key terms can frame—or help us to interpret—what we observe. Burke explains this point using an example from psychology, looking at the interpretation of dreams, but he might have applied it with equal justification to stories about human energy: "A man has a dream. He reports his dream to a Freudian analyst, or a Jungian, or an Adlerian, or to a practitioner of some other school. In each case, we might say, the 'same' dream will be subjected to a different color filter, with corresponding differences in the nature of the event as perceived, recorded, and interpreted."[8]

Like language expert Burke, Chevron executive Yarrow explains that Human Energy is "the filter through which to tell many stories—stories that illustrate how people come first. It unifies the stories of technology developed and applied by people."[9] As such, the term illuminates the resemblances among apparently disconnected stories—for instance, about the environment, community and society, and renewable energy—and their connections to what is fundamental to the organization. Samson explains:

The beauty of the term is, in part, that each storyteller gets to define the term a little differently but the audience gets the same takeaway—our internal pride in the standard of living we're helping to provide. "Human Energy" plays across the energy spectrum. We are in oil and gas but are also dealing with energy in many ways. Finally, "Human Energy" speaks to our ingenuity.[10]

Along with Chevron, several other companies work successfully with brand taglines that serve, among other things, as a "filter through which to tell many stories" and as a way to create coherence across apparently disconnected stories: Philips, General Electric, and Dow, among others. (Like Chevron's tagline, theirs also have a vital role in changing or reinforcing culture and in building strategic positioning—but these are topics for another study.)[11]

GE launched a brand campaign in 2003 with the tagline "Imagination at Work," which replaced the long-standing tagline "We bring good things to life." Gary Sheffer, executive director of corporate communication and public affairs at GE, comments on this shift:

The old tagline was associated with light bulbs and appliances—just a small part of our business now—but people wanted to see a connection between the things we do and the things the world needs, and they wanted an emotional connection to the company. We're also a company that's a collection of diversified businesses, some having nothing to do with others. We made "SeaBiscuit" which has nothing to do with aircraft engines, another business. The new tagline is about a company that's creative and innovative and can take ideas and put them to work for customers. "Imagination at Work" tells about a company with enormous brain power in the research center, a company that has the best scientists in the world but is also a blue-collar company with sweat equity.[12]

Under the umbrella of "Imagination at Work" appear stories about creativity and innovation across the company's products and services. These stories abound online, some with video clips and told in the voice of the GE employee who is engaged in the activity; and in print, on TV, and on the Web, in the United States and abroad. Other stories illustrate variations on the tagline, such as "Imagination Breakthroughs," new business concepts capable of generating $100 million in revenue in three to five years[13]; and "Ecoimagination," products and services that help the environment, like a solar-powered winery or an offshore wind farm.

As another example of successful branding and storytelling, consider Dow Chemical's brand campaign called "The Human Element," launched in 2006 with the announcement of a new (metaphoric) element called "Hu," an essential element to be added to those in the traditional periodic table. Chemistry should be linked to humanity, this tagline suggests: the right people working at Dow addressing the needs of consumers, including their environmental concerns. The intention of the campaign is to motivate current employees, recruit new ones, and reach out to customers. According to Catherine Maxey, public affairs director at Dow, the "human element" stands for the company and its employees' commitment to sustainability; namely, to addressing the challenges of having an adequate food supply, clean water, housing, safety, personal health, and a renewable energy supply.[14] Early stories focused on individual employees and the actions they had taken to achieve sustainability, as portrayed in the "I am the human element" stories, autobiographical excerpts that show the brand in action. More recent stories move out internationally to include employees' contributions to provide safe water to flood victims and aid to local communities, among other things.[15] Asked to comment on the tagline, CEO Liveris stated that "we are connecting the emotionalism of being a human being, the emotionalism of intertwining with our environment, with the notion that chemistry enables everything."[16]

At another level—and one at the core of storytelling—a brand tagline can work as a lesson learned or a moral that captures the meaning of a story, as in one of our oldest story types, the fable. (As early as 2000 B.C. fables were inscribed on clay tablets in ancient Mesopotamia.[17]) Think of *Aesop's Fables* and their time-honored lessons, like "You can't believe a liar even if he tells the truth," which frames the story of the boy who cried "Wolf! Wolf!" one too many times. When he sounded the alarm because a wolf had actually broken through the gate to kill the sheep, no one believed his warning. Consider the moral "Give assistance, not advice, in a crisis," which provides the lesson learned for the story about the drowning boy who begs a passerby to help rather than to scold him for his reckless swimming. And, finally, recall the commonplace "Necessity is the mother of invention," which makes sense of the thirsty crow and her ingenious plan to raise the water level in a pitcher by dropping pebbles into it so that the water would rise enough for her to reach it. Although fables often toss aside realism, placing the reader instead in a fictional world of talking animals, and, by contrast, Chevron's stories are fact-based, both types of stories share important similarities: they are brief, and they clearly link a narrative to its meaning.

As frames, brand taglines should be good enough to work with and cheap enough to put aside. Chevron is aware that the frame of "Human Energy" gives meaning to stories and provides insights, but, as with any frame if used excessively, it could restrict the number and kinds of stories told to the exclusion of important ones. "There are stories that don't fit the 'Human Energy' concept," explains Yarrow:

There's no platform that's perfect. In California we are talking about our legacy here. Though some of the stories about the "California Initiative" are Human Energy stories, such as our work with UC Davis on energy efficiency, others are static and backward looking, and we tell them anyway. Human Energy stories are forward looking, so Human Energy doesn't fit the legacy stories. No one should be held back by a platform. I believe in the 80/20 rule.[18]

As capacious and malleable as "Human Energy" is, not every story is an example of Human Energy. The framing power of taglines is substantial, yet they should not be the litmus test by which to select every story.

Brand taglines can also be generative of both stories *and* actions. The frame "Human Energy" has been called "an engine for storytelling, a platform that generates multiple storylines to support our business."[19] Members of the communication group and the business units meet annually to come up with lists of story topics to pursue across communication channels and keep an eye out for story opportunities. But in addition to generating new stories, a brand tagline can function as language that creates new understanding and motivates action. In the words of linguist George Lakoff, frames are "mental structures that shape the way we see the world."[20] They also "shape the goals we seek, the plans we make, the way we act, and what counts as a good or bad outcome of our actions."[21] In combination with the values articulated in "The Chevron Way," "Human Energy" has this capability, as a verbal representation of what the company stands for, to stimulate a line of action the company can take to discover new energy sources and build new technology through partnerships, cooperation with entrepreneurs, and collaboration with other firms, communities, and governments.

TELL STORIES TO MAKE THE BRAND
TAGLINE CONCRETE AND CREDIBLE

Human Energy stories give realism and credibility to the tagline, showing how the company has fulfilled its promise to address energy challenges, for at the most basic level, stories are about concrete actions performed and about the agents who perform them. Moreover, the agents who perform these actions often tell the story themselves, thereby creating even greater realism and credibility. As Ray Jordan, corporate vice president of pubic affairs and corporate communication at Johnson & Johnson, notes: "These stories [in which the teller and the chief protagonist are identical] can give people a sense of a company through voices that are not corporate leadership. The people who are telling the stories are closest to the activities. We have the credible voices of someone participating, who has a direct connection to the activity."[22] In addition, storytellers who have participated in the stories they tell show by example and invite engagement. If a Chevron employee can volunteer to work for a food bank and then tells this story, then the implicit question is, "Why can't the reader do the same?"

Chevron is depicted through stories—many of which are told by employee-participants—as setting an example: conserving energy (for example, its construction of a "green" LEED-certified building in Louisiana; its use of employee vanpools); searching for affordable and reliable supplies of energy (its production of natural gas in Barrow Island, Australia; deepwater drilling in the Gulf of Mexico); investing in geothermals (for which Chevron is the largest producer) and in alternative energy sources or "renewables"; showing respect for the environment (nature conservation on Barrow Island; protection of forests in Indonesia); taking responsibility as a global citizen (support for HIV/AIDS awareness; science education for girls; assistance for AIDS patients in South Africa); and providing energy literacy to the general public. Taken as a whole, such stories can demonstrate that a company has delivered on its promise. They can show that if a company has made bold claims, it can substantiate them by recounting how it has performed specific relevant activities.

Stories demonstrate brands in terms of human actions and spokespeople. Language expert Burke explains that key terms of a culture—like a brand in this case—are *performed* by members of that culture: "The various tribal idioms are *developed* by their use as instruments in the tribe's way of living."[23] In this specific case, the Chevron stories (lived and told) represent this organization's, or "tribe's," way of living the notion of "Human Energy." What then is the term's extended definition that emerges through its "use as an instrument in the tribe's way of living"? Composed of multiple stories, Human Energy means people performing acts of Human Energy—an engineer building platforms in the ocean, an employee working at a food bank, an ecologist protecting wildlife on a remote island, an engineer-entrepreneur finding new forms of energy, an AIDS victim experiencing the generosity of her local community's outreach—and expressing these actions in their own voices. People enact the brand narrative, which in turn is steeped in the company's values. In doing so, people become "brand evangelists" who can back up the company's claims about what it stands for.

Although the voice of each storyteller is distinctive, common elements are shared thanks to the corporate guidelines about voice. From the audience's point of view, a "Chevron storyteller" is a speaker who approaches a listener with what narrative expert Rita Charon calls "a virtual arm over the shoulder and comforting inviting presence. Other narrators are experienced as removed, skeptical, unforgiving, or judging."[24] "Other narrators," who would be antithetical to the voice of Human Energy, as described in the Voice Web guidelines, don't appear in Chevron's stories.

As a fluent storyteller, each of the multiple voices of Chevron's storyteller-participants, carries, as it were, a version of the "melody" called "Human Energy"—like the musicians in a jazz combo in which the piano player may introduce the melody, a sax picks it up, and the bass reinforces and moves it into another register. And like the music listeners, the audiences for stories can identify the melody and the multiple versions played by each instrument—or in this case by each storyteller and participant in each story. There are multiple storytellers and storyteller-participants and many topics, all of which demonstrate one or another facet of Human Energy.

DEVELOP STORIES THAT APPEAL TO
THE HEART AND ARE DATA-RICH
Like all good stories, Chevron's stories appeal to the heart (a key component of fluent storytelling), but unlike some, they are also fact based and

fact checked (a key component of authentic organizational stories) since the company is an engineering culture where data count and processes are meticulously detailed. Executive Helen Clark explains how scrupulous the company is in verifying data and assertions before launching a story:

We don't say anything unless we can say it's true. For instance, there is a sign-off process for every piece of advertising. It goes through four key areas: subject matter expert (e.g., on geothermal); strategy policy group (is the ad consistent with investment strategy, the future supply of oil?); the DC office for political ramifications; and legal, who ask if we can substantiate everything. The two-and-a-half-minute ad has twenty pages of substantiation. To prove the proposition "Oil, energy, and the environment: The story of our time," we had to go to [Dow Jones's] *Factiva* and ask for all the stories on this topic for this and previous years with those words in it, and then for the percentage of stories with those words. That's how we proved oil, energy, and the environment is the story of our time. We don't do hyperbole in our company.[25]

Not only do stories embed facts, but they also complement other communications, the primary purpose of which is to provide facts such as information and explanations about processes and policies. For instance, a fact sheet on geothermal energy is supported by stories that make it a tangible and even a human experience to people. Editorial manager Jeff Glover recognizes the importance of facts in combination with stories: "We're an engineering culture with a strong respect for numbers, but engineers are also hungry for stories. They want to know the story behind something, not just the charts and graphs, and they want a way to explain technology to their families."[26]

Using reliable data as the basis for the authenticity of stories is important to Chevron as it would be to any major company in the energy sector, especially since the notorious 1989 *Exxon Valdez* oil spill of 11 million gallons of crude into Alaska's Prince William Sound, an act that tainted the reputation of the industry as a whole and intensified the media's anti–big-business bias against companies in the sector; as well as the large 2010 oil spill by BP in the Gulf of Mexico. (When one company is under attack, all of those in the sector are often tarred with the same brush.) This media bias is intensified even further by the ease with which anti–big-business advocacy groups and individuals can express opinions online.

RECOGNIZE THAT STORIES MAY EVOKE AND APPEAL
TO THE SHARED VALUES OF THE BROADER CULTURE

Compelling branding stories may be those that seek common ground with audiences, their values, interests, and concerns. Headquarterd in California and founded over 130 years ago, Chevron has developed multiple stories that echo what we might call a uniquely American set of values, admired and appreciated by many worldwide (but also maligned and envied by some), namely, the romance and adventure of technology and exploration in tandem with American pragmatism. The United States is distinguished as a nation of visionary engineers who value teamwork—the first country to put a man on the moon—and one of inventor-entrepreneurs that dates back to Founding Father Ben Franklin and his invention of the lightning rod, bifocals, and the Franklin stove; to John and Washington Roebling, father-and-son builders of the Brooklyn Bridge, one of the oldest suspension bridges in the United States and much celebrated in the visual arts and poetry; and to Thomas Edison, inventor of the electric light bulb, the phonograph, and the motion picture and founder of a company that eventually became the multinational corporation General Electric.

Several of Chevron's stories reflect this unique set of attributes, especially those that show enormous structures described with pride and near-lyrical admiration by the engineers and geologists who work on these projects. These stories also speak to the pragmatic basis of creativity in the United States. At the 125th anniversary of the company, one of the seven CEOs who spoke about engineering challenges at a roundtable said, "I never saw a problem so big that a bunch of people with slide rules couldn't solve it sitting around a table."[27] Belief in the country's problem-solving capabilities also reflects a fundamental optimism. Chevron executive Yarrow summarizes this point aptly: "Human Energy helps to build confidence and hopefulness. The stories are solutions to problems that matter to people, and solving these problems is a matter of people sitting around a table and talking until they come up with solutions."[28]

NOTE WHAT'S LOST IN A BRANDING CAMPAIGN
WITH MINIMAL ATTENTION TO STORIES

Of course, companies choose how they communicate their brands, everything from celebrity endorsements, to sponsorship of events, to packaging design and brand signage—and a branding campaign can give minimal attention to stories. But at what cost?

Imagine a bare-bones summary of Chevron's story "Caring for South Africans with AIDS": "Chevron has worked with the South African-based Dunoon community to establish a program for home-based care for AIDS victims. The care is provided by trained local residents to AIDS patients, who are very grateful for this program as are community leaders. Senior management at Chevron realize the importance of this and similar programs." This succinct account is relatively accurate but lifeless. Much would be lost in translation: a palpable, concrete awareness of exactly what has been given to the community, a "felt understanding" of what the people involved experience that touches our hearts as well as our minds and encourages us to put ourselves in their shoes.

The absence of stories in a branding campaign can mean that an organization is a faceless monolith except for the presence of the CEO. And even in the case of an articulate CEO who is accessible on blogs and in town-hall meetings, even a leader who champions the corporate brand, consider what is lost. Employees, customers, and other beneficiaries of a company's actions would not be *present in their own voices* to tell their stories. Stories convey a unique, intimate view of a company that emotionally connects the tellers of these stories (often participants in them as well) to those interested in learning about their experiences. In doing so, stories put *faces* on an organization.

APPLY LESSONS LEARNED FROM THE
CHEVRON CASE TO YOUR WORK

Unlike some of Chevron's corporate communication professionals interviewed for this chapter, you may not be in charge or even be on the team developing the branding strategy for your organization, but you should find opportunities to tell stories, some of which are linked to your organization's brand. The Chevron case touches on a variety of ways that story and brand may be connected: how a brand tagline can frame stories, how stories can support the brand, how they should be data-rich and also appeal to the heart, and how they can evoke and appeal to the broader culture. Exhibit 6.1 provides a checklist and commentary that may assist you as you make connections between story and brand in your own work.

- *Consider whether your company has a brand tagline, and if so, whether it serves as a frame or filter for stories*: Does your company have a corporate brand that is credible and realistic? Does it express the company's core values as well as differentiating it from the competition, and is the brand tagline a memorable and succinct shorthand for what the company stands for? If so, are there stories that you use at work whose "moral" or main point is one or more aspects of the brand? For example, if creativity is a component of the company brand, do you tell stories about yourself or about others at work that exemplify this component of the brand? If not, are there potential stories that come to mind that are worth telling? To whom and on what occasions? Do other people, those internal and external to the firm (including the traditional media, bloggers, analysts, customers, suppliers), tell such stories? Taken as a whole, are these stories diverse in content but similar in message, and what if anything are the benefits of this?

- *Determine whether at least some of your stories or those of others support your company's brand tagline*: Do stories that you or others tell about your company's brand show how the company has delivered on its brand promise? Are there stories that derive from your work or personal experience that speak to and extend the brand? Are there multiple voices—many storytellers—who demonstrate in stories one or more facets of the brand? In at least some instances, are you able to work with video clips or pictures for your stories?

- *Identify stories carrying the brand narrative that are rich in accurate data and appeal to the heart*: These attributes apply more broadly to all stories, the former representing authenticity and the latter fluency in organizational storytelling. In the case of stories that you or others tell about your company's brand, do they fulfill these two criteria for successful organizational storytelling? In

EXHIBIT 6.1.   Checklist for Stories and Corporate Branding

some instances, are stories accompanied by other communications, such as fact sheets, descriptions of processes, or senior leader's addresses, that complement the story and corroborate the story's authenticity?

- *If applicable, assess the stories that evoke and appeal to broader cultural values*: If appropriate for your company, do you use brand stories that appeal to broader cultural values, values that may be admired by others and associated with the country in which you are headquartered or have a large presence? If, for instance, you produce jewelry or fashion in Italy, are there brand stories that evoke the artistic sensibility connected to many things Italian? If you are headquartered in Germany and sell high-end machine parts, do you evoke the German heritage of scientific excellence? If in the United States, do you use a rags-to-riches story that taps into the country's entrepreneurial and pioneering roots?

EXHIBIT 6.1.   Continued

Besides the multiple connections between stories and corporate brand, the Chevron case also brings to our attention the importance of voice in stories. Indeed, the issue of voice cuts across the development of all stories, not just those that are part of a brand narrative.

Chevron's corporate communication group offers guidelines on voice which employees are encouraged to use in their communications. The corporate voice includes qualities like "steer away from verbiage that is: dry, too cold and technical, stilted" and encourages an informal but respectful tone that displays the positive attributes of a people-focused engineering culture. (See Exhibit 5.1 for the full list of voice attributes.) At the same time, the guidelines leave room for individual expression, illustrating in this regard how authentic storytelling requires a balance between organizational and individual expression.

Does your organization have specific guidelines for voice? If so, consider when and how you can adjust your personal voice to reflect these guidelines. For example, if you are a computer scientist accustomed to using fluently the technical jargon of the field among your fellow specialists, and your company's guidelines for voice call for being "easy to understand" and "close to the customer," can you translate the language of bits and bytes so that users can understand what you're talking about? Can you show them how the technology serves their needs without making them feel lectured to or bored to tears by an elaborate discussion of technology for technology's sake? If your organization does not have guidelines, what do you know about the company's corporate branding, culture, and communications that, taken as a whole, suggest an organizational voice that might be emulated in your own stories without submerging or distorting your personal voice? This might require you to stretch beyond your linguistic comfort zone. Can you do this to respond to the needs of others with whom you're communicating without feeling untrue or inauthentic to yourself?

Brands and stories, the generalization and the specifics, complement each other. A brand frames stories, highlighting their meaning and showing relationships among them. At the same time stories anchor a brand in real actions and agents, giving the corporate brand realism and credibility, distinguishing the company from the competition, and encouraging an emotional link between the company and its stakeholders. Employees, communities, investors, partners, governments, and other stakeholders can all carry elements of the brand narrative.

In the opening of Chevron case, Helen Clark, manager of corporate marketing in the policy, government, and public affairs group at Chevron, explained the importance of Human Energy stories to the company: "Why stories? Because we are a people company and choose to show this. We want people to experience us from this perspective, and humans tell great stories. They don't just relate facts." Her insights apply beyond her own company. Regardless of your organization's size, stories can differentiate it from the competition, show your human side, and engage internal and external stakeholders intimately through inviting them to imagine the drama and details of the stories you choose to tell. Moreover, as the technology for producing visual stories becomes less and less expensive and as the authenticity of stories is increasingly linked to "employees telling their company's stories," the interesting and relevant stories of employees who are "amateur storytellers" open an opportunity for businesses of any size to reach important stakeholders.

In tandem with a corporate brand based on organizational vision, culture, and accomplishments—and not on a clever linguistic game of inventing flashy catchwords detached from a company's reality—stories can illuminate the many facets of a corporate brand and locate brand expectations in the company's actions and agents. At best, stories take the brand's promise and make it real, putting people and their experiences at the forefront.

DIGITAL STORIES

FOR BUSINESS: FEDEX

Trust and authenticity are driving the need for more storytelling because consumers are looking at character, values, and integrity of corporations beyond the thirty-second ad and slogans. Stories told by our own people through the Web, video, and commercials put audiences at ease who are comfortable with new technology.

—BILL MARGARITIS, corporate vice president, global
communications and investor relations, FedEx

REFLECTING ON THE SUBSTANTIAL CHALLENGES of building trust in organizations, Bill Margaritis singles out stories told by employees as the type of discourse best able to present the "character, values, and integrity of corporations" and notes the importance of technology to storytelling. Advances in communications technology have opened up heretofore unforeseen possibilities for digital stories, in this case online video clips and blogs, that extend stories beyond their traditional reach. Such stories can touch the minds and hearts of people worldwide through visuals as well as words, spreading instantaneously across platforms, and can encourage the engagement of stakeholders who respond to the stories and generate their own.

This chapter shows how the powerful convergence of three organizational capabilities can maximize the potential of digital storytelling:

advanced communications technology; knowledge and practice of the craft of storytelling, especially in this case the choice and presentation of significant details and the novel and unexpected; and a strong corporate culture that embodies "character, values, and integrity" and is often expressed in stories of employees as culture heroes.

As an extended illustration of several aspects of the storytelling framework, the FedEx case sheds light on the capabilities that characterize storytelling, which here especially include working with communications technology and crafting stories. The case also illustrates how stories can help companies achieve the general business objective of building trust and the specific objectives of strengthening culture and brand. Finally, the case underscores the challenges of producing stories that take into account the organization's point of view and expression, on the one hand, and the individual's, on the other.

Let's turn now to FedEx.[1] A global transportation company of 285,000 employees, FedEx operates four business segments: FedEx Express for time-certain delivery of letters and packages within one to three business days; FedEx Ground for inexpensive ground delivery of packages; FedEx Freight for "less-than-truckload" freight services; and FedEx Services, which includes FedEx Office, sales, marketing, information technology, and customer service support to the other segments.[2]

FEDEX AS A PIONEER IN USING TECHNOLOGY TO COMMUNICATE WITH KEY STAKEHOLDERS

Flash back to 1988 and you'd find a then state-of-the-art corporate television facility, FXTV, at the company's headquarters in Memphis. FedEx established the facility to connect employees located around the country and to provide timely information, company news, and training.[3] At that time CEO Fred Smith reflected on the benefits of an in-house broadcast function as an enabler of open communications:

From the early days of Federal Express, we have shared good and bad news and have answered our people's questions in a straightforward manner. As we saw it, we had no choice. We had to communicate to survive. Even as we've spread out around the globe, we continue to look for new ways to keep channels open to all employees.

Perhaps our most dramatic move was to deploy what has become one of the largest private television networks in the world: FXTV. This medium has proven invaluable in managing changes. We announced FedEx's acquisition of Flying Tigers to our employees immediately after we informed the financial wire service so that they would get the news from us first. Throughout the integration and merger, we used the network for live phone-in sessions between senior management and employees. Our people didn't mince words. They had a lot of hard-hitting questions. They got straight answers.[4]

From the start, FXTV saw robust activity. Smith gave his quarterly reports on the network.[5] Tom Martin, then managing director of employee communications, taped a short daily company news program,[6] and videos about employees' achievements and contributions appeared routinely.[7] Initially, original content was scheduled at least three times a week, but as the company grew so did the amount of video content. In addition to standard leadership messaging and training, the medium was used to engage employees in company causes through telethons and other volunteer and fundraising broadcasts.[8] To broaden the audience for these broadcasts, more channels were created. Employees could view the broadcasts on fixed monitors in break rooms, or on demand using video streaming.[9] According to then FXTV manager Joe Hopkins, by 2002 the operation connected two thousand sites worldwide. Hopkins explained that having their own TV channel was particularly good in crisis situations. In fact, on 9/11 the technology helped senior management who went on the air to calm people and inform them of the company's near-term actions.[10, 11] Although these technological capabilities may seem ordinary by today's standards, they were then state-of-the-art for corporate America, and the company received numerous awards for these achievements.

FEDEX, TECHNOLOGY, AND COMMUNICATIONS IN 2005 AND BEYOND

By 2005, Margaritis saw the need to take a closer look at digital storytelling as a vehicle for strengthening stakeholder engagement, as he observed an increase in consumer expectations that businesses be accountable and authentic. To lead the new effort, he hired Diane Terrell. Formerly a senior producer at MSNBC and ABC News, Terrell moved to FedEx as the managing director of global broadcast and interactive communications. Her assignment, in her words, was to "re-invent FXTV," which was "Memphis-centric and very traditional in approach."[12]

When Terrell arrived at FedEx, she found that there had been no significant investment in the broadcast technology for ten years. In addition to outdated equipment, the communications group continued to rely on old models of leadership communications: scripted material read to a teleprompter conveying policies and procedures. Terrell introduced a journalistic approach to employee communications: character-driven stories that informed through emotive narrative. In reflecting on this period, she noted:

We were growing more global, acquiring new businesses here and abroad, expanding our portfolio of service offerings—all of which began to shift the center of gravity away from Memphis, away from the Express business; at the same time, the media landscape had turned confusing and chaotic, eliminating traditional avenues to reach the customer; new media technologies dominated every conversation. . . . We (FXTV) did not want to be lost in the arc of all that.[13]

Over the next three years, the strategic plans of the communications group reflected leadership aspirations by laying out specific steps for "re-inventing" FXTV to address the new challenges. "FXTV, the broadcast team" became "FedEx One, the all media network" with greater focus on digital storytelling. Margaritis was also watching the evolution of social media very carefully for clues to its impact on the business world.

Vigilant about reputation management and measurement, in 2008 the company began to systematically track online audiences commenting about FedEx. "Experts in social media all agree—now!—that every corporation needs to listen to the conversations going on about them," explains Ryan Furby, manager of social media strategies, who was assigned to develop strategies for engaging people in social media: "We started listening in 2007/2008 when few companies were taking conversations in social media seriously. We were pretty basic in the beginning," he adds, "searching for key words, questions, and sentiments expressed about the company."[14]

Communications also joined forces with Russ Fleming, VP of marketing, to look at how social media tools and technologies could be applied to achieve business results; "monitoring" was the first step. Terrell comments: "In 2008, there were not many examples of Marketing and Communications collaborating in this space. More often than not, the two departments were rivals battling for ownership of Social Media. Russ and I were unique in believing that this was so big, so important, no one could own it."[15]

In the summer of 2009 Margaritis created a director-led communications team to work on enterprise social media strategy development. The new group was named "Digital and Social Media Engagement."[16] As Terrell explains:

The near-term objective [of the team] is to help modernize our business and culture by encouraging higher degrees of collaboration, participation, and engagement through social media strategies. We want people using the tools and technologies to connect with each other and the company, to collaborate more effectively, to participate in innovation across functions and hierarchies. We aspire to a more flattened, more open and engaged organization that is apace with generational and cultural trends.

The new team consists of a Director, Renee Horne, and three Managers:

Dianna [O'Neill] is responsible for identifying and implementing "next generation" content strategies that will continue to make FedEx One [formerly FXTV] a key global channel to connect critical stakeholder audiences.

Ryan's team [Ryan Furby's] is responsible for building an ecosystem of channels and platforms designed to move stories and information seamlessly in the digital and social space, comprised of FedEx internal, external, and 3rd party sites. These channels include the FedEx presence on Facebook, YouTube, and Twitter, as well as the FedEx Blog and About FedEx, which offers corporate information to audiences visiting fedex.com.

His team also creates education and adoption strategies helping team members understand the business value of commitment to social media and how to best leverage the channels to extract that value and achieve business objectives.

The focus of Pam's team [Pamela Roberson's] is to drive business results by creating an engaged workforce that understands the business goals, what actions to take to deliver results, and how those actions contribute to business success.[17]

In this new environment, Terrell's goals for strategic storytelling are to retain a role for the traditional broadcast while moving the company's internal and external communications out of the studio into social and digital environments; to include the voices of frontline employees alongside those of senior executives; and to develop more relevant, resonant content, especially stories. To achieve these goals, her team works closely with IT because, according to Terrell, "they have the tools, the technology, and the expertise to enable success."[18]

Terrell summarizes the effort in this way: "We went from an identity as a broadcast center (FXTV) whose role it was to support internal clients in a very linear way—tell us what you want, and we will deliver—to an identity as a 'media consultancy' with a focus on proactive problem solving. We now create content and channels to meet 'anywhere, anytime' audience expectations. That's where stories come in."[19]

WHY THE EMPHASIS ON STORIES AT FEDEX?

I want to create a collection of thousands of stories that will add up to The FedEx Story.

—DIANE TERRELL, Vice President, Strategic Communications

Why the emphasis on stories, in particular on digital stories? The rationale and road map for this focus was spelled out in several strategic planning documents for the communications group from 2006 to 2008 under the umbrella of "reinventing FXTV."[20] According to the planning objectives, digital storytelling would take a dominant position in communications to bridge the divides of a workforce that is "global, multi-cultural, and multilingual."[21] The company wanted to create "a shared global experience that isn't solely dependent on language."[22] The visual experience would be dominant. In contrast to other types of discourse, stories were singled out for their ability to "inform, educate, and entertain" while "creat[ing] empathy through visualization."[23]

Asked about the emphasis on stories, Margaritis identified several macrotrends that stimulated this interest: a number of social, political, economic, and cultural trends as well as the state of communications technology that impact a company's ability to conduct business. These trends included people's demand for authenticity in the institutions with which they engage, and their lack of trust in large institutions; the economic downturn and FedEx's position as a bellwether of the economy (since the company is a leader in the transportation of goods worldwide); and the growing role of digital media in communications.

From a strategic perspective, Margaritis saw the need for FedEx stories to fulfill multiple purposes:

- To demonstrate how the customer experience is one of the company's top business priorities.[24] Stories strengthen this value proposition with customers and reinforce the culture, showing through examples how the company provides reliability and speed in delivery of packages—and goes beyond this objective. Stories can show, in Margaritis's words, how "the company does more than move packages. It has a higher calling in terms of increasing the standard of living and the quality of life."[25]

- To enhance the company's brand and reputation by showing real people—FedEx employees, beneficiaries of their services, and customers—and real stories. As Margaritis explained, "stories are part of the effort to fortify the emotional elements of the brand, things like 'likely to buy' and 'customer focused.' Consumers are taking a bigger look at the brand. Its emotional appeal is the biggest attribute."[26]

- To display the company's thought leadership. Company stories help with public advocacy, raising awareness of FedEx's role in society, demonstrating how the company supports free trade and improvement in people's lives, how positive results occur when commerce flows freely, and how businesses grow with the company's assistance.

DIGITAL STORIES AT FEDEX

Digital stories tend to be brief, interactive, and accessible. A story that might run for thirty minutes on a traditional broadcast platform would be three and a half minutes or less in an online version, in recognition of users' short attention spans and speed in consuming information online.[27]

Access to stories—relevant content within easy reach—requires efforts on the part of content developers as well as technical experts in content distribution.

Stories are often user-generated and linked to other communications platforms. For instance, a blog on giving back to the community by one FedEx employee stimulates another to tell a story about working on Wall Street at FedEx Office and discovering that people who used to come in to copy financial documents are now showing up to have their resumés copied: could the company offer a day on which people can have their resumés copied for free? This is just one example of how social platforms at FedEx allow employees to participate more directly in business decisions.[28]

Compelling digital stories are likely to "go viral": Stories about FedEx employees, either first-person reports captured by video crews or stories by the employees themselves using flip cams or Webcams, cascade from the intranet to the Web, appearing on employees' Facebook or YouTube pages.

The company also understands that channels are not under its control. As Diane Terrell notes: "No one can own the organization's voice. Authentic stories in the voice of actual people telling them will work their way into this new social culture with or without us."[29]

CULTURE, STORIES, AND HEROES

According to Bill Margaritis, FedEx has built its culture in part around heroic stories, the enormous lengths to which employees will go to deliver "golden packages,"[30] such as a FedEx truck driver who pulled an elderly man out of his car in a flood,[31] or a team of employees who successfully delivered 90 tons of artifacts from the *Titanic* destined for an exhibition in Atlanta but stranded in southern Italy.[32] Stories of these discretionary efforts by employees who have prevailed in the face of substantial obstacles are, Margaritis adds, the centerpiece of communications about culture:

Seeing and hearing heroic stories become self-fulfilling. People are rejuvenated through stories. They hear heroic stories and want to emulate them. You can't legislate the heart, the extra step people will take. No training or rule book defines whether someone goes above and beyond. No training or rule book can force someone to be loyal and motivated. Employees are our ambassadors and represent and promote the company. If you create the right context for employees, they will pass this experience on, showing outsiders about it through their social networks. Stories are the emotional part of all this. We don't forget the scenes in certain movies.[33]

Eric Epperson, the director of workplace communications (and a direct report to Terrell), is responsible for reinforcing the company's core values with the workforce. At the heart of his efforts is instilling the "Purple Promise," employees' commitment to making every FedEx experience outstanding. Purple Promise awards are given to recognize employees who go above and beyond to provide excellent customer service and to motivate others to do so. Such acknowledgment is based on the FedEx philosophy of "People-Service-Profit" (PSP): treating employees well—putting them first—ensures that they will give the discretionary effort which, in turn, leads to profits.[34]

Many of the Purple Promise stories placed on the Internet are about heroes; for instance, the story of a shipping agent who rescued a neighbor attacked by a large dog,[35] or that of a ramp agent and senior operations support specialist who volunteered their vacation time and personal equipment to transport couriers and packages between Sanibel Island and the Florida mainland when the connecting bridge was closed for emergency repairs.[36]

Epperson sees an important role for stories in reaffirming the culture and, in doing so, enhancing the company's revenue and reputation through the efforts of employees. Asked to explain how stories accomplish this, he remarked:

My job is to get employees to embrace the values of the company. FedEx is in a highly competitive service industry. We're at parity [with our competitor] in pricing. Customer loyalty depends on service experiences. We need to ensure that customers are well taken care of. Discretionary effort counts, and this means individual decisions every day by people who work here: the courier who goes off his route to do an unscheduled delivery, or the guy who picks up the phone at 5:01 when he's officially finished with work. Stories are something to inspire other employees. They evoke the emotional part of the job. Let's take the story about the national speaker on the road who sends his material by FedEx from place to place so that he doesn't have to carry it himself. He gets to a city where his materials are in storage until the next day, so he wouldn't get them in time for his presentation. He speaks to a FedEx employee about his problem, and the employee asks a friend who lives in the city where the speaker is to work to go to the warehouse, track down the package, and deliver it to the speaker. We tell and celebrate this story.[37]

To follow up the Purple Promise program, "I am FedEx" was introduced in 2009. It was the new media version of Purple Promise, a culture initiative to celebrate employees by giving voice to their role as the face of the company. "For employees, the Purple Promise is about what they do," explains communications manager O'Neill. "'I am FedEx' is about who they are."[38] Some stories are told by Purple Promise award winners like FedEx Express courier Joe Gauthier, who searched tirelessly after hours for a customer's lost medication.[39]

"I am FedEx" was especially important in the wake of reduced compensation and the layoffs of several hundred people during the severe economic recession of 2008 and 2009. As Terrell notes: "We lost some of the trust we had built with employees over the years and team member recognition became our number one priority. But we couldn't offer the financial rewards we had in the past so we had to get real creative."[40] A recent module, "Everyday Acts," asks coworkers to nominate a peer who consistently performs at a high level and whose work is then celebrated in a short video clip.

"I am FedEx" was designed to create a seamless narrative about the company, to build a single, powerful story about FedEx through the many diverse stories of its employees. In practice, this approach gives employees latitude for creating their own story while guiding their thinking about what topic to choose and how to develop it (see Exhibit 7.1). In addition, the approach allows the company to use the accumulation of stories under each topic to project a consistent profile of itself and its corporate values. For instance, all the stories listed under the topic "My Commitment" demonstrate that FedEx is a socially responsible citizen that gives back to the community. The company shows this through the stories of good works performed by individual employees, such as CIO Rob Carter telling about teaching algebra to ninth-graders—an effort he describes as more challenging than

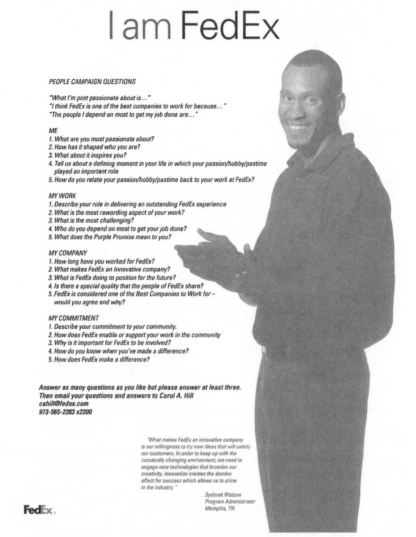

I am FedEx

PEOPLE CAMPAIGN QUESTIONS

"What I'm post passionate about is..."
"I think FedEx is one of the best companies to work for because..."
"The people I depend on most to get my job done are..."

ME
1. What are you most passionate about?
2. How has it shaped who you are?
3. What about it inspires you?
4. Tell us about a defining moment in your life in which your passion/hobby/pastime played an important role
5. How do you relate your passion/hobby/pastime back to your work at FedEx?

MY WORK
1. Describe your role in delivering an outstanding FedEx experience
2. What is the most rewarding aspect of your work?
3. What is the most challenging?
4. Who do you depend on most to get your job done?
5. What does the Purple Promise mean to you?

MY COMPANY
1. How long have you worked for FedEx?
2. What makes FedEx an innovative company?
3. What is FedEx doing to position for the future?
4. Is there a special quality that the people of FedEx share?
5. FedEx is considered one of the Best Companies to Work for – would you agree and why?

MY COMMITMENT
1. Describe your commitment to your community.
2. How does FedEx enable or support your work in the community
3. Why is it important for FedEx to be involved?
4. How do you know when you've made a difference?
5. How does FedEx make a difference?

Answer as many questions as you like but please answer at least three. Then email your questions and answers to Carol A. Hill
cahill@fedex.com
973-565-2383 x2300

"What makes FedEx an innovative company is our willingness to try new ideas that will satisfy our customers. In order to keep up with the constantly changing environment, we need to engage new technologies that broaden our creativity. Innovation creates the domino effect for success which allows us to shine in the industry."

Sydorek Watson
Program Administrator
Memphis, TN

FedEx.

EXHIBIT 7.1.   "I am FedEx"
SOURCE: Courtesy of FedEx Corporation

presenting to a business group of a thousand people[41]—and by employees working together to build or restore "green" areas in cities,[42] transport food to those in need,[43] or march to support children's charities.[44]

Employee stories can be shared through the "I am FedEx" Web site in several ways. Employees can upload a photo they've taken along with a caption or short text of two to three lines (though occasionally an employee writes a longer narrative); upload a video they've shot, typically about two minutes; or participate in a video shoot or photo portrait that the FedEx digital and social media team produces.

Culture heroes emerge not only in the individual vignettes of "I am FedEx" but also in blogs by employees who develop a following. One such individual is Sheila Harrell, vice president of customer service operations. People know Harrell, even if they haven't met her, because of her blog. The oldest of four daughters raised in a small town in Missouri, she describes herself as gregarious by nature—her father was an auctioneer—and as a "collector of stories" from an early age, when she spent time at St. Jude's Ronald McDonald house listening to people in the hospital tell their stories while she waited for her sister to return from treatment for cancer. A thirty-two-year veteran of FedEx, Harrell has held multiple positions—in the first call center, in courier planning, in various roles in technology, and in ground service. In 2008, she became the head of customer service operations. With a mandate to get to know the eight thousand people who report to her and to strengthen customer service, she turned to blogging as a tool to bring people close to each other through stories and to reflect on her life experience as it's connected to theirs. Her first blog, which was about work/life balance (posted externally as well as internally) drew responses from both FedEx employees and "Mommy bloggers". Their common interests, initially articulated in her life story, created an online community of people within and outside the organization. Harrell has extended the theme to include sharing customers' stories about their challenges, along with the ways that FedEx can help them; for instance, by delivering a "golden package"—a precious gift—in a snowstorm during Christmas or by helping a small company like Memphis's "Rendezvous BBQ" deliver ribs around the world. Harrell has moved more and more from telling her own stories to telling those of others, both employees' and customers', underscoring the connection between engaged employees and happy customers: "I try to use the technology to celebrate people every week. I send out three stories every week which show what people have done to serve a customer, and I name them."[45]

Another culture hero and fellow blogger with a following, Mitch Jackson, who is the vice president of environmental affairs and sustainability, uses his blog to tell stories about the company's "green" initiatives, such as spearheading the electrification of commercial vehicles, and to reflect more broadly on sustainability and environmental stewardship. Jackson weaves thought-provoking quotations into his blog from the likes of the American writer Washington Irving and biologist Stephen Jay Gould ("Nothing is more dangerous than a dogmatic worldview—nothing more constraining, more blinding to innovation, more destructive of openness to novelty").[46] Jackson also comes up with puns that blend the formal and the colloquial in his distinctive personal voice. Note, for example, the title of his blog entry "Innovation: Knickers in a Twist" followed by a quotation from Washington Irving, aka Diedrich Knickerbocker, in which Jackson urges businesses to see risks not as dilemmas—finding their "knickers in a twist"—but as opportunities to create innovative approaches to environmental challenges.[47] His unique style of expression in storytelling shines through while he shows his thought leadership in the broader conversation about these issues both within and outside of the company.

Communication professionals working internationally underscore the importance of stories in the creation and maintenance of a united culture of 285,000 people working worldwide. Sharon Young, communications advisor of global communications, reflects: "The more a company is global, the more it needs to work with stories. Someone in LA does not quite understand the attitude of someone in Asia, but can understand this through stories. People feel part of a bigger whole when they can see the person loading a package at one end of the world that's then delivered to another end of the world."[48] Similarly, Dianna O'Neill points out: "How do we link the courier delivering packages in Iceland to the one in Manhattan? The answer is sharing experiences about delivering excellent service."[49]

AUTHENTIC STORYTELLING: HONORING PERSONAL
EXPRESSION WHILE FULFILLING ORGANIZATIONAL GOALS
FedEx stories address organizational goals like building a more engaged workforce but leave ample room for individual expression and interpretation. The company balances the personal and the organizational through the use of story topic categories and specific questions linked to each topic. Take the "I am FedEx" program, in which the company "seeds" stories, inviting employees to celebrate themselves by creating their own stories while selecting one of four broad story topic categories and responding

to questions for the topic selected. Exhibit 7.1 identifies the broad topic categories—"Me," "My Work," "My Company," and "My Commitment"—under which appear questions to "prime the pump," to engage the imagination, to help generate content, and to bridge between the personal and the organizational. "People like to talk about things in this order: me, my job, my company and my life," says Diane Terrell (a quote she readily admits to having borrowed from CIO Rob Carter). "We organized 'I am FedEx' storytelling around these foundational pillars to help elicit authentic participation and engagement for our subjects."[50]

Note how a category like "Me" gives more weight to the personal—an employee's passions or a defining moment in his life—than to work life but nonetheless encourages the creation of a link between the personal and organizational with the last question: "How do you relate your passion/hobby/pastime back to your work at FedEx?" The category "My Commitment" focuses more on corporate social responsibility, such as improving or creating "green areas" in communities,[51] but also includes the stories of individual employees asked for personal reflection on their work. Ultimately, the campaign, launched on the Web in January 2010, serves as a recognition platform. It is an approach in which people are not scripted; rather, they are guided but speak in their own voice.

FLUENT STORYTELLING: CRAFTING STORIES

Of the many choices about story elements that need to be made in crafting a story, FedEx corporate communication professionals give special attention to choice of significant details and choice and development of the novel or unexpected. These professionals help their colleagues who are not necessarily skilled in storytelling to gain mastery of these elements of fluent storytelling.

Focusing on Significant Details

I keep looking for the Tabasco in the drawer.

—DIANNA O'NEILL, Manager, Digital Content & Social Media Engagement

Before joining FedEx, Dianna O'Neill worked as a national news and documentary producer on topics like women on death row and blues music in the Mississippi Delta. Her filmmaker's visual imagination, especially her eye for detail, informs her work in story development at FedEx. Asked to create a story about engineers who study flight patterns to improve operations, she spent time in their bunker-style facilities, the nerve center for global operations, and tried to engage them in conversation about their work, a difficult challenge due to the technical jargon they typically use—for instance, "angels" (a common unit for altitude), "heading" (true or magnetic), "touch-and-gos" (practice takeoffs and landings by student or test pilots), and the "great circle route" (the shortest distance between two locations on a sphere such as the globe)—as well as their unfamiliarity with the use of storytelling in their professional lives. As O'Neill observed, in her initial conversations with them, "The talk was clearly professional and informed—but flat from a storyteller's perspective. There was no rhythm, no tone, no pulse."[52] As a result, she searched for a detail that would help her craft an engaging story for an audience unaccustomed to discussions about aerodynamics and advanced computer systems but potentially interested not only in the work of these technical experts but also in who they were as people. She found that connection in an unusual place. One day she noticed a file cabinet drawer labeled "Pending Jepp Revisions." It would not have caught her attention but for an incongruous detail. The drawer had fallen open to reveal not a "Jepp Revision," which O'Neill had never heard of, but bottles of hot sauce (Exhibit 7.2).

When she asked an engineer about it, he replied, "Oh, that's the condiment drawer; it's off-limits," laughing about the group's secret hot sauce stash and their shared meals, and confessing that it was deliberately mislabeled with the name of a tedious administrative task in an effort to keep others from discovering the group's prized hot sauce collection. It was this small detail that created an opening for O'Neill to connect with the engineering team on an emotional level. From then on, the conversations took a more energetic and lively turn as the group began discussing their shared meals and comradery and displaying a relaxed and spontaneous enthusiasm for the first time. O'Neill captured this human side to the group's activity in her story: "When I asked the engineers initially to talk about how they liked working in the unit, their answers were the model of talking-point efficiency—dedication to service—but I kept looking for

EXHIBIT 7.2.   Significant Detail: Hot Sauce
SOURCE: Courtesy FedEx Corporation

the Tabasco sauce too. That's the critical factor in making the story stick. It says something personal and memorable, and it creates a point of engagement with the audience."[53]

"Tabasco sauce," a significant detail that becomes the focus of a story, appears in many of the FedEx digital stories. Not surprisingly, given the importance of culture and employees, a specific detail often illustrates the culture while illuminating the personality of the employee whose story is told: a young, high-energy courier who bounds with enthusiasm as she moves through her customer stops while commenting on losing her shyness as a result of the job[54]; a talkative driver with a unique way of describing himself: "I'm a natural. I'm the king of gab."[55]

Discovering Novel Topics and Developing Stories
Corporate communication professionals work in multiple ways to identify topics for stories and to craft, or help to craft them. Some topics have inherent emotional appeal; for instance, the story of the rescue and return of the penguins from the Audubon Aquarium of the Americas in New Orleans

after Hurricane Katrina,[56] or the multiple stories about the pandas' voyage home to China after spending years in the zoo in Washington, DC.[57] Among these stories are the ones about employees as culture heroes who go to enormous lengths to deliver "golden packages."

When assisting employees in telling their stories, these communication professionals may select a setting or storyline. Consider, for example, two international stories launched under the guidance of commuications advisor Sharon Young. One features Eddy Chan, born in Hong Kong; and the other, Raj Subramaniam of Mumbai.[58] Young brings each of them back to his birthplace and asks him to tell his story against this backdrop, an approach that stimulates both memories—the sights and sounds of childhood—and reflections on the economic progress that has occurred over his lifespan, growth that is linked to the increased presence of FedEx as a bellwether of trade in his native land. Each story is autobiographical and, in Young's terms, a series of "pulse points" that mark both personal life and global change in Asia. For Eddy Chan, now a senior vice president for FedEx Express in China, his first job out of college was with FedEx in 1985, and his progression through the ranks parallels the company's growth in China. Eddy concludes his story with the lessons he learned about teamwork and humility at FedEx that capture the meaning he attributes to his story: "A humble soul equals an open mind." Raj Subramaniam, now senior vice president of international marketing, tells his story about growing up in an Indian culture that values high energy and entrepreneurship, and about the changes he has witnessed. He sees a growing, vibrant business environment with global market reach that promises a bright future for Indian business and for FedEx. For these stories, Young explains, "Each had a few bullet points to work with, but we got the story from the heart."

Corporate communication professionals also work to create an unthreatening environment for storytelling in which employees can tell their story (or have their story told) in a natural, uninhibited way. For instance, since Young is aware of the cultural reticence in China to talk about one's feelings, she takes an indirect approach in her interviews. Instead of asking her interviewees to talk about their work, she has them respond from an outsider's point of view: What do your friends say about your work? What do your friends tell you about what a good job is? What did your mother say when you got the job? Young also has a Chinese cameraman working alongside her who helps her understand cultural nuance.

A strong corporate culture exemplified by employees who are heroes, communication professionals with expertise in the craft of storytelling who work alongside those in advanced communications technology: these are ingredients for authentic, fluent digital storytelling that convey what Bill Margaritis identifies as the "character, values, and integrity of corporations." In the process these stories build trust and strengthen brand and culture. "Content is king," Margaritis adds, "so build content around authentic stories." While their primary purpose is to convey serious and inspiring messages, such stories can amuse and delight—and they can stimulate more and more employees to participate as storytellers.

8   FEDEX: LESSONS LEARNED

T HE FEDEX CASE SHOWS that digital storytelling in business benefits from the expertise of corporate communication professionals.
They are experts in the craft of storytelling, able instructors of others less
skilled in the craft, experienced users of communications technology to
support digital storytelling, and good collaborators with high-tech experts
who can help them produce and distribute stories. All of these qualities
were in place in the FedEx case along with the company's recognition that
authentic storytelling requires room for individual expression as well as
corporate representation and should give a central place to stories of employees as carriers of the corporate culture.

This chapter offers an analysis of the FedEx case supplemented by examples from other organizations and from experts in storytelling who work
in the arts or in business. The initial objective is to introduce the best practices in fluent storytelling that can be drawn from the case. These include
elements associated with the craft of storytelling, like choosing compelling
topics for stories, focusing on significant details, featuring characters, and
looking for the novel and unexpected. Next, technology and storytelling
underscore the opportunities for innovation and the need for coordination
between those who develop content for stories and the high-tech experts
who work on disseminating them. Although the quality of digital stories

in business benefits from the expertise of corporate communication professionals and high tech experts, every business professional interested in learning about storytelling can extrapolate practical lessons from the case.

USE A TOPICS-AND-QUESTIONS APPROACH
TO "INVENT" STORIES

Effective storytelling for business often draws on personal experience while linking it to specific business purposes. Such stories leave room for individual expression as well as corporate representation. The "I am FedEx" program introduces an approach using topics and questions to help employees find and develop stories that link the personal to the organizational. One story is that of the FedEx employee who tells about his experience as a football coach in an inner city. "Ironically," explains communications manager Dianna O'Neill, "in representing himself personally, he became a more engaging ambassador for FedEx."[1]

Working with topics and questions may alleviate the concerns of employees who resist storytelling, for the approach gives people the freedom to choose a topic they're comfortable discussing in public and to decide how to develop it. Many of the baby boom generation (whom I've worked with in my consulting) resist using stories, preferring instead to stick to more familiar forms of business communication, such as PowerPoint presentations of data and analysis. Some think that working with stories necessarily means revealing intimate details and may be unwilling to risk too much self-disclosure. A topics-and-questions approach like the "I am FedEx" guidelines helps a businessperson find a topic that's authentic yet is neither too intimate nor embarrassing.

By contrast to some of the baby boomers, many Millennials (born between 1981 and 1992) are quite accustomed to digital storytelling on platforms like YouTube and Facebook. They enjoy the self-expression it affords and place stories online before getting their first job. Two Millennials whom I know quite well—my son, Benjamin, and my nephew, David—shot YouTube videos typical of the quirky humor and personal stamp of members of their cohort group. Benjamin appeared in "The Great White Flake." He cast himself as the "Flake" because of his broad, peeling, sunburned back, a result of surfing for days in Costa Rica. David starred as the "Christmas Tree"—he's quite tall—in his Ultimate (Frisbee) team's holiday greeting card. A study reported by the Center for Media Research found that one out of five Millennials has posted a video of themselves online.[2] "This latest generation new to the job market," FedEx communication manager Eric Epperson explains, "does not want to be a cog in a wheel. They complain that culture can be homogenized, and they want it to be personalized."[3] The Millennials need very little, if any, encouragement to put their stories online.

FOCUS ON SIGNIFICANT DETAILS DOWN TO THE INDIVIDUAL WORD AND PHRASE

In business decisions and communications, value is often placed on scrupulous attention to data, especially the details of numerical analysis, but significant *human* detail is often unwittingly or purposely ignored. Yet, it is the human detail—the gesture, intonation, dress, pictures, and the awards on an executive's office wall—that gives vibrancy and power to stories for business.

Literary critics like Alfred Kazin revere the significant detail as an opening to the human heart and mind: "The detail is the clue. The human mind and heart are labyrinths we never get the better of. All we have are a few details. Remember Ariadne's thread? The famous going through the labyrinth? You don't reach the end. . . . But you have to have the detail."[4] It is what O'Neill calls "the Tabasco in the drawer." This detail can evoke emotions, memories, and desires and stimulate the visual imagination of those on the receiving end of stories. Similarly, screenplay writers talk passionately about the importance of detail to their work.

Significant details are one of the hallmarks of great fiction as well. The twentieth-century French novelist Marcel Proust is reported to have interviewed a member of the British delegation to Versailles during the signing of the peace treaty that ended World War I. The novelist would ask: How do the delegates walk in?[5] This interview occurred before the publication of his great opus *Remembrance of Things Past*, a work that captures the details of fashion, verbal expression, and gesture that bring to life his characters and the fictional universe they inhabit. Proust's interest in detail carried over in his private life to his loathing of clichéd expressions, "examples of the most exhausted constructions whose use implied little concern for evoking the specifics of a situation."[6]

No one would expect or want a story for business with the length and the verbal complexity of Proust's work—but the human details matter in business stories. As we have seen, the significant detail illuminates FedEx's digital stories. This is the case for customers' stories that appeal to the five senses: a vat holding a 70-pound batch of cream filling for candies and the machines that coat the cookies drenched in chocolate[7]; a craftsman drilling holes in antlers to make chandeliers and table lamps[8]; a maker of musical instruments stretching the skin of a drum over a lacquered plywood frame.[9]

Communications advisor Sharon Young emphasizes the importance of focusing on the five senses: "If I'm getting a story from a truck driver, I'd ask, 'What's cool about this truck?'" In a story she developed about FedEx NASCAR driver Danny Hamlin, she recalls asking him: "'When you're sitting in the car during the race, what does it sound like?' The answer is fabulous: 'When you're in the car, the faster you go, the slower you see the crowd.'"[10]

One does not need to be a novelist to be a close observer of detail, but these mental faculties, part of what we might call a "storyteller's sensibility," are perhaps best expressed by one, in this case the nineteenth-century French short-story writer Guy de Maupassant:

Talent is lengthy patience. It is a question of looking at anything you want to express long enough and closely enough to discover in it something that nobody else has seen before. In everything, there's something waiting to be discovered, simply because we tend to look at the world only through the eyes of those who have preceded us. The most insignificant thing contains something of the unknown. Let's find it.[11]

FEATURE CHARACTERS IN STORIES

Stories about corporate life, especially about corporate culture, need to focus on people who in this age of significant distrust of business are perceived to be the chief corporate truth tellers. The best stories often start with one character. The American novelist Henry James admitted that he built his novel *The Portrait of a Lady* with "a single small corner-stone, the conception of a certain young woman affronting her destiny."[12] Literary critic R. P. Blackmur comments on James's approach, singling out his extraordinary powers of attention: "Subjects never came ready-made or complete, but always from hints, notes, the merest suggestion. Often a single fact reported at the dinner-table was enough for James to seize on and plant in the warm bed of his imagination."[13] Novelists like James may build their fiction around a single character, the relationships she develops, and the complications these create. The narrator of Nobel Prize-winning Czech novelist Milan Kundera's *Immortality* reflects eloquently on the birth of story through detail of character. A writer himself, the narrator tells of observing a woman in her sixties taking swimming lessons from a young lifeguard:

I was watching her from a deck chair by the pool of my health club, on the top floor of a high-rise that provided a panoramic view of all Paris. I was waiting for Professor Avenius, whom I'd occasionally meet here for a chat. But Professor Avenius was late, and I kept watching the woman; she was alone in the pool, standing waist-deep in the water, and she kept looking at the young lifeguard in sweat pants who was teaching her to swim. He was giving her orders: she was to hold on to the edge of the pool and breathe deeply in and out. She proceeded to do this earnestly, seriously, and it was as if an old steam engine were wheezing from the depths of the water (that idyllic sound, now long forgotten, which to those who never knew it can be described in no better way than the wheezing of an old woman breathing in and out by the edge of a pool). I watched her with fascination. She captivated me by her touchingly comic manner (which the lifeguard also noticed, for the corner of his mouth twitched slightly). Then an acquaintance started talking to me and diverted my attention. When I was ready to observe her once again, the lesson was over. She walked around the pool toward the exit. She passed the lifeguard, and after she had gone some three or four steps beyond him, she turned her head, smiled, and waved to him. At that instant I felt a pang in my heart! That smile and that gesture belonged to a twenty-year-old girl! Her arm rose with bewitching ease. It was as if she were playfully tossing a brightly colored ball to her lover. That smile and that gesture had charm and elegance, while the face and body no longer had any charm.[14]

Despite the mild distractions of anticipating the arrival of a colleague and having his attention diverted momentarily by an acquaintance, the narrator remains focused on this woman. She later emerges out of the narrator's dream state and becomes the character Agnes, "the heroine of my novel."[15]

Media entrepreneur Avi Savar advises companies to "lead with 'people stories,' not 'product stories.'"[16] Though intended for practical business purposes like building a culture of exceptional service—and not for aesthetic ones—stories for business that focus on characters, real people in this case, provide multiple benefits to business. Among these are inspiring greater efforts on the part of employees, and building trust through displaying the actions of a key asset of an organization: its employees. Tom Kowalski, vice president of corporate communications for BMW of North America, notes: "Every day employees have a chance to do great work, to do things that contribute value. Some of their actions will, and some won't. Communication provides the opportunity to help employees make decisions to drive more value in their work."[17]

So strong is the appeal of people stories over product stories that "Abe's Market," an e-commerce venture launched in October 2009, has created a business around providing a space for CEOs who sell green products to tell "getting acquainted" and founding stories that make connections to a potential customer base and build trust by illustrating the challenges and passions they experienced in building their firms. Richard Demb, cofounder of Abe's Market, explains the appeal of the site: "People want to buy from other people. There are very few opportunities to meet the people who make your markets. We look at Abe's Market as a limitless farmers' market."[18]

Perhaps an even better way to build trust is to have customers tell their stories online about their experience with a company, as FedEx, Dell, and JetBlue have done. These are the visual counterpart or supplement to traditional customer testimonials, typically written statements only. Customer stories at FedEx include that of a rose grower from Colombia who tells the story about transporting his flowers worldwide,[19] and a manufacturer of uniforms designed in Indianapolis and shipped from China to customers globally.[20] Dell's "take your own path" campaign features enthusiastic customers who volunteer to tell their stories of how Dell's products and services helped them conduct business. According to Erin Mulligan Nelson, senior vice president and chief marketing officer, these stories communicate Dell's authenticity to insiders as well as outsiders; as a result, the brand is less nebulous, and the employees become more personally engaged by seeing the results of their work in the success of others.[21] At JetBlue, people who are real customers and not celebrity endorsers talk in online video clips about what is uniquely attractive to them in their flying experience on the airline.[22] Like FedEx customers and employees who tell their stories, JetBlue's customers are not scripted.

As noted in the FedEx case, some company stories are truly heroic. When heroism—on the part of individuals or teams—is a realistic aspect of a business enterprise, even greater engagement by stakeholders can be expected because the stories tap into deep emotions. The most basic of these heroic stories may be the successful *quest* for a worthwhile goal in the face of significant obstacles, a plot line that is as old as the ancient epic tradition. Think of Homer's *Odyssey* and the struggles the hero faced in making his way home. Conflict—the battle against the one-eyed monster Cyclops, the multiheaded creature Scylla, and the powers of nature in the form of the whirlpool Charybdis and of the fierce winds subject to the whims of the god Aeolus—and especially conflict with a positive resolution, add dynamism and intensity to these stories. Examples abound at FedEx: employees who risk and succeed in the face of natural disasters, such as a FedEx truck driver who saved an elderly man by pulling him from his car in a flood[23]; or the team of employees who faced complex obstacles in transporting precious cargo like whales and dolphins[24]; or the odyssey of the Washington, DC, pandas—a return home to China—orchestrated by another team.[25, 26]

LOOK FOR THE NOVEL AND UNEXPECTED IN STORIES
Every movie's a suspense movie, even a romantic comedy. There's a need for anticipation and surprise. These are essential.
—NEIL LANDAU, Screenplay writer and Visiting Assistant Professor,
UCLA School of Theater, Film, and Television

Filmmakers, arguably the world's experts in visual storytelling, know that stories must surprise and delight to bring viewers to the screen and hold their attention. The novel, the unexpected, is sometimes discovered by corporate communication professionals who themselves have had training and experience as documentary filmmakers or journalists. Dianna O'Neill, formerly a national news and documentary producer and now in charge of content development at FedEx, persists in asking questions of her interviewees until she finds the unusual, the "hot sauce." For example, an employee for FedEx Ground, a "take charge" guy who appears to be all business in setting work objectives and focusing on service, unveils a personal side one would not have anticipated. He's known to his coworkers as a joker and a gifted impersonator.[27] To make his point, he breaks out into a dance routine, an imitation of "Carleton," Will Smith's cousin in the TV show *The Fresh Prince of Bel Air*.[28] An African American vice president of information technology with the poise of a professional dancer tells her story to a rap beat and doesn't unveil her corporate role until the end of the story.[29] This story became the prototype for the "I am FedEx" stories that followed.

Clichés and artificiality, antithetical to the novel and unexpected, are stripped out of stories. "If I'm asking someone what it's like working at an operating company," O'Neill explains, "the standard reply is, 'We are dedicated to service,' but that doesn't really tell you anything. Everyone is dedicated to outstanding service, so the statement evaporates. You have to keep looking for the Tabasco sauce in the drawer, the nuance or unexpected moment that creates the staying power of the story."[30] Note, for example, the authentic voice of truck driver Bill Bridges of FedEx Freight in describing his efforts to find a lost customer package, an accomplishment that resulted in his receiving a Purple Promise Award: "I wasn't trying to get [an] award, I was just trying to keep a customer and let them know we want their freight. We want to be able to haul it for them and they can depend on it."[31] "People detest memorized corporate speak," FedEx communications manager Young remarks. "I edit it out and ask questions to get beyond it."[32] And as Katie Delahaye Paine, CEO of a public relations firm, notes: "Blogs become popular because they reflect the real personalities and values of the people writing them. No one reads a blog to get more corporate speak. They read blogs to get the information *behind* the corporate-speak."[33]

FIGURE OUT HOW BEST TO USE SOCIAL
MEDIA FOR DIGITAL STORYTELLING

Social media experts Charlene Li and Josh Bernoff offer a systematic approach to tapping into what they call the "groundswell," "a social trend in which people use technologies to get the things they need from each other, rather than from traditional institutions like corporations."[34] The approach applies broadly to all types of communications, not just to stories, but is also useful in thinking about digital storytelling for communicating with a large number of important stakeholders. Li and Bernoff ask businesses to first identify the goals they want to achieve by using social media. Among these are listening to customers, talking to them, energizing those that like the company to spread the word, and supporting them by providing social media tools to help them communicate with each other.[35]

At FedEx, to achieve the goal of *listening* to customers, social media manager Ryan Furby tracks stories online produced by outsiders who comment—through these stories—on the company.[36] *Talking* encompasses support for employee-generated blogs and videos. *Energizing* involves presenting the stories of customers and of beneficiaries of the company's philanthropic efforts (for example, the Red Cross, the New Orleans zoo, relief efforts in Haiti) who can, through their stories, communicate the company's accomplishments to their peers. *Supporting* is perhaps best exemplified by customers and employees sharing information and advice on blogs like Sheila Harrell's on work/life balance and Mitch Jackson's on sustainability.

ENCOURAGE INNOVATIVE DIGITAL STORYTELLING
RELEVANT TO YOUR BUSINESS PURPOSES

There are multiple examples of innovation in online narrative to date, and more are likely as communication professionals become more familiar with the capabilities of the technology and as technology experts reach across the aisle to communication experts. At Kodak, employees craft stories for customers that focus on how to take and share photos.[37] Siemens has used "jamming," online blogging focused on interactive storytelling, to discuss and shape the company's core values, like responsibility, excellence, and innovation, and to get buy-in for these values through the process. These stories came alive through real-time interaction between senior managers and employees and convey lessons about culture. The CEO of Siemens USA kicked off a three-day session, moderating and laying out the story; other senior managers took turns in one-hour slots. Final tally: there were 26,000 hits and 450 discussion comments. Stories extracted from the blog and illustrating corporate values were then included in the company's magazine.[38]

At PepsiCo, digital stories can take the form of a competition, the "PepsiCo Refresh Project." People pitch their stories on the Pepsi Web site on a social cause they are passionate about. Then others vote online for what they believe to be the most worthwhile story, and that cause receives a grant. The company sees the online game as a way to increase consumer reach and engagement, and ultimately to build brand by contributing to the things people care about. PepsiCo is giving away $1.3 million a month.[39]

COORDINATE CRAFT AND TECHNOLOGY, "CONTENT DEVELOPMENT" AND "CONTENT DISTRIBUTION"

Reality is the convergence of content and technology. It is not gadgets for gadgets' sake but sharing information with friends, families, and storying.

—RYAN FURBY, Director, Workplace Communications

Innovations in technology notwithstanding, the focus of digital storytelling should be the story, which has greater reach than "pre–social media" storytelling thanks to the technology. "Combine the power of storytelling plus the connectivity of the Web to tell a richer, more resonant FedEx story," advises Diane Terrell.[40]

As we saw in the FedEx case, advances in communications technology occurred in tandem with the company's communication strategy for engaging important stakeholders. Beginning in the 1980s, the CIO and CCO worked together closely in these endeavors. This cooperation intensified as social and digital media began to dominate. In fact, FedEx developed an enterprise-level strategy for social media, one with the goal of creating what Terrell calls "a single, unified approach to Social engagement and also drives 'social media-fication' of our business culture. To succeed, we clearly required an organizational locus for this activity, a team accountable to guide and enable employees by bringing the best tools, technologies, platforms, and strategies into the workplace, and educating folks on how to apply them in the context of the global business."[41] Other companies noteworthy in this regard include PepsiCo, Ford, Dell, and Toyota.[42]

APPLY LESSONS LEARNED FROM THE
FEDEX CASE TO YOUR WORK

You can reap the benefits of the work conducted by experts in storytelling at FedEx without having to be a specialist in the field. FedEx offers its employees a topics-and-questions approach to "invent" stories, that is, to discover topics of interest to themselves and to their organization and to turn them into stories. As we saw in the FedEx case, these topics are Me, My Work, My Company, and My Commitment (see Exhibit 7.1 for the full list of topics and questions). Some of them may help you generate and develop stories of your own for business. For instance, look at the questions under the category Me:

> What are you most passionate about?
> How has it shaped who you are?
> What about it inspires?
> Tell us about a defining moment in your life in which your passion/
> hobby/pastime played an important role.
> How do you relate your passion/hobby/pastime back to your work
> at FedEx [substitute the name of your company]?

How would you answer these questions? What story can you compose based on your answers? When and why would you use it? Review the other topics in "I am FedEx" (Exhibit 7.1) and see whether any of them stimulate your thinking about a story for a specific business objective that you can tell, write, and possibly record as a video clip for use on a personal or organizational Web site.

Note that the topics and questions can be used flexibly. For instance, My Work includes the prompt "Describe your role in delivering an outstanding

FedEx experience." Adapted to your own work experience, this might be something like "Describe your role in delivering an outstanding experience to your company's customers." To prepare to put together such a story, take detailed notes after your customer meetings and, as Jeff Hunt, principal and cofounder of PulsePoint Group (a consulting firm for strategic communications), recommends to his clients, use a phone-app to take pictures of the client meetings to supplement your notes. Then develop the story. Consider too whether the story would have more impact if it were told from the point of view and in the voice of the customer than from your own. If so, can you encourage your customer to tell the story about superior service?

Under this same category of My Work, the last question—"What does the Purple Promise mean to you?"—may stimulate your thinking about whether your organization has core values that provide norms of behavior and, if so, what they are. What values are prominent, and what actions have you taken that represent these values in a powerful way? Is there a story to be told about this?

FedEx corporate communication professionals also offer employees assistance in developing fluency in storytelling. In addition to choosing topics using the "I am FedEx" topics-and-questions approach, this includes learning how to focus on significant details, to feature characters, and to find the novel and unexpected. Exhibit 8.1 presents a checklist that identifies questions relevant to these aspects of the craft of storytelling. Similarly, in Chapter 10 you'll learn how to apply what Philips corporate communication professionals teach about fluency to your own practice of storytelling.

Although few organizations can deploy the human resources of FedEx in service of creating and disseminating digital stories, advances in technology are making it easier for businesses with even a modest budget to encourage employees to try their hand at storytelling. The activity opens up the creative side of people, their imaginations and unique voices, and taps into the tribal experience of telling tales sitting around a fire.

The stakes in all this for corporate reputation are large. As Terrell tells us, "A corporation is really just a collection of people, so employees telling

- *Identify the "hot sauce" in your story*: Is there a significant detail that can appeal to your audience's emotions, perhaps evoking similar memories and stimulating their ability to imagine seeing, touching, hearing, even tasting and smelling the concrete detail in the story? For example, let's say that the story is about (mis)managing your self-presentation at a formal public event. The significant detail in your story is a white T-shirt for working out that you had to wear to a formal wedding—the public event—because you forgot to pack the white lace blouse that goes with your long formal skirt. Can you talk about the T-shirt's cheap, washed-out fabric, the whiff of laundry detergent, the frayed sleeves and your attempts to conceal the shirt under a long shawl—and how difficult this was to do with a glass of wine in your hand? Can you include a couple of additional details, perhaps about the setting or storyline, that provide a fuller picture of the situation? For instance, that it was a formal military wedding held at Arlington National Cemetery, complete with a horse-drawn carriage and a ceremonial guard of soldiers with crossed swords under which the couple walked to the church? Can you describe how you felt wearing the T-shirt on that occasion? Awkward? Off-balance? Annoyed with yourself? Don't just mention the T-shirt; help people see it, understand the discomfort you felt, and imagine themselves in a similarly embarrassing situation. (Of course, the T-shirt story is my own.)

- *Figure out how to do "lead with people stories," stories about characters*: Besides yourself, are there others you should feature in your story? What about a customer's experience with your firm? From a sales perspective, it is more effective to develop a scenario about actual customers' experiences with a product than to enumerate the product's features. The former allows

EXHIBIT 8.1.   Checklist for Building Fluency in
Storytelling Based on FedEx Practices

prospective customers to tell about the benefits they'd enjoy from using the product.

- *Search for the novel and unexpected*: Where are the "aha" moments in the story that may surprise and delight, grab and hold people's attention? What's the news in the story, not the background but the foreground? What elements of the story are counterintuitive and can drive your point home? This may be a significant detail (the hot sauce), or a novel character (the FedEx vice president of information technology with the poise of a dancer who tells her story to a rap beat), or even a novel expression. Edit the story to strip out jargon, clichés, and corporate speak. Remember that people are likely to be turned off and to tune out of stories that appear to be inauthentic.

- *If the story is digital, think about whether it will go viral*: Have you engaged people's minds and hearts? Is the topic timely and relevant to those you want to reach? Have you done a good job of crafting the story—weaving significant detail into the story, focusing on people rather than products, and including the novel and unexpected? Can you push the story out to friends, family, and business associates, some of whom may take up the topic and spread the story? Who might be the likely champions of your story?

EXHIBIT 8.1.   Continued

inspirational stories about themselves, their work, their colleagues, all enable outsiders to see a corporation from a different, more emotive, vantage point."[43] Moreover, with the online migration of stories from corporate Web sites to individual ones (through the decision of individual employees), businesses have the opportunity to gain—or to lose—through digital storytelling.

9   STORYTELLING WORKSHOPS
FOR CHANGE: PHILIPS

Before the workshops, company communication was much more about broadcasting
functional messages about technology, about semiconductors, lumens per watt,
ballasts and bulbs. Our people were not thinking about how our technology
could really help people's lives.

—MARIKE WESTRA, vice president, corporate
communications, Philips Lighting

AS THE EXECUTIVE WHO LEADS PHILIPS'S initiative for storytelling, Marike Westra emphasizes its central role in communicating
the shift in the company's strategic direction from "lumen" to "human,"
from a technology-centric to a people-centric approach to the market with
an emphasis on how technology and innovation can help improve people's
lives. "At the workshops we ask people to open up, to move away from
'corporate speak' to something personal and authentic. My job is to teach
our leaders how to find that in themselves. How to move from lumen to
human."[1] She also credits storytelling with communicating related changes
in branding and culture.

What can a large organization do to help its employees understand
and accept major changes, make sense of them in their own terms, and
then act as the company's goodwill ambassadors to convey these changes

to others both inside and outside of the firm? The subject of this chapter is how storytelling workshops can be the means to achieve these ends as well as the chief vehicle for dealing with the practical issues of building employees' fluency as storytellers.

This chapter presents a two-part business case, the first on the Philips Healthcare sector, where the storytelling initiative began, and the second on the Philips Lighting sector, whose initiative benefited from the earlier efforts. These efforts represent a kind of organizational inheritance passed on from one sector to the other.[2]

Each part of the case shows the central role of workshops as a systematic approach to getting buy-in for storytelling at the enterprise level and as a launchpad for extending the reach of stories beyond the workshop. Each shows how stories can communicate change in an organization's business model (or strategic direction), in its corporate and sector brands, and in employee behavior and culture.

As the storytelling framework identifies, changing or strengthening strategy, branding, and culture are three specific business objectives that storytelling can help an organization accomplish. The Philips case shows how workshops that offer instruction in authentic and fluent storytelling to the company's employees can become an "engine" for stimulating and fortifying organizational change.

The Dutch company Royal Philips Electronic was founded in 1891 in Eindhoven, a small city in the south of the Netherlands, as a light bulb manufacturer. Over the course of the twentieth century, the company developed a reputation for technological innovation and became a household name in television, radio, and other consumer products. Early in the new millennium, Philips identified itself as a "diversified health and well-being company"[3] focused on three key markets: Healthcare, Lighting, and Consumer Lifestyle. The company employed 116,000 people and had a presence in sixty countries.[4]

CEO GERARD KLEISTERLEE'S CALL FOR CHANGE

Gerard Kleisterlee, appointed CEO in 2001, believed at that time that the electronic components for which the company was known were fast becoming a commodity business. As a result, the company would need to shift its strategic direction and then develop the appropriate branding to communicate the shift and inspire internal and external stakeholders alike to embrace the benefits of the change and its implications. Reflecting on this period, Geert Van Kuyck, Philips's chief marketing officer, explained that for Kleisterlee "it was important for the company to know how the technology fit in people's lives. The CEO hired marketing people from consumer-based companies who could understand this need and define the brand."[5]

The company's shift in strategic direction was marked by a focus on helping people to have better lives, what Philips calls "health and well-being." Everything from product development to sales and service would look to meet customers' needs on the basis of consumer and end-user insights. "Health" referred not only to meeting people's medical needs but also to their needs for developing and maintaining a healthy lifestyle; "well-being," to their quality of life, in particular to "a sense of comfort, safety and security people feel in their environment—at home, at work, when shopping or on the road."[6, 7]

To align with the new focus on "health and well-being," Kleisterlee sold the semiconductor business, organized the company into three sectors—Healthcare, Lighting, and Consumer Lifestyle—and in the fall of 2006 purchased Respironics, a medical equipment manufacturer that specializes in sleep therapy and could move the company into the home healthcare market. Classic Philips products in consumer electronics took a small position within the Consumer Lifestyle division.[8]

While the company undertook organizational restructuring, acquisitions, and divestitures, Andrea Ragnetti, the first chief marketing officer at Philips, introduced the brand campaign "Sense and Simplicity" to communicate the company's new emphasis on end users' needs and aspirations.[9] The branding effort was intended to be a unifying link across the three sectors and a wide range of business processes, everything from product development to after-sales care. Conceived in 2004 as more than a brand tagline to replace the then nearly decade-old "Let's make it better,"[10] "Sense and Simplicity" underscored the transformation of Philips.

Asked to elaborate on the implications of the brand campaign, Van Kuyck explained:

When you have a brand promise like "Sense and Simplicity" you have to find the connection for all of the Philips businesses. For example, how does this relate to healthcare? We have moved away from the notion that we're making health-care machines. Instead, we're saying that we are a company trying to simplify healthcare and healthcare decisions. Suddenly, people think that makes sense. We've done the same thing in lighting and we're doing the same thing with our consumer products. We have to make a connection. . . .

We used to have a technology-focused view about what we do, and that has changed. The Philips of old probably would have talked about lumens per watt.[11]

In 2007 senior managers met to discuss their understanding of "Sense and Simplicity" and how it applied to their business units. Following this session, a number of "Simplicity Days" were launched that brought to-gether more than 100,000 employees and set up working groups to assess whether and, if so, how different departments were putting into play the three key elements of "Sense and Simplicity": "designed around you" (de-sign products that people want), "easy to experience," and "advanced" (build technology to address people's needs).[12]

BUILDUP TO THE STORYTELLING WORKSHOPS
FOR THE HEALTHCARE SECTOR

While the "Sense and Simplicity" campaign was progressing, Philips's CEO shared his observations with Andre Manning, the vice president of external communications, that each Philips person who spoke on TV had a different story about the company. Kleisterlee wanted everyone to tell the same story and knew that achieving this goal would pose substantial challenges in a culture dominated by engineers and in an organization that was a conglomerate of ten to fifteen acquisitions,[13] and had five business units and sales and services in one hundred countries.[14]

During this same period, communications executive Marike Westra was assisting senior leaders in Healthcare to manage stakeholder relations and traveling across the globe with the CEO, who would talk about healthcare issues to government representatives and patient groups, among others. The CEO of Healthcare was also doing his own storytelling, and would himself tell a personal story about his father having a heart attack and its impact on him.[15] He also spoke about the importance of storytelling to country managers, approximately fifty senior leaders responsible for the business in a particular geographical region, including sales and service across the three sectors. In the course of these travels, Westra and Healthcare's senior leadership became aware that the country managers were uncomfortable talking about health issues in terms of people's needs, preferring instead to continue to embrace the norms of one-way "broadcast" communication with a focus on the technical excellence of products.

The leadership also recognized the need to define and tell a new organizational story for the Healthcare sector given the shift from a focus on technological innovation per se to one on people.[16] This change would require helping employees talk about healthcare in a nontechnical way and think about the end consumer—for instance, a patient who is diagnosed using Philips's MRI equipment—even though the company, in this and many other instances, sells to a business, a hospital. Employees would need to provide to the customer (the hospital) the technical specifications of the MRI machine but also engage the customer emotionally in what the equipment could do for the patient.

The challenges for Philips: how to communicate the shift in strategic direction along with the change in branding and culture, and how to stimulate employee engagement and related changes in behavior. How might this be accomplished? How would Philips get people to think and act differently?

The initial response to these challenges began with pictures rather than with words. Philips hired four photographers in 2007 to take pictures of health and well-being around the globe—and to avoid putting machines in them. This effort resulted in an exhibit of four hundred photos in 2007 that appealed emotionally to the visual imagination and set in motion a shift in perspective and attitude about Philips's role in healthcare (see Exhibits 9.1 and 9.2).

THE STORYTELLING WORKSHOPS FOR HEALTHCARE

In 2008, Westra used the photos to launch the first storytelling workshop, which was offered to communication professionals who were expected in turn to roll out this effort with Healthcare executives and country managers. Before the workshop, participants were asked to submit personal photos they associated with health and well-being to stimulate their

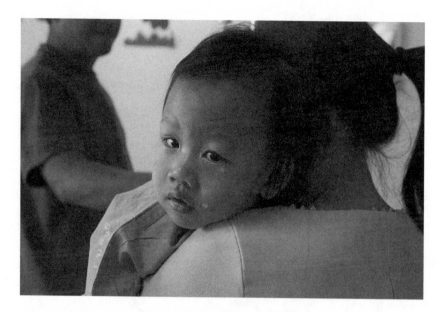

EXHIBIT 9.1.   Responding to a Child's Tears
SOURCE: With permission of Philips B.V.

EXHIBIT 9.2.   Caring for the Sick
SOURCE: With permission of Philips B.V.

thinking about a personal experience or case study about healthcare. (One manager from Israel turned in a picture of chicken soup.) One workshop leader explained the importance of the photos: "Their purpose was to instill in communication professionals that behind every solution there is a patient, a real patient."[17]

In this and subsequent workshops, photos feature prominently in the first phase of a three-phase workshop. The first phase is called "Passion," or the motivating force of "a powerful or compelling emotion," and is intended to support the belief that the participants, as representatives of Philips, can make a difference in the health and well-being of people, and should strive for excellence in carrying out this mission. This phase is followed by "Action," or "start doing something," and finally "Commitment," or "our collective investment."[18]

"Passion"

In reviewing the photos at the workshop, participants are asked to respond to a number of prompts:

- My favorite image
- How many images from my territory do I recognize?
- What personal memory or patient experience does this image trigger?
- Images I could use to tell a story
- Images I would cite in a press conference/TV appearance
- Identifying images with no obvious geographic clues[19]

They are then asked to come up with a personal story about health based on their own experience or on one of the photos that is meaningful to them—and to share the story. As one participant reflected on his experience, "People had to do a personal exercise on how healthcare affects them, and the personal photos they brought to the workshop evoked deep emotions. I witnessed people looking at photos, and they might talk about their granddads or parents while they, the speakers, are in a professional setting at an international conference speaking before colleagues."[20]

Photos may trigger personal memories, but they may also express the shared human condition of health and illness while highlighting the differences in access to healthcare and in the concept of healthcare across the globe. As one participant noted:

There is universality to the photos. Even when pictures were obviously about healthcare issues from another country—people waiting for help at a clinic in Africa—participants might translate that back to their own society and think, "How much better things are in my setting. It's likely I'd have difficulty here in this setting if I had healthcare issues." The photos opened people's eyes to what things are like in Africa.[21]

This same participant added: "Storytelling helps to see how health and well-being work across cultures. It means different things to different people. In Eastern Europe, it means being well off, having luxuries. In North America it means access to healthcare, including medical equipment."[22]

The communications facilitator who runs the workshop then describes "passion" to participants as a significant cultural value that unifies the global business units, galvanizes employee efforts worldwide, and permeates each employee's mission, as well as the organization's. The main objective of the workshop is then identified: to give employees the tools to carry out their work in advancing the company's mission, which is specifically linked to the brand tagline "Sense and Simplicity"—that is, to solutions that are designed around the user's needs ("designed around you") and are easy to use ("easy to experience").

In this phase of the workshop, the communications facilitator also talks about Philips's overarching brand story and draws upon what people have said earlier about their individual stories on health and well-being as illustrations of the brand story. The goals here are to help the participants feel comfortable with the brand story and begin thinking about how to use it, in particular by attaching it to realistic scenarios that call for stories. The latter goal is at the heart of the second phase of the workshop, "Action."

"Action"

For the second phase, "Action"—"to start doing something"—participants apply newly acquired storytelling capabilities to real situations they encounter. They discuss various stakeholder groups they are likely to meet, and their needs, and then develop stories that anchor the brand "Sense and Simplicity" to the specifics of these situations—and they practice. For instance, a Philips employee from the patient monitoring division who sells MRI equipment used by radiologists is asked to imagine meeting a doctor at an ultrasound conference to assess the doctor's needs and interests vis-à-vis what Philips can offer, and to craft a story on the basis of this assessment. In this case, the employee considers what he or she should say to the radiologist, including the proof points—research or anecdotal evidence—that can be used. The employee might talk about a pregnant mother who goes into labor prematurely and the medical attention she can receive in the ambulance, such as heart monitoring. The employee then crafts this story and practices.

To increase flexibility in telling a story and in making it relevant in different situations, once the participants put together their story, they revise and tell it from multiple vantage points for different audiences, for instance as an interviewee on a British chat show with an aggressive host, in a formal press conference in Asia, or in a roundtable for stakeholders in Europe. They later present a more polished version in a plenary session.

To gain further insights about health needs from an outsider's perspective, participants meet in small groups facilitated by communication professionals and interview healthcare experts and spokespeople, who are themselves patients and skilled storytellers, on their experience with illness. In one instance, this is a nurse who has diabetes, and in another, it is a patient who suffers from multiple sclerosis (MS). The latter is Bjorn

Bjørn Anders Foss Iversen's perspective
We have asked mr. Anders Foss Iversen to share with the participants what multiple sclerosis means to him in his general life; how it influences or even interferes with his daily activities and how he deals with this. We asked him to emphasize his concerns and fears as a person and father and what he expects from healthcare and the professionals working in it. Importantly, he has been exposed to various high-tech tools to diagnose his condition and probably monitored with it regularly. He has to use drugs on a regular (daily) basis to avoid flare-ups of the disease. The participants need to understand the impact and consequences of all this for him as a person. We have asked him to bring his injection set to the meeting to show delegates what this looks like. One of the things Mr. Anders Forss Iversen mentioned during an earlier telephone call, was that according to him, a treatment will not be successful unless there is a relationship, a rapport, between the patient and the physician.

Relationship to Philips activities
Multiple sclerosis is diagnosed by using MRI and CT. Areas of diseases activity can be monitored with PET as well.

EXHIBIT 9.3.   Bjorn Anders Foss Iversen: Notes to set up the interview
SOURCE: With permission of Philips B.V.

Anders Foss Iversen, who is an advocate for the Volunteer Norwegian MS Society.[23] Iversen was interviewed by a small group who were then asked to write (in pairs) a press release based on the interview (see Exhibit 9.3 for the notes the workshop facilitator used to set up the interview and storytelling exercise). Iversen's bio was also shared with the workshop participants (Exhibit 9.4). As one participant recalled in the interview

Philips
Global Corporate Communications Forum

Background Information
Workshop Experts

Bjørn Anders Foss Iversen   **Booth C**
Volunteer Norwegian MS Society

Multiple Sclerosis patient since 1998
Norway

Personal Biography
Bjørn Anders Foss Iversen is 37 years old, married and living at Spydeberg in the South-East of Oslo in Norway. He is a father of three children, aged four, eleven and thirteen years old. Bjørn works as volunteer for the Norwegian MS Society.

Bjørn suffers from Multiple Sclerosis (MS), which was officially diagnosed almost ten years ago, in October 1998. The illness, however, most likely started manifesting itself a decade earlier.

The first four years after the diagnosis of MS, until 2003, Bjørn led a very active life and was involved in such sports as handball. However, Bjørn now very often suffers from fatigue. The most important element in dealing with his illness is to listen to what his body tells him and, subsequently, to do what it tells him. In terms of treatment, Bjørn has to give himself an injection of Beta-Interferon every other day, which helps to prevent MS attacks. When an attack does happen, the illness manifests itself through overwhelming fatigue and a loss of balance, sometimes even forcing him into a wheelchair.

In Bjørn's opinion, the relationship between a physician and the patient is essential. A treatment or procedure cannot be successful if there is no trust or confidence between a healthcare professional and a patient.

Background of Medical Area
Multiple Sclerosis is an uncommon, slowly progressive brain disease. Its exact causes are unknown, but the patient becomes ill because the body's own immune (host defence) system erroneously attacks the insulation sheets in the electricity wiring within the brain. Clearly, this can lead to unpredictable currents and 'short-circuiting' with devastating consequences ranging from blindness and incontinence to paralysis and severe pain.

Multiple sclerosis is not continuously active and most patients deteriorate during disease attacks (active phases). Most patients have a normal life expectancy. Treatment options are limited and focus on avoiding new attacks by the immune system and reducing the consequent further brain damage.

EXHIBIT 9.4.   Bjorn Anders Foss Iversen: Short biography
SOURCE: With permission of Philips B.V.

with Iversen: "I kept coming back to Bjorn's statement that 'you have to be strong to cope with being ill.' As I interpreted it, strength meant to me being able to cope with the kinds of information coming your way when you have a tough medical condition."[24]

The interview with Iversen focused on his own story and on the larger context of the disease and how people cope with it. To broaden the participants' perspectives, he asked them to talk about friends or family members who had the disease before writing their stories about him, which were then read and discussed by other members of the small group. Then he chose the story that represented him best: "Smiling with MS" (Exhibit 9.5).

One of the authors of "Smiling with MS," Marie-Helene Azar, talked about her experience as a participant in the workshop. Only three months into the job at the time, she had anticipated that the workshop would be just a required professional exercise, but as she moved through it she understood how powerful and personal it was:

Bjorn spoke about the effect of his MS on his children and his marriage and that relaxed me. Early on, I thought that the task was to write a press release/article—basically the story—but that melted away. I begin to see the need to portray people realistically in stories. Otherwise it's futile. We need to be relevant and to do so I needed to participate in this discussion with Bjorn.[25]

After an interview conducted with a nurse who has diabetes, this same workshop participant talked about the importance of working with patient and healthcare experts face-to-face rather than using written case studies: "The person interviewed redirected us if we felt sorry for him. He made it clear that he was not to be seen as a victim."[26] Another participant reflected on how the live interview encouraged authentic storytelling: "The nurse was critical of what he felt embellished the facts: 'I can't see myself in this story.' So we had to revise it."[27]

This phase of the training was based on the belief, expressed at a communication planning meeting, that "to speak authentically, Philips' employees need a chance to hear the language of people-centric healthcare first-hand, and interact with those on the frontline of healthcare."[28] Face-to-face interaction allows them to test their stories with patients and medical experts who can discuss what their needs are, what their experiences have been, and how patient-centric medicine changes the experience

Smiling with M.S.

The most common images that come to mind when people hear the words "multiple sclerosis" are bed-bound patients and wheelchairs.

Although this uncommon neurological condition can have a significant impact on the lives of affected individuals, it is not all about disability and despair. Indeed Bjørn Anders Foss Iversen, an MS patient himself, has happily dedicated his life to shattering negative perceptions of MS. Bjørn refuses to be a victim of circumstance and has responded to the challenge of MS by turning his life around, choosing to live life to the fullest, and working to change the public face of MS.

"My life is not better because of MS," says Bjørn, "but it's much richer." After struggling to come to terms with his diagnosis, Bjørn realized that his engrained love of life was more powerful than his disease. He even chooses to see the humor in his condition and is able to laugh at himself as he has never done before. He has appeared a number of times on Norwegian comedy shows kidding about in a wheelchair dressed in drag and smashing guitars decked out in a punk costume, all things he would never have imagined himself capable of before he was diagnosed with MS. He even met his wife through his MS.

Bjørn's secret to a happy life with M.S.? An open and trusting relationship with his doctor is key, but so is his belief that no doctor can prescribe a thirst for a happy life. As an employee working for the Norwegian MS Society, he counsels patients coping with their recent diagnosis. His best advice? Always seek new opportunities, don't focus on limits... and "remember to smile."

EXHIBIT 9.5. "Smiling with M.S."
SOURCE: "Smiling with MS," Horizons in Healthcare, February 14, 2008, 4. With permission of Philips B.V.

of illness, since these medical "frontliners" would themselves tell their personal stories, partially based on the photo exhibit and on their understanding of the meaning of patient-focused medicine.[29]

In this phase, participants are also introduced to the "care cycle" model, an approach to dealing with healthcare that takes into account the full life of the patient rather than focusing narrowly on treatment—and in doing so, provides the potential for good stories.[30] Louis Hakim, then country manager for Philips Middle East, explained the storytelling potential of the care cycle in this way:

Cardiac arrest is one of the top three causes of death in the Middle East. In the past we'd look at solutions at different points of contact—for instance, in the ambulance, the emergency room, the cardiology center—and these were seen as isolated locations. Now we look at how these experiences are interrelated and how we can reduce pressure on the hospitals; for instance, looking at how to instill a healthy lifestyle, providing a feedback monitor at home, and having the ability to send this information to the doctor. There's a box at home connected to the TV that can check blood pressure and weight and send this information to the doctor or healthcare professionals. They in turn can give the patient a call to come in to be checked if the data indicate this need. So with the box at home, you can communicate your data and get feedback. These are good stories in which to approach the market and it's better than talking about an MRI. We become partners with the hospitals and healthcare professionals and not just suppliers. The Philips salesperson goes to a hospital to sell a product but talks about how to work together with the hospital to improve their operations. We discuss the total operations and the gaps we can fill. We discuss the healthcare cycle framework, thinking about the patient's experience and the cardiologist's experience.[31]

"Care-cycle thinking" focuses then on the *patient's* "journey" in stages. As Jois van den Hurk, general manager of cardiology care cycles at Philips Healthcare, describes it, for the cardiac patient these stages are prevention (for example, advice to give up smoking and take up exercising); screening to identify if there are problems (patient response to a questionnaire focused on risk factors); diagnosis or further analysis to detect if there is a suspected disease (EKG, treadmill test, ultrasound); treatment if there's a suspected disease (statins, angioplasty); management of the consequence of treatment (change in diet or exercise); surveillance and, if necessary, subsequent treatment. Stages may involve different technological capabilities that Philips can offer, but the focus is on the patient.[32]

"Commitment"

As described by communications facilitator Lindsey Mosby, who has led many of the healthcare workshops, the third phase of the workshop, "Commitment," means "getting everyone to put skin in the game. This can be filling out a card declaring what they will do, or having me or someone else skilled in storytelling come and speak to the participant's group. This is a wrap-up part of the workshop, and we want them to think about how they can ingrain the work."[33]

To support and encourage storytelling beyond the workshop experience, participants are introduced to various resources on the Philips intranet. These include presentations on topics like the care cycle, the company's core competencies, women's healthcare, oncology, and imaging, along with supporting photographs.

Sample stories and a template on the elements of an effective story (that might be used in full or abbreviated form in writing or speaking) are also placed on the intranet. See, for instance, Exhibit 9.6, the story about a sumo wrestler who suffers a heart attack. Note how the template in Exhibit 9.7 offers a checklist of questions to assess the story's effectiveness. The story, which appears in the first two sections of a larger

Philips weighs in against obesity

Yukio Hiraoka slammed into his huge opponent. Weighing in at a staggering 215 kilos, it was a devastating blow. Nevertheless, his challenger stood his ground, grasped Yukio around his thick neck and squeezed. It was only a demonstration match but the proud sumo warrior was determined to win. Sweat erupted on his forehead and dribbled down his cheek. He tasted the salt on his lips. He grabbed for his opponent's thong and grappled with his enormous weight, trying to throw him out of the 4.55m diameter ring. Suddenly his chest exploded. >>>

Every minute counts

The next thing Yukio was aware of, he was lying on a hospital bed, a tube running up his nose. All around him was a frenzy of activity. Because of his layers of fat, the doctors couldn't make clear scans of his heart, making it difficult to diagnose the severity of his condition. Every moment counted and Yukio condition was deteriorating fast. Fortunately, he arrived in hospital in time and the doctors were able to make a diagnosis in time and treat him properly. However, precious moments could've been saved if the hospital had been able to make clear images of his heart.

Obesity; a weighty problem

Obesity is one of the biggest health problems facing Europe and North America today. Being overweight causes a variety of health complaints, ranging from diabetes to heart problems. Obesity can also cause unexpected, indirect health problems such as making it difficult to produce sharp images for medical scans. The Philips C5-1 PureWave transducer is the answer.

Clarity is crucial

When is comes to scanning patients, obesity is a problem because thick layers of fat under the skin and around internal organs obscure details. This means sonographers often have to push harder to gain adequate penetration and produce a useable diagnostic image. This can cause patients discomfort or even pain. Furthermore, if hospitals fail to get the images they need, they may have to arrange for a CT or MR scan. This not only prolongs the patient's diagnosis and potentially causes them extra discomfort – it also costs the hospitals more time and money.

PureWave, pure image

The C5-1 PureWave transducer corrects the distortion of ultrasound waves that occurs in overweight patients. This results in improved pictures, which allows for more...

EXHIBIT 9.6.   Philips Weighs In Against Obesity
SOURCE: With permission of Philips B.V.

Does your story ...

- Inspire the reader?

- Contain verifiable facts about Philips?

- Touch people's lives?

- Have global or regional relevance?

- Generate interest over a longer period of time?

- Contribute to speaking about Philips' business highlights?

- Have related materials (images, video, audio)?

EXHIBIT 9.7.   Storytelling Template
SOURCE: With permission of Philips B.V.

piece—including "Philips Weighs In Against Obesity" and "Every Minute Counts"—presents the dramatic moments of the heart attack and the immediate aftermath. The story is followed by scientific data: sections that dispassionately explain the health problems associated with obesity, including one problem that Philips can address using its heart scans. The last three sections delineate the specifics of the Philips technology for addressing heart disease and scientific proof of effectiveness. Story thus opens the discussion of obesity, establishing the focus on people and drawing the attention of the listener or reader to the health crisis experienced by a single human being. The introductory story is followed by supporting data and explanation.

Among the resources on the intranet are "proof points," or stories of research about healthcare, sometimes funded by Philips. One example is a five-country survey of managers and their sleep habits that identifies who suffers most from lack of sleep, how the economic downturn affects people's sleep, and how work and family problems can be attributed to loss of sleep—ultimately drawing attention to "health and well-being" when people aren't sleeping enough.

Let's turn now to the extension of storytelling as a cultural norm and practice in the Philips Lighting sector, and to the role of storytelling in expressing and communicating the sector's new business model and brand.

LIGHTING'S NEED FOR BUSINESS TRANSFORMATION

Philips commercialized the first light bulb 120 years ago and enjoyed success in the business for over one hundred years, facing only three or four major competitors and building solid relationships with customers and government regulators. Despite this history of success, the core business of bulbs is giving way to something dramatically new due to the transformational changes in the industry brought about by the introduction of LED in the new millennium. LED is a disruptive technology that holds the promise of energy efficiency, a longer lifespan than traditional bulbs (incandescent or fluorescent), and variety in the hues and intensities of light, among other attributes. According to an internal Philips study, LED is expected to capture at least 50 percent of the market by 2015 and 75 percent by 2020.[34]

The Lighting sector's new business model, formulated in mid-2008, represented a radical shift from a focus on products, their attributes and development, to one on the sector's leadership as a service and solutions provider for a range of customers with lighting needs. To achieve this strategic repositioning, Philips executed a series of strategic acquisitions that gave the company expertise and presence across the "value chain" for Lighting—everything from lighting components (for example, light sources like LEDs) to solutions and applications (software and remote devices to control lights) to services (centralized energy management systems for retail chains). As Jeannet Harpe, senior director of corporate communications (Consumer, Lighting), describes this strategic shift:

With our new business model, we focus on providing solutions, actually doing turnkey projects—working, for instance, with architects and designers—and provide a package of consulting services like energy audits. We also help people understand LED technology, tell them about its benefits, like a longer life cycle for bulbs and the ability to change color and tone. Our product used to just be bulbs. Now we're talking to new people in a consultative selling process that's open and collaborative. We're also operating in a new competitive space with growing and diversifying competition.[35]

By late 2008, Philips Lighting was undergoing major changes: a dramatic shift in its business model along with a need to respond to the CEO's call for a company-wide focus on "health and well-being" and the related company-wide branding focus on "Sense and Simplicity." But what would this mean to Lighting, and how would it translate into a new Lighting story?

CREATING THE "ONE LIGHTING STORY" FOR THE NEW BUSINESS MODEL

In September 2008, Marike Westra joined the Lighting sector and was given one hundred days to come up with a recommendation for the CEO, Rudy Provoost, on how the communications function could best support the business. Westra observed that she was facing a similar challenge to the one she had addressed in the Healthcare sector, namely, employees' ability and desire to address the human benefits associated with Philips products while supporting the brand positioning of "Sense and Simplicity." Building on what she had learned from her work in Healthcare, Westra devised a plan that would help Lighting sector employees use storytelling about the new business model and formulate a new story for the Lighting brand for its key external stakeholders. She also had to gain buy-in for the plan from the Philips board of management on behalf of the Lighting sector management. Her challenge: Philips Lighting lacked a cohesive story of its added value for the future, had only a tenuous link to the company's overall focus on health and well-being, and was perceived as a "lamps manufacturer" that overemphasized functional product attributes and technological achievement.[36] "Lighting," according to Westra, "was ready for the future, one that was not just about light bulbs. They knew what they weren't, but not what they were."[37] In addition, Lighting employees felt little or no connection to "Sense and Simplicity."[38]

At the outset, several conditions set the stage for a positive outcome to the storytelling initiative. Lighting's CEO, Rudy Provoost, who announced that the sector needed to move away from seeing itself as only a lamps player, clearly understood the psychodynamics of storytelling and the importance of defining a vision of the future for both employees and the market. Westra knew then that she could build support for the storytelling initiative by drawing upon the CEO's understanding along with her recent experience of rolling out the storytelling workshops for Healthcare and the consensus among Lighting's leadership that strategic change, now a real objective, still needed to be clearly expressed.[39]

Early in 2009, Provoost and his senior leadership team launched an initiative to craft a unified story for Lighting—a "One Lighting Story"—to find the language that would translate Philips's overarching brand story of "Sense and Simplicity" to Lighting, to show how the Lighting sector fulfills the corporate goal of enhancing "health and well-being," and to express the business model, the sector's strategic differentiation from the competition and its unique benefits to customers. The twenty-five senior leaders in the Lighting sector got together to brainstorm about the topic. They participated in exercises to come up with individual stories about the personal meaning of light and the associations and memories it triggered for each of them.

Through this process, they became aware of the need to link lighting to people's lives. As they moved collectively toward defining a "One Lighting Story," the next step was to agree upon what they called a "North Star" scenario, that is, a guiding vision to help them identify where they were "located" as a sector and, ultimately, to serve as a way to judge whether a specific strategic decision the company was contemplating was relevant to the sector's overall strategic direction. Several of these scenarios were developed on the basis of discussions in the Lighting Leadership Team and were then used as the basis of a "North Star" workshop at a Global Lighting Leadership Conference, an annual meeting where the top 150 global leaders in the Lighting sector came together to discuss key business strategies for the coming year. The following emerged as the Philips Lighting North Star Scenario:

Bring light and life together

Unleash the power of light to create and inspire. Empower people to fashion their own environments, to shape their moods, to care for themselves. Light—harnessed—sustains, nurtures, and heals.[40]

The leaders then asked themselves a number of questions that would influence strategic business decisions based upon this scenario:

Who will we be if we do this right?

Who are our customers and what's in it for them?

How does this tie back to Royal Philips?

What are the risks of doing this? Of not doing this?

Is this a capability we currently have? How valuable would this be to the market?

How long do we think it will take us to get there?[41]

As a result of discussion about these business questions, the North Star scenario, and the personal stories people shared about lighting, the top 150 leaders cast votes to determine the best branding story: should it be "Take Lighting to the next level"? "Superior experience. Inspired creations"? "Bring light and life together"? or "Simply enhancing life with light"?[42] Rather than deciding on the basis of internal assessment only, Lighting sought to validate its new direction by seeking the opinions of outside stakeholders about what version was most compelling to them. In particular, Lighting spoke to a group of general opinion leaders and legislators, including the media, government regulators, and CEOs, and to a group of those who make purchasing decisions about lighting, such as architects, installers, facility managers, urban planners, and lighting designers. The first group was surveyed online with participants located in the UK, the US, China, and Italy. A sample from the second group was interviewed face-to-face in the UK.[43] All those interviewed were asked to respond to the following questions:

Is the message understood?

Is the message relevant in a lighting context?

What does the story mean (in depth)?

Do stakeholders resonate in an emotive way, and with which parts?

Does it inspire stakeholders? (to what?)

Does it fit with our brand promise of sense and simplicity?

Does it fit with/change the perception of Philips Lighting?

Is this expected from Philips?

Do stakeholders believe that Philips Lighting (can) deliver on it?

Does the message differentiate from other lighting suppliers?

What are the likes and dislikes?[44]

"Simply enhancing life with light" emerged from the research as the "One Lighting Story" along with several key findings: the North Star scenario accurately communicated what Lighting represents, elicited positive emotional responses, expressed the company's efforts to collaborate with customers about their needs, differentiated Philips strategically from the competition, and depended for its credibility upon specific evidence and examples relevant to users' needs (see Exhibit 9.8 for the fully elaborated

Light has long been taken for granted: something to switch on or off. It is simply there—in the background, and only really noticed in its absence. But light is so much more than this.

At Philips we believe light is potential. Light is possibility. And we have a unique and powerful approach to the way we work with you.

We are people focused

We begin by observing and listening to people to ensure that we address their needs and aspirations in life.

We are partners in innovation

Great partnerships encourage great results. With our collective passion, expertise, depth, and reach, we open up new possibilities powered by advanced technology.

We develop meaningful solutions to today's needs

Together we create meaningful and valuable solutions that enhance the quality, use, and experience of light.

Together we transform environments, create experiences, and share identities. With light, we uplift and inspire. With light, we comfort and heal. With light, we create safety and spectacle.

EXHIBIT 9.8. "One Lighting Story"
SOURCE: With permission of Philips B.V.

"One Lighting Story"[45]). "Simply enhancing life with light" was also specifically linked to the company's brand promise of "Sense and Simplicity" (just as "People focused. Healthcare simplified" of Philips Healthcare is linked to the company's brand promise) with each key term of the Lighting story associated with a facet of "Sense and Simplicity: "'enhancing' asserts that we are about value and innovation; 'life' speaks to the domain of 'health and well-being'; and 'light' is, of course, what we do."[46]

THE STORYTELLING WORKSHOPS

To ensure that the Lighting story would have vitality and application beyond the deliberations of the leadership team, Lighting then launched a series of workshops to communicate the story, especially to help employees make sense of it *in their own terms* and discover or construct links between the story and their work. The storytelling workshops were initially offered to members of the Lighting leadership team, who in turn led workshops for their management teams and other members of the sector. By early 2011, about 70 percent of the employees in the sector had participated in the workshops.

The workshop I observed in mid-January 2011 is fairly typical of these sessions and followed the sequence articulated earlier in the Healthcare sector: "Passion" (called "Inspiration" here), "Action," and "Commitment." The twenty participants represented a mixed group from legal, research, strategy, and design. Some people knew one another; others did not.

The communications facilitator and leader for the workshop, Marike Westra, opened the session by announcing its purpose—"To tell you what the Philips story is and to help you make it your own"—and then reviewed the larger strategic context from which the story emerged, going beyond the facts and figures to connect emotionally to the group by emphasizing the fundamental human needs that the Lighting business addresses. She highlighted technological innovations in lighting, the strategic shift at Philips to a focus on customer needs in lighting, the importance of changing stakeholders' perception of the company as a household name based only on televisions and light bulbs. She then showed an "Inspiration" video that displayed how LED-based lighting has transformed private and public settings.

Westra then introduced an "Inspiration" exercise. She shared associations to lighting offered by research respondents, such as "Light is a kiss from the sun" and "Light is the smile on my daughter's face," and invited the participants to reflect on and share their own experiences with light. This exercise had first been practiced by the leadership group in creating the "One Lighting Story," and a version of it had been practiced earlier in storytelling workshops for Healthcare. The emotional intensity and mental concentration in the room rose as, one by one, volunteers began to share personal stories about experiencing light: taking a deep-sea dive and emerging into the light as a kind of rebirth; walking through Paris at night and suddenly coming upon the Eiffel Tower ablaze in many colors; listening to a church choir with heightened pleasure when it's bathed in light;

observing a newborn who's placed under a white light to prevent her from turning yellow; experiencing a feeling of humility when seeing the Milky Way through a photographic lens for the first time. The participants were quiet, respectful, and attentive while listening to each other's story.

Following this exercise, Westra moved back to the "One Lighting Story" in the "Action" phase of the workshop. She elaborated on the three "key pillars" or strategic differentiators that, according to Philips, distinguish it from the competition: "people focused," "partners in innovation," and "meaningful solutions." As she explained, "people focused" means that the company is moving out of a closed environment and focus on research and development, products, and product innovation per se to reach out to customers and consumers, observing and listening to them, to their needs and aspirations for safety, efficiency, improved health, even inspiration. "People focused" also means taking into account that light can reduce winter depression, mitigate the experience of a stressful environment like a hospital, or stimulate alertness at work.[47] "Partners in innovation" refers to building long-lasting relationships with stakeholders, such as city governments responsible for addressing lighting needs, but also governmental leaders involved in regulating the use of lighting to promote safety and efficiency. It also means teaming up with creative and technical people who design spaces in which lighting is required. These partnerships should begin with an awareness of partners' needs for planning, economizing, and renovating and then use the creative energy of collaborative efforts to get results.[48] "Meaningful solutions to today's needs," which results from the focus on people and partners, refers to collaboratively created solutions to problems that partners want to address through imaginative uses of lighting, such as lighting that is able to create greater security, better learning environments, safer streets, increased productivity, and hospital environments that are more conducive to healing.[49]

Westra then introduced general manager Garrett Forde (executive vice president of Philips Lighting in Europe, the Middle East, and Africa), who gave a presentation to the group that demonstrated how he adapts the "One Lighting Story" in his conversations with different stakeholder groups and uses different proof points. For instance, he referred to a research study of lighting's effects on how children work and play when he talked to those who plan educational facilities—but not when speaking to others. A longtime employee at Philips, Forde expressed the pride he feels for the contributions the company is making in developing countries by bringing the gift of mobile solar-powered light to places that up until then had been shrouded in darkness once the sun set or limited to the light provided by kerosene lamps. A brand evangelist, he described the ability of LED technology to transform public and private spaces by offering a wealth of colors to establish mood and by making it possible for architects and light designers to create an aesthetics of place unencumbered by the old constraint that light had to be projected from the ceiling or from lamps. Because of LED's capabilities, he explained, "we become the architect's best friend. We walk in and help create solutions." He added almost as an afterthought that "it's paint companies that should fear us because we can change colors quickly and easily through LED-based lighting capabilities." Throughout his talk, he conveyed his passion for this mission and expressed his desire to "be able to tell my grandchildren what I did to help the planet."[50]

To increase the participants' acceptance of and comfort with the practice and to introduce the second—and final—storytelling exercise, Westra raised and dispelled some of the myths about storytelling: that it's an unnatural habit, a capability that no one possessed in the organization, and a practice unknown in the business community. She also discussed the specific links between the "One Lighting Story" and the company's overarching brand promise of "Sense and Simplicity": that "Simply enhancing life with light" captures the human and emotional aspects of lighting that are simple and relevant to people; "enhancing" speaks to what is valuable and innovative about the work; "life" is the link between Lighting and the overall corporate domain of "health and well-being" and delivering human benefits; and "light" refers to the work of this sector.

For the final exercise, each participant constructed a story for one of the scenarios (see Exhibit 9.9) that best matched a work or informal situation he or she is likely to encounter. One participant imagined a scenario involving a chance meeting with a prospective customer—the CEO of a construction company that has just won a building project for the next Olympics—when seated next to him on an airplane. In a role play with another member of his group taking the part of the CEO, the participant asked questions to learn about the CEO's needs for the new project and

1. You bump into the CEO of a building corporation which has just been awarded a government grant to rebuild the city center.

2. You are a factory manager speaking to your employees at a Talent lunch.

3. You happen to run into the Mayor of X city as s/he comes out of a TV studio.

4. You happen to run into an old friend, and s/he asks you whom you are working for now and what you do.

5. You are in the capital city of your country at an Industry Renovation meeting and you meet the Minister of Education in the hall.

6. You are in a preliminary meeting with the CEO of a prospective Energy Services Specialist company that we would like to acquire. We are in direct competition with Samsung.

EXHIBIT 9.9. Storytelling Scenarios

SOURCE: "Philips 'Sense and Simplicity': The Philips 'One Lighting Story' Training— 'Simply Enhancing Life with Light,'" September 9, 2009, slide 37. With permission of Philips B.V.

then fluently introduced the story of Philips's involvement in the Beijing Olympics, especially the high point of orchestrating the light show at the opening ceremonies in the newly built "Bird's Nest" Olympic stadium. The group observing and critiquing the role play advised the participant to focus on the CEO's lighting needs for construction of a new stadium rather than on the experience he might have as a spectator at the events; to listen more than to talk; and to focus less on pushing Philips's capabilities in a pressurized sales pitch and more on the story, the goal of which is to "network" with his old friend, who might in turn become a goodwill ambassador for the company.

At the conclusion of the workshop, a few participants shared their stories with the larger class and received comparable feedback. All the participants were urged to retell and adapt their stories with the help of colleagues in their own work groups and to consider what they need to "start, stop, and continue" in telling Philips's "One Lighting Story" in their own words and on their own terms.

FOLLOW-UP TO THE STORYTELLING WORKSHOPS
Philips Lighting took a number of steps to ensure that storytelling would
both permeate and be relevant to the many business units within Lighting. Storytelling trainers and employees who tell lighting stories have
online access to continually updated sets of frequently asked questions
and answers about the "One Lighting Story." These cover topics like the
need for the story, its basis in research with stakeholders, the authority it
derives from both research and decision making by the leadership team
that created it, its importance as a new strategic message, and the specific
meaning of each of the words in both the "Sense and Simplicity" tagline
(for the company as a whole) and "Simply enhancing life with light."[51]

Employees also have separate guidelines and materials tailored to each
of the nine customer segments (home, outdoor, office, industry, healthcare, shops, hospitality, entertainment, and automotive). These materials
help to generate and present stories, reinforcing the link between what
the division sells and what end users need. For example, Exhibit 9.10

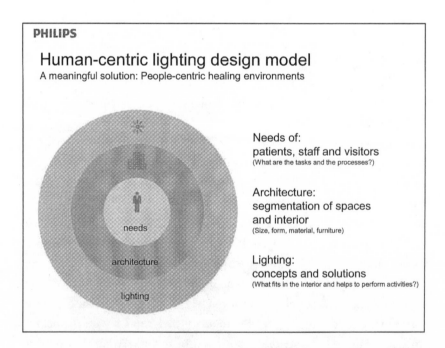

EXHIBIT 9.10.   Human-centric Lighting Design Model
SOURCE: Healthcare Lighting, "Simply enhancing light with light," slide 22. With permission
of Philips B.V.

Delivering the ultimate arena experience: Focused on people

Leaders of La Caja Magica, a novel sports complex in Madrid, Spain, hoped their center could successfully play multiple roles—a high-profile sports site, a hard-hitting performance venue, and a business event space. "On big projects like these, people want solutions that meet all of their needs, not just products that address only one or two of them." (slide 25)

Delivering the ultimate arena experience: Partners in innovation

"Philips was equipped with flexible and integrated solutions."

Developing a comprehensive arena experience, we provided the latest in sports, LED façade and video lighting, as well as advanced controls and integrated systems for remote adjustment based on use of the space at any given moment. (slide 26)

Delivering the ultimate arena experience: One company. One advanced, multipurpose solution

"The added value from Philips was having an expert partner for the integration of LED screens, LCDs, lighting."

Philips' unique system delivered La Caja Magica a "one-stop shop" experience. And more importantly, the freedom to use their space as they wish. (slide 27)

EXHIBIT 9.11.   Lighting's Sports Division
SOURCE: "Sense and Simplicity," communications update, Marike Westra, Corporate Communications, Lighting MRM, August 24, 2009, slide 27. With permission of Philips B.V.

("Human-centric Lighting Design Model") shows employees who work in the Healthcare segment of Lighting how to conceptualize their work: to look first at people's needs, then at the hospital space, and finally at the ways in which lighting solutions can "enhance life with light" for patients and medical professionals in that space. See also Exhibit 9.11, the storyline for the outdoor business unit of Lighting's sports division. Some of the materials for the different business segments are created by members of that business who attend the same storytelling workshop.

Besides the training they receive in the workshops, lighting communication specialists who work across the different markets are provided with their own supplementary material called "toolkits" for developing communication plans, including stories to convey the new Philips brand and strategy. According to Jeannet Harpe, senior director of corporate communications (Consumer, Lighting):

We needed the toolkits to build up an experienced communications team. Given the new strategy, communication tasks are now different. Rather than announcing a new light bulb, we talk about complete projects. Rather than just a press release, we invite the media to new installations where we tell the story of enhancing life with light. We invite the mayor of the city to the event and show how energy consumption can be reduced in a city and how lighting can help a city have an identity at night that increases tourism and reduces crime. We never had to do this when we were just selling light bulbs.[52]

Each toolkit begins with an assessment of the macrotrends influencing the specific customer segment and moves on to provide quotations from that segment's customers; a narrative that weaves this information into the Philips "One Lighting Story"; "reasons to believe," or evidence that Philips has "lived" the story; and specific objectives and components of that segment's communications plan. For example, "Simply enhancing life with light . . . in *livable cities*"[53] first identifies the trends of increased urbanization and the related concerns about "quality of life (urban safety, security, health and well-being)"[54]: the use of public space for recreation and cultural events, the desire on the part of municipal leaders to create a unique urban identity for their city (with the resulting increase in tourism and other economic activity), and the interest in environmental issues. A "Trends" section is followed by quotations attributed to key target customers, for instance architects and urban designers, which provide immediacy and insight about these trends. A section called "Our Story" turns the data into a coherent narrative about these urban challenges and Philips's approach to addressing them and includes specific examples of successful projects. A concluding section, the "Communications Plan," focuses on the need for stakeholder engagement—dialogues with stakeholders such as tourist and heritage authorities, utility companies, city planners, national governments, mayors, and municipalities, with an eye to enhancing the reputation of Philips as a thought leader in improving urban environments. The toolkits are available through the intranet, and Philips is now working on how the supplementary material can be used across different markets.

FROM THE COMPANY AS A WHOLE TO HEALTHCARE TO LIGHTING TO . . .

Storytelling at Philips was set in motion by the transformation of the company's business model to a focus on "health and well-being" and the accompanying need to build understanding and support for it among employees and other stakeholders. The storytelling efforts in the Healthcare sector were a logical extension of the company-wide shift from "health and well-being" to healthcare. For Lighting, the connection to "health and well-being" was less obvious but became clear once the "One Lighting Story" was created (see Exhibit 9.12) and storytelling workshops became an organizational practice. In fact, asked about the differences

One Lighting Story - Survey

- total number of listed trainings	117
- total number of trained people	2555
- total number of people who filled in the survey?	781

Participant	Average
How do you rate the following elements on the Our story intranet site on a scale of 1-10?	
How well do you understand our new One Lighting story?	8.6
How inspired are you by our One Lighting story?	8.1
How did you experience the 'inspiration' section of the training?	7.9
How did you experience the 'action' section?	7.8
How did you experience the 'commitment' section?	7.8
How would you rate the overall training?	8.0
How comfortable do you feel in telling Our story to family/friends/customers/other stakeholders?	8.1
How do you rate the following elements on the Our story intranet site on a scale of 1-10?	
The One Lighting story itself	7.7
The One Lighting story overview presentation	7.9
The segment modules	7.7
The ease of finding relevant materials	7.6
How likely are you to recommend the 'Our story' intranet site to a colleague?	7.8
How likely are you to recommend this One Lighting story training to a colleague?	7.9
Will use in daily job?	90,9 % say yes

Facilitator	
Did you use the pre- and post-workshop survey cards during the training?	0,34% say yes

EXHIBIT 9.12. "One Lighting Story" Survey
SOURCE: With permission of Philips B.V.

between the storytelling workshops for Healthcare and Lighting, both Marike Westra and Lindsey Mosby, who created the overall program and led many of the storytelling workshops, noted an improvement in the storytelling workshops from Healthcare to Lighting. The Lighting initiative was more comprehensive, including the systematic creation and testing of the "One Lighting Story," the extensive training materials, and the efforts to track and monitor the adoption of storytelling across the sector. The third sector—Consumer Lifestyle—is at the time of this writing the next (and last) to engage in these storytelling activities. Given the rollout in the other two sectors, one can expect the Consumer Lifestyle effort to be even stronger.

Philips's extensive use of storytelling workshops for changing and strengthening strategy, branding, and culture demonstrates how the practical, intensive immersion of employees in storytelling exercises can yield dramatic positive results. Along with building authentic and fluent storytellers, the workshops themselves became a valued cultural norm, a set of behaviors that employees appreciate and enact. Storytelling is also a capability that was bequeathed by one sector, Healthcare, to another, Lighting, with the likelihood that this organizational inheritance will be passed on to the third sector, Consumer Lifestyle.

10 PHILIPS: LESSONS LEARNED

STORYTELLING WORKSHOPS ARE AT THE HEART of Philips's efforts to communicate the shift in the company's business model and the changes in branding and culture that need to accompany it.[1] As with any large organization, there are substantial challenges to making this happen:

- How does an organization ensure that storytelling is authentic to its business model, branding, and culture, on the one hand, and to the experience of individual employees, on the other?

- How does an organization assess and build organizational readiness for stories?

- Who are the best champions of storytelling?

- Once storytelling is introduced through the workshop, how is the momentum sustained?

- When might storytelling better communicate strategy than would other types of communication?

Once a company identifies a new business model, workshops can help the company develop its brand story and help its employees craft their own stories to explain the business model, to convey the brand, and to do all this with authenticity.

Storytelling workshops also help companies deal with practical matters that go beyond communicating change in strategy, brand, and culture. For example, in a company like Philips that has a large technical staff, storytelling helps them build a bridge between their specialist knowledge and a nonspecialist's limited understanding of technology. The challenge here is this:

• How does an organization address the special challenges of storytelling in a corporate culture that values engineering and, in general, technical expertise?

Let's now take up each of these six challenges through an assessment of storytelling at Philips and related examples, and consider how you might address these challenges should similar circumstances arise in your organization.

DEVELOP STORIES AUTHENTIC TO THE ORGANIZATION AND TO THE STORYTELLER

There is a general story about Lighting, but it doesn't do the trick for people at the lower levels of management: "What does it have to do with my work?" You need the workshops to address this question.

—GUIDO MOUWS, director of customer care for Europe at Philips Lighting

As Mouws points out, an organization as a whole may have a story, but individual employees still need to *own* that story in their own terms. If an organization uses a workshop approach, it must be designed to do more than pay lip service to the individual and the personal. In fact, in the absence of exercises that provide room for people to explain and share, to interpret and connect emotionally to an organization's change, organizational storytelling is likely to be no more than corporate speak. Expressions like "Sense and Simplicity," "People focused. Healthcare simplified," "Simply enhancing life with light," "partners in innovation," or "meaningful solutions" would be mere rhetoric.

As the Philips case demonstrates, storytelling workshops can encourage employees to discover their authentic voices. They can be imaginative, even freewheeling and quite personal in developing emotionally compelling stories about healthcare or light in a risk-free environment while feeling unconcerned in these "Inspiration" exercises about how their personal stories might be linked to the organization's. The impact of these exercises is powerful. As an observer of one of the Philips workshops, I noticed the immediate involvement of the participants when they were asked to respond to the question, "What does Lighting mean to you?" and then even greater involvement when volunteers shared their personal stories with the others, who listened with respect and close attention. In addition, the photo displays of health and light at these workshops appealed to the visual imagination and evoked people's emotional responses as well as stories inspired by these responses.

Organizational storytelling requires more than the personal. Indeed, as discussed earlier and shown in other best-practice cases, it's a balancing act between the personal and the organizational. Depending on the specific purpose, the story an employee tells may concern a company's brand, its business model, or the business of the particular unit to which the employee belongs, as well as the needs of customers. The challenge is to balance elements that are authentic and personal to the teller with ones that are authentic to the brand story, the strategy of the organization, and the business unit.

The ebb and flow of the personal and the organizational in the workshops helps to achieve this balance. When the communications facilitator and business manager-storyteller take center stage at the workshop, they model this balance by explaining the changes in the business and in the brand story and by anchoring these larger changes in terms of the participants' specific work responsibilities. Participants are asked to develop stories that require them to weave the brand story into their personal experience, to respond to typical business scenarios they face, and to include proof points from research and customer testimonials.

As discussed earlier, authenticity in organizational storytelling is inherently social and flexible. Not just about the teller, it is open to significant others, their needs, concerns, and interests, and requires the storyteller, whether an entire organization or an individual, to begin the activity by listening. At Philips, this was evident in the formal process of creating the "One Lighting Story." During this effort the company sought the responses of senior leaders and important external stakeholders to versions of the brand story before one was chosen. This was evident as well at the workshops where the participants interviewed healthcare experts before crafting stories, which took into account the interviewees' experiences and insights, and in workshop exercises in which the participants imagined the audience for their story before shaping a version of it to suit that particular audience—the aggressive British chat show host, the reporters at a press conference in Asia, potential customers and their healthcare or lighting needs. Finally, this was evident in the company's willingness to listen to employees' personal stories, which in some cases had no more than a tangential link to the company's goals but were personally quite significant to the storyteller.

Listening needs to continue through the telling of the story. As my observations at a Philips workshop and my own work with clients and students confirm, the storyteller should observe nonverbal cues from an audience, signs of confusion, boredom, interest, and excitement. On the basis of this observation, the teller improvises by rearranging parts of the story, eliminating some, and strengthening others. From this vantage point, storytelling is never insular or rigidly bounded. It has a kind of semipermeable membrane and resembles speech more generally as it has been characterized by the Russian philosopher Mikhail Bakhtin: it is fundamentally social, "constructed while taking into account possible responsive reactions."[2]

ASSESS AND ENCOURAGE ORGANIZATIONAL READINESS FOR STORIES

Is there organizational readiness for storytelling? The answer is often, "Look to the leadership." As the Philips case illustrates, the support for storytelling from senior management is essential to getting the effort off the ground. In fact, without support, the likelihood of success in building storytelling capabilities is quite limited. Reflecting on the early initiatives to encourage storytelling, Marike Westra, vice president of corporate communications, underscored the importance of spending time up front to get senior leaders' support: "The extra time getting buy-in will pay off."[3]

At Philips, the CEO believed in the power of storytelling. He championed its introduction across the organization and understood its importance to the strategic transformation of the company from a focus on products to one on "health and well-being." Recognizing that people had difficulty understanding the new business model, he saw the need for the explanatory and emotional power of stories to convey the meaning of the model that applied to individuals, be they employees, Philips's customers and their customers' customers, government representatives, suppliers, communities, the media, or NGOs, among others.

Success in one sector of an organization can also pave the way for success in another. The campaign for storytelling workshops in Lighting benefited from the earlier efforts in Healthcare as well as the experienced communication leader who moved from Healthcare to Lighting and took the lessons learned from one sector to the next. The earlier experience assisted the senior leadership group in Lighting to engage in a "story-creating" process for the sector's new branding story. The leaders in Lighting were ready for this activity, Westra explains, because "Lighting was in a transition phase strategically.In creating the Lighting story, leaders discussed different versions of the story, and while sorting them out, they negotiated and refined the meaning of the brand; "owned" the change in the business model and brand by participating in this activity; and learned the value of storytelling. The productive outcome of this exercise helped persuade them of the power of storytelling.

FIND THE BEST CHAMPIONS FOR STORYTELLING: EXPANDING THE REACH OF THE WORKSHOPS

Senior leadership has a prominent role as champion for storytelling, but it is often the manager most closely linked to employees who has the biggest influence on behavior. Note the important role of the business manager in the storytelling workshops at Philips. It is the business manager who is likely to have the strongest credibility with the attendees because he or she is known to them directly or by reputation; is intimately aware of the specific business challenges faced by the group; can model the use of storytelling in typical scenarios, for instance meeting with customers, talking to a government rep, or chatting with a neighbor; and can show the relevance of the brand story to these scenarios, providing practical examples of when and how to use stories that link the specific business challenges to the overarching brand story. Living proof of the power of storytelling, the manager models the practice—telling stories—he or she wants to encourage and is the best person to follow up with attendees to build momentum for the practice, to check whether they are following through, and to address difficulties in implementing the new learning.

A business manager who is initially skeptical about the uses of storytelling and then "converts" through the workshops into a supporter may be the most convincing champion of the practice. Such is the case of Frank Van der Vloed, Lighting country manager for the Benelux. Vloed, who has four hundred people reporting to him, was uncomfortable with and uninterested in working with stories before attending a storytelling workshop. He explains his resistance in this way: "I was used to speaking to customers in terms of numbers, projects, and products."[4]

Vloed now speaks in glowing terms about moving away from his old approach, showing office visitors art books full of magnificent photos of cityscapes and famous architectural sights illuminated and transformed by lighting. He uses stories to encourage dialogue with current and potential customers about their needs and to encourage increased sales. He now promotes storytelling workshops to his direct reports and serves as the business manager-presenter at the workshops for members of his organization.

SUSTAIN THE MOMENTUM FOR STORYTELLING WITH SUPPLEMENTARY MATERIAL

Organizations that recognize the importance of storytelling can sustain the momentum by creating and deploying supplementary material, including collections of stories. Employees can draw upon the material as they put together their own stories for the different stakeholders they reach out to. As we have seen in the Philips case for Lighting, supplementary material is provided for *each unit* in Lighting: explanations of how to connect the

"Sense and Simplicity" corporate brand to the "One Lighting Story" and then to the segment; proof points, or evidence, that can back up stories; and analysis of specific stakeholders in each customer segment who can be reached through storytelling. Taken as a whole, this package of information for all employees provides compelling detail, including beautiful visuals, as well as ways to adapt it in stories to different stakeholders. In addition, Lighting communication professionals in the countries receive supplementary materials for using stories to build external PR and communication plans. All of this is available on the intranet.

As new technology has made tracking, collection of, and access to information easier, organizations are increasingly using archives of stories and supplementary material to sustain momentum for organizational storytelling. Think, for instance, of the many digital stories available on the Chevron and FedEx Web sites that can be brought into talks and other communications. Moreover, as personal computing devices become ubiquitous, they too increase collection of and access to stories. Jeff Hunt, principal and cofounder of PulsePoint Group, a consulting firm for strategic communications, has the executives he works with at Dell use an iPhone app to take pictures and add notes right after a meeting with a customer. The executives are then trained to turn this material into stories when talking to potential customers about how Dell's products address people's needs. "The collection of stories," Hunt remarks, "provides vivid and reliable evidence for these discussions and involves emotion, certainly when compared to a discussion about megabytes and speed."[5]

In instances when stories about a company's past are important to business, companies may take a systematic approach to creating and collecting historical information. At Kraft Foods, associate director Becky Haglund Tousey is in charge of the archives, preserving company-generated records that have enduring business value. "We are the corporate memory bank and the keepers of the history of our many brands,"[6] Tousey explains. Materials may be retrieved for brand anniversaries, speeches by the CEO, and special events, among other things. "For a formal 'Innovation Day' when scientists brainstorm about possible new products," Tousey adds, "they frequently tap into the archives for information about past products. Marketing folks look at graphic design evolution for packaging. They look back at the history of a particular product in order to understand how to move forward."[7]

At Johnson & Johnson, manager of corporate communication Margaret M. Gurowitz (who trained as a historian) is in charge of the company archives, which represent more than a century of legacy. Gurowitz notes: "Our archives are incredibly valuable. They are a record of the culture. Without it, new hires and others would not be able to experience the longevity of our culture firsthand."[8] Gurowitz frequently talks about the company's past to new employees as a way to introduce them to Johnson & Johnson's Credo, a codification of company values that speaks to its responsibility to stakeholders, and she maintains a blog on the topic. The company has also published a collection of stories by employees and retirees about the meaning of the Credo to their personal and professional lives, a book that demonstrates the staying power of the company's mission and reinforces the importance of cultural values.[9]

As another example of the power of stories about the past, Staples celebrated and reinforced its commitment to businesses, large and small, by collecting stories about the founding members of the company for its twentieth anniversary in 2006. Paul Capelli, then vice president of public relations, reflects:

The date of the twentieth anniversary, 2006, made us realize that we needed to stop and look back at our history and, if we didn't do this now, those involved— the founding people—would eventually be gone and their stories along with them. We needed to record the history. We put together a catalogue of interviews about the early years and how the company started. The theme was, "We have entrepreneurial roots and we helped small businesses—and now small and large businesses—to thrive."[10]

A cautionary note: although stories about the past can provide valuable supplementary material to illustrate current initiatives, working with historical material is much less helpful—and can even be counterproductive—when a company's change in strategy marks a *break* from the past. This was the case with Philips as it shifted from a traditional emphasis on products as its strategic differentiation (with the exception of the business group that still creates light bulbs).

RECOGNIZE THAT STORIES CAN BETTER COMMUNICATE A STRATEGIC FOCUS ON SERVICES AND SOLUTIONS THAN CAN OTHER TYPES OF COMMUNICATION

Don't think in terms of a brochure or fact sheet but about what lighting can do, how it's linked to people's experience.

—FRANK VAN DER VLOED, Lighting Country
Manager, Philips Lighting, Benelux

An organizational strategy focused on products is communicated well by product specification sheets and brochures, but a strategy focused on services and solutions to customers' problems is conveyed much more powerfully and appropriately by storytelling that begins with dialogue with the customer. Note how communications at Philips morphed from an emphasis on product specs to one on stories when the company's strategy shifted from a focus on products to one on services and solutions. Talk about product specs gave way to listening to customers' stories about their health or lighting needs and then to the Philips rep creating "revised and improved stories about the future" in which those customers' needs are identified and addressed. In this regard, storytelling is a collaborative, consultative process: the customers (and in many instances, the customers' customers since Philips sells to businesses that serve end users) begin the process by expressing their needs (or those of the end users), and the Philips rep listens to their story—about a patient suffering a heart attack who needs immediate attention en route to the hospital, or about people who don't feel safe walking down a city street. After listening, the Philips rep creates a "revised," solutions-based story—about the heart attack victim who's monitored in the ambulance, or about pedestrians who feel more secure when street lighting that's well placed and well timed helps guide their way.

Solutions-based stories that begin with listening to the customer or end user apply to anything from handling customer complaints to addressing the needs of large healthcare systems. Consider, for example, the story that Guido Mouws models for his direct reports who are responsible for addressing complaints from customers. In the past, Mouws explains, his staff would tackle the specific technical problem, for instance a breakdown in part of a lighting system and the steps to repair it, perhaps telling a "death story" about eight other customers who had the same problem. As a result of the training in storytelling, his staff are now likely to turn this problem into an opportunity to help the customer envision a story about the future, often supported by photos, on how enhancements in a lighting system can help the customer improve safety, aesthetics, and business.[11] Consider too a story offered by healthcare executive Jois van den Hurk. At a branding event in Russia, he told the story of a sixty-year-old woman who, while walking her dog in a park in Moscow, collapses from a heart attack. A bystander calls emergency services who show up twenty minutes later. The woman's heart muscle is already dying, but emergency services, because they have Philips equipment on board, are able to do the initial diagnosis in the field and alert the local hospital to assemble a medical team with ballooning and stenting capabilities. Surgery takes place ninety minutes after the heart attack. The benefit of having Philips equipment in the emergency vehicle, van den Hurk concluded, is to save time—and often a life—by diagnosing the patient en route. Van den Hurk told his story to a mixed audience: laypeople who would identify with the patient in crisis, Philips's distributors in Moscow who can use the story to sell the equipment, and physicians who recognize the importance of timely, accurate information about a patient who arrives at the hospital for emergency treatment.[12]

ADDRESS THE CHALLENGES OF STORYTELLING IN A
CULTURE THAT VALUES ENGINEERING AND TECHNOLOGY
Companies that, like Philips, differentiate themselves partially through technical excellence in fields such as engineering or medicine yet want to communicate to nonspecialists through storytelling, face special challenges:

- Can the company deal effectively with some employees' old habits of communicating that may be at odds with storytelling?

- Can the company find technical experts, either employees or outsiders, who are powerful storytellers capable of translating their knowledge in story form and modeling this capability for other members of the company?

Employees' old habits of communicating as technically trained professionals can be quite rigid, even in the face of a need for change. These old
habits—in this instance, a resistance to telling stories—are a condition that
language expert Kenneth Burke called "trained incapacity": "One adopts
measures in keeping with his past training—and the very soundness of this
training may lead him to adopt the wrong measures."[13] Burke goes on to
say that "their [people's] past training has caused them to misjudge their
present situation. Their training has become an incapacity."[14] Functional in
one context, such as a company with a product-focused strategy in which
there's a need to describe the technical features of products, these habits of
communication are dysfunctional in other contexts. Yet the inertia—people's
tendency to fall back on the types of communication they're accustomed
to—is quite powerful. As country manager Vloed explained earlier, he and
his staff were accustomed to talking about product features, which reflected
Philips's old strategic focus on products. Country managers in healthcare
had a similar resistance to storytelling. They too preferred to rely on the
familiar discourse of describing the technical features of products. Andre
Manning, vice president of external communications in Philips Corporate
Communications, concluded: "Country managers had difficulty telling the
healthcare story. They can tell a story about a TV but are scared to tell a
healthcare story, its impact on the lives of patients, the products' benefits,
and how healthcare issues are related to social trends."[15]

My own experiences as a communication consultant mirror those of
Vloed and Manning. Many of the business professionals whom I've worked
with and who were trained as engineers are accustomed—as a result of
their technical education—to writing and talking about product features,
even when it would be preferable to turn to storytelling, for instance to
identify a product's benefits to a customer or the company's strategic differentiation from the competition to a prospective investor. Indeed, the
shift to storytelling can be difficult.

The corporate communication function at some companies helps their
engineers translate their technical expertise so that they can convey to
nonspecialists the excitement and commercial application of new discoveries. At Google, Matthias Graf, head of engineering communications,
explains, "You don't want to lose the stories that the engineers can tell. I

help them develop as spokespeople. They're the inventors and have interesting stories. We also tell the culture story about what fosters innovation. Engineers can spend twenty percent of their time on any project they like as long as it's related to their work. That's how Gmail and Google News were developed."[16]

The second challenge—finding technical experts who are powerful storytellers capable of translating their knowledge in story form and modeling this capability for other members of an organization—may be easier to address than the first because it's a matter of identifying or building talent rather than changing engrained behavior. Philips addressed this challenge quite well in sessions at the Healthcare workshops that featured doctors, nurses, and public officials in healthcare policy who told personal stories about their own medical condition and its impact on their lives while providing a broader context and data about the specific diseases and their management.

In addition to inviting specialists in a technical field to participate in storytelling workshops, organizations should encourage discussion of stories written for nonspecialists by and about scientists as well as discussion of filmmakers interested in science and storytelling. The roster of scientist-storytellers is quite robust and continues to grow.[17] Think of neurologist Oliver Sacks, who in his recent collection of stories, *The Mind's Eye*, shows yet again how he can break the boundaries of the dry medical "case history" and shed light on the emotional drama of those who are struck down exactly "where they live," yet remain resilient. The collection includes a story about a novelist who suffered a stroke that made him unable to read but was able to painstakingly recover this capacity, and continues to write; a concert pianist, similarly challenged in her ability to read music, and the ways she compensates for her loss by relying on her auditory memory to play musical pieces; and a cultured, gregarious woman who can no longer speak but can communicate by using a language of eloquent gestures. Sacks himself tells his own story of suffering from a tumor in his right eye, a cancer that may ultimately blind him, yet he nonetheless tracks this life-altering experience with the persistence, curiosity, and attention to detail that he gives to the others' stories while observing his complex emotional responses to his condition:

5 P.M.: A sudden stabbing pain in my eye, then a turmoil of raying purple forms, starfish, daisies, expanding outward from a multitude of separate points. This turmoil seems to fill the whole visual field. It fascinates and frightens me. Is something adrift, askew, amiss in the eye? Or is it my brain filling in, generating visions, in reaction to the cutting off of vision in my operated eye?[18]

Consider too the personal stories by Nobel Prize-winning physicist Richard Feynman (who was also revered for what physicists consider to be the most elegant, authoritative, and readable lectures for the freshman physics course at CalTech). Feynman's stories capture the grand adventures of finding out how things work. Insatiably curious, brilliant, and flamboyant—he played the bongos and defended a local topless bar's right to do business—he comes across in his stories as a man who asks profound questions and lacks even an ounce of pretension. Here's a glimpse of the episode leading to his pioneering discovery for which he received the Nobel Prize, a period when he was teaching at Cornell University but unable to jump-start his research in physics:

Then I had another thought: Physics disgusts me a little bit now, but I used to *enjoy* doing physics. Why did I enjoy it? I used to *play* with it. I used to do whatever I felt like doing—it didn't have to do with whether it was important for the development of nuclear physics, but whether it was interesting and amusing for me to play with. . . .

So I got this new attitude. Now that I *am* burned out and I'll never accomplish anything, I've got this nice position at the university teaching classes which I rather enjoy, and just like I read the *Arabian Nights* for pleasure, I'm going to *play* with physics, whenever I want to, without worrying about any importance whatsoever.

Within a week I was in the cafeteria and some guy, fooling around, throws a plate in the air. As the plate went up in the air I saw it wobble, and I noticed the red medallion of Cornell on the plate going around. It was pretty obvious to me that the medallion went around faster than the wobbling.[19]

This "Frisbee" moment was the inspiration for the work he eventually did in quantum electrodynamics (QED) for which he received the Nobel Prize.

To Sacks and Feynman one can add a growing list of scientist-storytellers who might inspire those technically trained and working in industry to turn to narrative: evolutionary biologist Stephen Jay Gould, "translator" of geological phenomena John McPhee, surgeon Richard Seltzer, and biologist Lewis Thomas, among others. This is surely a feast of great storytellers who bring the craft of storytelling to communicating science and technology to the general (though curious) reader.[20] Their stories may then serve as inspiration or even models for technically trained businesspeople who are novice storytellers, uncomfortable experimenting with the form, perhaps afraid of failure, and in some instances unconvinced of the usefulness of stories.

Yet another source to inspire technically trained business professionals to turn to storytelling are stories *about* scientists. See, for example, Kraft's historical collection of stories about inventors called *The Greatest Thing Since Sliced Cheese*.[21] Based on more than two hundred interviews with Kraft inventors, the book focuses on the human drama of the obstacles they faced and overcame. As Melanie Villines, coauthor of the Kraft book, notes, "Engineers are so sharp. One of them looked at a piano leg and was inspired to create a method for manufacturing cream cheese."[22] The same can be said for the inventors of instant coffee, macaroni and cheese, "Stove Top" stuffing, malted milk, and (of course) sliced cheese.

Perhaps an even more compelling case for stories about technical topics than the stories written by and about scientists are the insights of filmmakers who have an interest in science and technology. Chief among them is James Cameron of *Avatar* and *Titanic* fame. Asked by a group of faculty and students at CalTech how to gain support for space exploration, Cameron urged the audience to tell stories that are artful and that inspire: "There's a need to project human consciousness into the solar system—a protagonist with two eyes." He called for a show of hands in the audience to indicate how many people read science fiction. Hands shot up from three-quarters of the audience. "Science fiction taps into curiosity," Cameron added. "There's more intensity if we're facing an enigma and if we bring human consciousness to a place." Asked how to improve science education for children, he urged the audience to "make science aspirational for kids. Show them a young scientist at CalTech who's a cool person, a juggler. Tell about your personal excitement. You need to be a real human being first."[23]

Despite the examples of scientist-storytellers and filmmakers like Cameron, it may be prudent to downplay the term "storytelling" in workshops for technically trained businesspeople who may still regard storytelling as a "stigmatized" discourse. Jennifer Hoover, senior strategy manager at Philips Lighting, takes this conservative approach in her storytelling workshops for engineers in research and development at Philips. Called "technical innovation workshops"—and not storytelling workshops— these sessions invite participants, in Hoover's words, to "take a solutions approach to creativity, to embed customer needs in the creative process." Hoover has them consider the "three pillars": "people focused," or listening to and inquiring about people's needs; "partners in innovation," or imagining working with them to come up with options to meet those needs; and "solutions" to the needs. Although the innovation workshops downplay the "One Lighting Story" and omit the term "storytelling," they are in fact a variation of the storytelling workshop and result in participants developing stories about technical inventions that respond to users' needs.

Whether to highlight or omit the term "storytelling" in workshops designed to encourage this capability may depend on an assessment of the participants' receptivity to the practice. As Frank Van der Vloed explains: "People in finance and administration find storytelling hard. Product managers also have difficulty. Those best at using storytelling are marketing people. Lighting application specialists embrace it. They'll ask potential clients about space requirements, aesthetics, and the functions of lighting: Is the light just for a desk or should it affect a social area?"[24]

APPLY LESSONS LEARNED FROM THE
PHILIPS CASE TO YOUR WORK

Fluent storytelling at Philips is not random; rather, it is built into the culture on a consistent foundation of workshops, exercises, guidelines, and supplementary materials. Many of these can be adapted to your own circumstances for telling stories.

Exhibits 10.1 and 10.2 distill the instruction in storytelling at Philips into two summary checklists you may want to review as you plan your own stories. The checklists are supplemented by additional questions

- *Find a picture, a video clip, or a personal photo that stimulates your imagination for creating a story*: A picture may trigger a memory or a set of associations that generate a compelling story. Choose a visual and think about why you chose it and whether you would use it—the actual picture or photo—in the story, since pictures are a kind of "universal language" that can engage the minds and hearts of even those who lack a complete understanding of the written or spoken language.

- *Develop a story that is responsive to people's needs, concerns, and knowledge*: What is the best story you can offer that is responsive to people? For instance, can you tell a solutions-based story to prospective customers, a story about a current customer for whom your company's services solved that customer's problems? Better yet, can you first listen to your prospective customer's specific needs and tell a story about how your company's products or services can address these needs? If you are a technical expert speaking to nonspecialists, can you build your story by picturing them as intelligent and inquisitive people who are willing to give you a brief opportunity to engage their attention and address their needs? Be sure to strip technical jargon out of the story.

- *First identify the various occasions on which you might talk to people about work, choose your story topic, and then develop different versions of the story to suit each occasion*: The scenarios at the Philips workshops present real situations that employees may encounter for which a story would be a powerful response, such as talking to a customer or speaking to an employee. (See Exhibit 9.9 for the full list of scenarios at Philips.) What are the typical scenarios in which you would tell stories? Meeting with a supplier? Interviewing a job candidate? Talking to a local government representative? What stories would work in these situations? How

EXHIBIT 10.1.   Checklist for Building Fluency in
Storytelling Based on Philips Practices

would you modify the story to suit your purpose and assessment of people for each scenario? What do you know about their needs, concerns, and knowledge of you and your firm? Can you interview them to learn more? Would you change the length, the details, the language, the emphasis in the storyline as you consider using the story with different people? Would you strengthen your story by including supplementary material that would enhance its authenticity, for instance metrics and customer testimonials (ministories)?

• *Rehearse, receive feedback, and then revise the story*: The Philips workshops build in time for participants to receive critiques of the content of their story and their performance. See if you can enlist trusted colleagues to work with you on improving your storytelling capabilities. If so, provide your colleagues with the details of the scenario in which you plan to use the story. This should include the story's purpose, audience, and norms about anything from length to tone. Ask them to listen to (or read) the story carefully first, putting themselves in the place of the intended audience and paying attention to when they are interested and when and why they are bored, confused, or otherwise resistant to listening. If you know the vulnerabilities in the story that you may not as yet have addressed to your satisfaction, ask them to comment on these weaknesses. Ask them as well to give their overall response to the story and to comment on other specific elements of the story.

EXHIBIT 10.1.   Continued

and comments based on my work as a consultant. The Philips workshop approach deals with many practical issues about storytelling beyond its uses in achieving the three specific business objectives of changing and strengthening strategy, brand, and culture. In fact, the approach provides multiple ways to build fluency in storytelling.

Does your story ...

- Inspire the reader?

- Contain verifiable facts?

- Touch people's lives?

- Have global, regional, or local relevance?

- Generate interest over a longer period of time?

- Contribute to speaking about your company's business highlights?

- Have related materials (images, video, audio)?

And I would add to this list whether your stories ...

- Gain and hold people's interest?

- Express the storyteller's genuine voice (not corporate speak)?

- Provide a powerful opening or closing to a talk?

- Have a place and function in another part of a talk or written document?

EXHIBIT 10.2.   Checklist for Storytelling

SOURCE: Adapted from Philips Storytelling Template
(cf. Exhibit 9.7). With permission of Philips B.V.

In the larger business culture that values numbers and analytical models over stories and may even label them as "bedtime stories"—the stuff of fairy tales—even a CEO who supports storytelling and a corporate communication group experienced in the practice cannot assume that employees will embrace this effort. This is where storytelling workshops come in. They can introduce the practice of storytelling systematically through the ranks, demonstrate its relevance to people's specific job responsibilities, energize and train people to be fluent storytellers, explain a company's business model and branding story—and ultimately establish storytelling as a cultural norm while building the business.

ENDING WITH

A BEGINNING

THE RESEARCH AND WRITING for this book was a four-year journey that put me in touch with dozens of professionals engaged in organizational storytelling. In this last chapter, I'd like to share with you a retrospective look at what strikes me as the most memorable takeaways and trends to keep in mind going forward. In doing so, I will take you "behind the scenes" to what has impressed me most in my discussions with business professionals and in my consulting work.

If you are considering the potential for storytelling in your own work, I also offer a first concrete step for building the practice of storytelling: formulating your "signature story," a personal story (and versions of that story) about a significant experience, relationship, accomplishment, or failure that has given you insights about who you are as a person and a professional.

PROFESSIONALS WHO VALUE ORGANIZATIONAL STORYTELLING ARE ITS CHAMPIONS

Across the many interviews conducted for the book, primarily with corporate communication executives, I was struck by how many of them expressed a passionate commitment to the practice and, in some cases, a belief in its ability to transform people's relationships at work. We saw in the first chapter that the climate is right for organizations to turn to storytelling. It can reach hearts as well as minds, garner support for initiatives, and help to articulate and strengthen core business concerns like corporate strategy, culture, and brand. The practice can also mitigate the lack of trust in business, cut through the competition from a proliferating number of sources for "mindshare," and address people's hunger for engagement at work.

It is this last point, the hunger for engagement at work, that may explain how frequently my formal interview process—after all, this was management research—became something approximating an intimate discussion with a friend. By and large, an interview began as a conversation with a stranger, but by the end I would often feel I knew my interviewee as a person beyond his or her role and formal position at work. It was as though the questions I asked about storytelling pulled a string that opened up memories and reflection, emotional places in people's lives and the stories that gave meaning to them. For instance, one woman, a senior vice president of corporate communication, told me a story about growing up in a household of three daughters with a mother who was a physicist interested in explaining the marvels of science to her daughters, two of whom became science educators while she herself became the head of the communication department for a high-tech engineering company. Another interviewee, also a corporate communication executive, explained with great animation how a story circulating rapidly in his firm about the new CEO revitalized the workforce while signaling a big change in leadership. The CEO had taken a look at a new product the company was about to launch and declared, "This is the ugliest thing I've ever seen. Don't produce it." The employees thought the CEO would not get his way, but he responded to their lack of confidence in his ability to execute on his decision with "Says who?" A button was then created that employees wore proudly, which said "SAYS who." The button, along with the story, became emblematic of the CEO's direct management style, the boost in employee morale, and the company's renewed competitive position in the marketplace.

A comparable level of passion for and engagement in storytelling prevails among professionals in storytelling workshops, especially when they're members of the same organization. When a participant at a workshop volunteers to tell a story that he or she might use at work, all of a sudden the competing computer screens and cell phones are ignored by the audience, and the room turns into a group of attentive listeners who wait until the story runs its course before responding to it. A coworker is likely to respond to the story by exclaiming with surprise to the storyteller whom he or she has worked with for years, "I never knew that about you." A version of this response is also commonplace in executive coaching sessions on communicating strategic initiatives as a form of persuasive storytelling when participants are telling stories about a future they conceive of and advocate for their organization (akin to the Schering-Plough approach to strategy as a "story in chapters"). The storyteller's audience of workshop participants, taking on either the role of the intended target audience for the strategic pitch or as communication consultants, responds with acute but respectful comments on everything from vulnerabilities in the storyline to decisions about details and language. The passion, attentiveness, and respect that greet these performances bode well for the future of storytelling in organizations.

BEST-PRACTICE ORGANIZATIONS ARE STORYTELLING ENTERPRISES

At best-practice organizations, storytelling has *depth* as well as *reach*, an accomplishment that other organizations can aspire to.[1] What makes for the depth of the practice at these organizations is its connection to one or more core activities of the business, such as helping to build and strengthen the organization's strategy, culture, or brand. Authorized by senior leadership as important to these activities and gradually embraced by much of the organization, storytelling evolves into a valued organizational norm and part of the conversation at work about how best to communicate with people. Though as a researcher I asked a series of questions about storytelling at these companies, much of the time I felt that I was simply entering a setting to listen in on an ongoing conversation about the topic. Moreover, rather than an exclusive in-house activity siloed in a communication group, stories appeared to be owned and shared by many of the company's relevant players. Such was the *reach* of stories.

To promote this reach, corporate communication professionals—the chief protagonists in each of the best-practice cases—act as storytelling "guides." They plan and implement storytelling activities, bring others along (some of whom need little coaxing and others who are skeptical and resistant), and help people develop fluency through workshops, consultations, guidelines, and modeling of the craft themselves. As taught, storytelling is neither a scripted activity with a rigid set of rules for composition and use, at one extreme, nor a sporadic, haphazard outpouring of tangential personal anecdotes by members of the organization, at the other. Instead, instruction strikes a balance between personal and organizational expression.

DEVELOPING FLUENCY IN STORYTELLING IS WITHIN EVERYONE'S GRASP

The elements of fluent storytelling identified in the second chapter are taught at best-practice companies, but the skill set is within everyone's grasp, even if you are working independently on it. Revisiting the checklists in Chapters 4, 6, 8, and 10—exhibits in each case's "lessons learned" chapter on applying the case and commentary to your own work—would be a good place to start. As you may recall, each checklist distills the particular elements of fluency in storytelling highlighted in that company's efforts to identify what makes for successful stories and, in some instances, to train their people in storytelling. By extension, these lists may help you make good choices about a variety of story elements. I encourage you to refer to the lists as they apply to a specific situation you may face that calls for stories.

Looked at from this perspective, the "Checklist for Using Stories to Support Your Strategic Initiatives" (Exhibit 4.1) provides practical advice about persuasive storytelling. The checklist identifies a number of questions to consider in assessing whom you want to influence, including their biases, potential competing agendas, values, knowledge, and concerns. It also asks you to think about how to modify your story on the basis of the different goals you want to achieve with different audiences, and to judge in advance what aspects of the initiative you are willing to open to negotiation, whether the story would be strengthened by supporting material, who the best champion for the story is, and what timing and setting for communicating it are best.

The "Checklist for Stories and Corporate Branding" (Exhibit 6.1) focuses on some of the links between stories and branding, prompting you to evaluate whether your organization has a brand tagline and, if so, whether it effectively frames the organization's stories that are intended to focus on strengthening corporate brand. The checklist has you consider as well whether at least some of the stories that you and others in the firm tell support the brand and whether those stories are both rich in data and emotionally compelling.

The "Checklist for Building Fluency in Storytelling Based on FedEx Practices" (Exhibit 8.1) emphasizes how to build stories that center on key characters; that look for the novel or unexpected, which results in stories capable of surprising and delighting your audience; that find the significant details for a story to draw and hold your audience's attention; and that are good candidates for going viral.

The "Checklist for Building Fluency in Storytelling Based on Philips Practices" (Exhibit 10.1) emphasizes the importance of visual imagery in stories and reiterates the need to focus on creating an audience profile (the audience's knowledge, values, concerns, and so on). This was brought up in the Schering-Plough checklist (Exhibit 4.1) but is presented here with attention to specific scenarios—the settings, people, and purposes for different versions of a story. The emphasis on audience assessment here and in the Schering-Plough checklist underscores the importance of knowing your audience when planning stories that can engage hearts and minds. Here too are recommendations for using rehearsal and revision in crafting stories, ideally involving constructive criticism by trusted colleagues.

Although working with technology—an increasingly important component of fluent storytelling—is not directly addressed in the checklists, the clear trend in technology innovation is toward making cameras and social media platforms for developing and sharing stories cheaper, easier to use, and capable of greater quality (for instance, high-definition video, CD-quality audio, 3-D). Taken as a whole, these advances translate into more power for individuals to create and distribute their own stories. One can't predict exactly how technology will develop, but the rapid progress of the last few years suggests that a return trip to the best-practice companies will show changes in digital stories, their development, and their uses, and it promises an easier job and better results for anyone seeking to create digital stories.

This has not been a how-to book on organizational storytelling, yet between the checklists, which give explicit attention to skill development, and the cases, lessons learned, and storytelling framework you should have multiple resources to draw upon in developing fluency in the practice.

SIGNATURE STORIES CAN REVEAL MUCH ABOUT WHO YOU ARE AND INFLUENCE OTHERS

Rediscover your storytelling roots. What is memorable? It's the stories. You need to know your stories.

—JULIE HAMP, Chief Communications Officer, PepsiCo

If you are planning to use storytelling in your work, the place to begin is by putting together your signature story. Much like your signature, your "signature story" is unique to you and is probably the most personal of stories you'd share in business settings. It may reveal something about your character—what you value—and take the form of an autobiographical excerpt; that is, a personal story (and versions of that story) about a significant experience, relationship, accomplishment, or failure that has given you insights about who you are as a person and a professional.

Finding and Developing Your Signature Story

How do you take up Hamp's advice to "rediscover your storytelling roots"? Finding a topic for a signature story and creating that story (and versions of it) may be a relatively simple task for some of us, especially if we have been surrounded by storytellers all our lives and have observed their efforts. This can also be the case if we're avid readers or film enthusiasts who analyze what makes for a good story while enjoying these pastimes. My friend and colleague Nelson Gayton, who is a filmmaker and academic, talks about the storytellers he encountered during his childhood. They were the "old men," the refugees from Cuba who frequented a place called "Domino Park" in Miami, Florida, where they played dominoes and regaled each other with stories about pre-Castro Cuba. Through stories, they were able to relive their youth and convey to the younger generation the cultural legacy of life in that time and place. (The old men Gayton describes have much in common with the whittling cowboys McMurtry describes in the small west Texas town of his youth.) "Domino Park" became not only a signature story for Gayton but a film he produced that, in his words, "celebrated where I came from, a place that was alive to me in 'Little Havana' in Miami, an ethnic enclave where old men passed on the Cuban culture in their stories."[2]

Gayton had the good fortune to have been surrounded by models for storytelling in his youth, but in the absence of such inspiration and implicit instruction early in life—or even in addition to them—how is it possible to take up Julie Hamp's recommendation to create your signature story?

I have found in my work as a consultant that the following questions can "prime the pump" to help you find a subject for your signature story or, in Hamp's words, "to know your stories":

- What specific experiences have you had with a mentor, a family member, a teacher, friend, boss, colleague, or significant other who has had a substantial impact on who you are as a person and a professional?

- What major challenge have you faced in your personal or professional life? What choices did you make, and what insights did you gain from this experience?

- What stories told to you, read in a book, or seen in a film move you,—and what does this say about you as a person and a professional?

Now consider when and why you'd use your story: In front of what audiences? For what purposes? How would you change the story (for instance, the details or word choice) as your purpose and audience change? Think too about whether you'd use your signature story as a stand-alone story or embed it in a longer communication (for instance, as an introduction to a talk) or as part of a series of communications (for instance, in conjunction with a letter of application and resumé for a job). There are numerous occasions for using your signature story, so it is worthwhile to spend time crafting and revising versions of it for different audiences and purposes. Exhibit 11.1 provides a checklist for reviewing your signature story that reflects both this and earlier discussions of what makes for a successful story.

1. What is the purpose and who is the audience for your signature story?

2. In light of your answers to Question 1, has the story achieved your purpose(s) with the intended audience?

3. Does the story tell your audience something significant about your "lived experience"—your character, values (what you care about), heartfelt convictions, accomplishments, failures?

4. Have you connected emotionally with your audience? Does the experience conveyed seem authentic, and is it told in a voice that is genuine (not corporate speak)?

5. Does the story gain and hold your audience's interest? Does the story contain the novel and unexpected? When (if at all) are *you* bored?

6. Is the story "too personal" for the intended audience? Are they likely to be embarrassed or feel you are just being self-indulgent?

7. Though necessarily personal, is the story sufficiently connected to the business objective you are trying to achieve?

8. Is the story the appropriate length given what you know about your audience and purpose? Would anything be lost in shortening it? If not, what should be condensed or eliminated?

9. Does the story have concrete details that help the audience see, hear, feel (even imagine smelling or tasting)?

10. Does the beginning of the story immediately catch your attention? Do the parts that follow have a logical sequence, a kind of inevitable movement from "a" to "b" to "c," building suspense along the way?

11. How might you use the story in the opening of a talk or as part of a longer communication or a series of communications?

12. If you do not intend the story as an online communication, would you consider placing it on a company Web site or Facebook? Do you think the story would go viral? What changes should be made to enhance its chances of going viral?

EXHIBIT 11.1.   Checklist for Reviewing Your Signature Story

Examples of Signature Stories

Business professionals at all stages of their careers use signature stories for a multitude of purposes and audiences. One celebrated story is Apple founder and chairman Steve Jobs's in three autobiographical excerpts that he presented as his commencement address at Stanford University in 2005. The story allowed him to teach without preaching, to advise students to "pursue the authentic life." Taken as a whole, these excerpts illustrate how he pursued his passions through a combination of self-knowledge, curiosity, and circumstances beyond his control (Exhibit 11.2).

Like Jobs, Tena Clark, CEO and chief creative officer at DMI Music & Media Solutions, used her signature story in the opening of a commencement address she gave at her alma mater, the University of Southern

In the first excerpt, Jobs talked about his humble beginning as the adopted son of working-class parents, and how he dropped out of college and "dropped into" a calligraphy class that gave him insights he applied ten years later in designing the Mac, "the first computer with beautiful typography." In the second excerpt, a story about "love and loss," he talked about being fired by Apple's board, starting Pixar, which produced the first computer-animated film, and meeting his wife. In the third, he disclosed his diagnosis of pancreatic cancer, thought to be an immediate death sentence, only to learn that he had a rare form that could be treated by surgery. In concluding, he offered the following words of wisdom:

> Your time is limited, so don't waste it living someone else's life. Don't be trapped by dogma—which is living with the results of other people's thinking. Don't let the noise of others' opinions drown out your own inner voice. And most important, have the courage to follow your heart and intuition. They somehow already know what you truly want to become. Everything else is secondary.

Interestingly, Jobs's final reflection is an eloquent statement about authenticity.

EXHIBIT 11.2. "You've Got to Find What You Love"
SOURCE FOR QUOTED MATERIAL: http://www.youtube.com/watch?v=UF8uR6Z6KLc, June 12, 2005

Mississippi, to inspire and teach the graduates. Clark captured the subject of her story—her tenacity and drive to distinguish herself from the environment in which she was raised—in the title of the address, "That's Just the Way It Is But Don't You Believe It," and her portrayal of herself as a salmon fighting against the current, an image that opens and closes the story (Exhibit 11.3). As she explained to me: "I started my talk with this story. I wanted to honor the people who had achieved the great accomplishment of graduating, and I wanted to be true to myself and to why they had asked me to deliver the talk."[3]

Jane Wurwand, CEO of Dermalogica, a skin care products company, used her signature story to motivate employees and aspiring entrepreneurs, showing too that she had faced difficult circumstances in early life that may allow her listeners to identify with her experience. The story's central character is Wurwand's mother, who was her role model (Exhibit 11.4).

Wurwand told me this story while we were sitting at a café in Westwood, California. Looking down the block at the long row of storefronts,

I am a salmon. I go against the current and push the limits. When I was four years old I lived on a farm my parents owned in Mississippi. I was much younger than my sisters so I was basically an only child. During pecan season Blacks would come on the farm to pick the pecans. One day when I was running and laughing in the fields with a little Black girl, my mother screamed and called my name: "Tena, get in the house. Why, don't you know that Black people have germs?" (My mother actually was sympathetic to Black people.) She began scrubbing my hands, and through my tears I asked her: "So then Virginia can't brush my hair, cook my meals, and scratch my back if she has germs?" My mother answered, "That's just the way it is." The title of my talk is "That's just the way it is but don't you believe it." I am a salmon. I continue to fight the fight.

EXHIBIT 11.3. Tena Clark's Signature Story:
"That's Just the Way It Is But Don't You Believe It"

SOURCE: Interview, April 20,2010

My Mum was widowed at age thirty-eight with four daughters when my father died suddenly of a massive coronary. I was two years old, and this was Edinburgh, Scotland. Mum had no mortgage security and no family support so she had to figure out what to do. She had trained as a nurse but left work when she got married. She pulled herself together and called a friend who was the matron at the Edinburgh Western General Hospital and said, "I need a job and I need to work nights." She worked from 7 PM to 7 AM in the morning. My sisters came home at 3:30 PM, and my elder sisters made dinner while Mum went to work. Mum told us that life is not about balance. It's about resilience: "Be strong and physically fit. You need a skill set so you can put food on the table." Two of my sisters became nurses, a third a laboratory technician, and I went to beauty school.

EXHIBIT 11.4.   Jane Wurwand's Signature Story
SOURCE: Interview, April 14, 2010

she challenged me in a friendly way to estimate how quickly I could find a job if I were out of work. "For me," she said, "I can walk down the street here and find a beauty salon that would hire me to do skin care in an instant." Her challenge to me reinforced the point of her signature story, the need for a practical, portable skill, which was her mother's legacy to her.

At the other end of the spectrum from established business professionals is Alex Thibault, a young entrepreneur who left a secure, prestigious job as a lawyer. To gain financial backing for his entrepreneurial ventures, Thibault tells his signature story to potential investors about why he left a successful career for a risky one (Exhibit 11.5). "Spinach" is Thibault's version of "hot sauce," or the telling detail that can propel a story forward.

These signature stories provide you with concrete examples of the variety of expression and purpose of this kind of story. Central to each of them is the attempt to be truthful to who the storyteller is and what he or she values, what might be called the authenticity of signature stories.

> I was assigned to do legal work for a growing small business in Canada,
> a spinach farm. Though I am neither a vegetarian nor attracted to the
> rural life, I realized how happy I was tackling all aspects of the business.
> Then came the moment when I knew I wanted to be an entrepreneur
> and not a lawyer: "Spinach," I thought. "I don't even like to eat spinach.
> If I can be passionate about the spinach business, then entrepreneurship
> is for me."

EXHIBIT 11.5.   Alex Thibault's Signature Story
SOURCE: Interview, April 2010

The Authenticity of Signature Stories

For signature stories, being true to who you are gives center stage to feelings, a notion of authenticity bound up with thought about individual identity that has its roots in late eighteenth-century Romanticism.[4] To the then quintessential advocate of authenticity, French Romantic writer Jean-Jacques Rousseau, authenticity had to do with experiencing and expressing his unique, heartfelt convictions about himself, his belief in the importance and celebration of his deepest feelings. Rousseau offered his autobiography, his *Confessions*, to the world as a model of self-disclosure, and as a portrait of his innermost nature: "the sequence of feelings that characterized the successive states of my being."[5] His autobiography is often glaringly oblivious to facts, a weakness that he readily admits to but sees as inconsequential. In the tradition of Rousseau, the contemporary American writer Joan Didion might say that the autobiographical fragments she captures in her writer's notebook are authentic because they don't put a premium on accuracy in the details. "I always had trouble distinguishing between what happened and what merely might have happened,"[6] she reflects. Rather, she is authentic—true to her feelings—in that she represents how things felt to her at the time.[7, 8]

Being "true to your *feelings*" can trump being true to the *facts*, a fundamental requirement for authenticity in organizational storytelling; however, there are important caveats to the claim that feelings are superior to the facts in signature stories since they are communications for business purposes (and not the autobiographical pieces and fiction by writers like Rousseau and Didion). Notwithstanding that the authenticity characterizing signature stories focuses on feelings, this priority is tempered by the realities of functioning in the business world. What are the important caveats?

First of all, being "true to your feelings" doesn't mean that there is one true version of your signature story. Let's take my "Nana Betty" signature story as an example. It's not coincidental that the version of the story I told to corporate communication professionals at PepsiCo emphasized media relations (my grandmother's inviting me to talk to her neighbors, the "press") and corporate advertising (my grandfather's asking me to judge the quality of the ad for his company that he wanted to place in the *New York Times*). By referring to these business activities that are a routine component of this group's professional responsibilities, I placed my audience on familiar ground and hoped to move them quickly into my story, to have them identify with my experience and understand the point I wanted to underscore about how our mentors can give us courage to take risks so that we can grow personally and professionally. For a different purpose and audience, I'd focus on different details of plot and character. For example, in a workshop for executives planning to work abroad, I'd drop the reference to media relations per se and the entire piece on my grandfather and focus on "meeting the press" as a successful cross-cultural encounter. The emphasis in this version of the story would be the ethnic diversity of the neighbors I met who were often nonnative speakers of English. These aspects of my signature story might encourage the workshop participants to think about their experience (or lack thereof) in talking to strangers and what this suggests about the ease or difficulty of their upcoming transition to a foreign work environment. This version of my signature story would also convey to them that I feel very much at home among strangers, in fact, that I enjoy "meeting the press."

We all need to make decisions about which versions of ourselves to project with different groups. These choices don't make us less authentic or make the story a fabrication. Rather, since we are multidimensional, we can genuinely bring out different aspects of ourselves with different people depending on circumstances, and the versions of the signature story reflect how we use our stories strategically and how self-expression is tempered by the realities of functioning in the business world.[9]

Being "true to your feelings" also doesn't mean that your signature story is a "tell all" story. Even in the relatively risk-free environment of a storytelling workshop, businesspeople don't see these opportunities for narrative as a chance to spill their guts and divulge every personal story or every intimate detail. In a public setting, professionals are strategic in their choice of the stories they select to tell and in the details they emphasize or discard. In plain terms, we all function in social worlds in which there are things we choose *not* to tell. I am reminded in this regard of an interview I conducted with a CEO who mentioned how she told her signature story to a group of business students, a story about the unflattering evaluation she received from a headhunter early in her career when she expressed interest in running a high-fashion company. "You don't look the type," he said. "I can see you running something in home building, but not high fashion." The director of public relations for the school who heard about her story asked her if she'd be willing to record this story for the school's Web site. She turned him down, she explained to me, because she didn't want to be *defined* by that particular story in an online public forum, although she had been willing to share the story with students in the informal setting of the classroom because the story might encourage them to ignore attempts from authorities to stifle their professional dreams.

Though feelings can trump the facts in a signature story, especially for high-profile businesspeople, it is prudent to get the facts right even in this most personal type of story. CEOs may know this best. Even a trivial detail—"He lied about wearing a blue tie; it was really purple"—can stimulate negative publicity from self-appointed or establishment critics who may use this lie to build a case for the CEO's dishonesty. As one of my interviewees explained, "The press puts senior execs under a microscope and then broadcasts the slightest imperfection with a megaphone." Especially if the content of the story involves business accomplishments, it is wise to check the accuracy of the details.

Finally, "being true to your feelings" does not mean having a license for narcissistic self-promotion. For this reason, I prefer the term "signature story" to "personal branding" story, a term that's gained popularity;

the latter often devolves into vapid emotionalism and self-advertising with little or no reference to one's accomplishments, values, and the truth of one's experience. The word "branding" in "personal branding" is also problematic, raising ethical issues because it suggests that we humans are commodities whose surface features—our "packaging"—are of paramount importance.

The earlier discussion of signature stories suggested how to develop your story and how and when you might use it, issues of what I have called fluent storytelling. The sample stories in this chapter illustrate how business professionals have successfully used their stories. They may stimulate your thinking about what to include and how to develop your own stories. The last discussion—on authenticity—underscores the importance of tapping into genuine feelings, though doing so is qualified by important considerations that have to do with the public presentation of these stories for achieving business objectives.

In this final chapter we have returned to square one, the original inspiration for this book and the very first story presented—a story about my relationship with my storytelling and story-listening "Nana," my beloved grandmother. Nana welcomed me into her community by inviting me to tell my story-of-the-moment to her neighbors, who were until that moment strangers to me. It is a story that in its many renditions became my signature story.

This book has focused on storytelling at the enterprise level, but storytelling starts with a single unit in relationship to another unit or units, each of us engaged in listening to and telling stories to others. In ending with a beginning, I conclude as I began but with a slight revision: my decision to address you directly. I invite *you* to find and develop your own signature story, and to "meet the press."

REFERENCE MATTER

ACKNOWLEDGMENTS

Many thanks to the professionals, whom I personally interviewed, who shared their insights with me about storytelling in business.

FROM BUSINESS

John D. Bergen, Senior Vice President–Corporate Affairs and Marketing, Siemens Corporation

Anne C. Bucher, Associate Principal Designer, Packaging R & D, Kraft Foods

Angela A. Buonocore, Senior Vice President and Chief Communications Officer, Xylem Inc.

Paul Capelli, Vice President, Corporate Communications and Community Affairs, QBC; former Vice President, Public Relations, Staples

Tena Clark, CEO and Chief Creative Officer, DMI Music and Media Solutions

Beth Comstock, Senior Vice President and Chief Marketing Officer, GE

Ron Culp, Partner, Ketchum

Michelle Daniels, Executive Communications, Dell Inc.

Valerie Di Maria, Principal, the 10 company

Richard Edelman, CEO, Edelman Associates

Bob Feldman, Principal and Cofounder, PulsePoint Group

James J. Finn, Chief Marketing Officer, Groovy Corporation

Greg Gable, Senior Vice President–Corporate Public Relations, Charles Schwab & Company

Andy Gilman, President, Commcore Consulting Group

Steve Goldstein, Executive Vice President, Public Affairs and Marketing, TIAA-CREF

Gary Grates, Principal, WCG Worldwide

Eric Greenspan, Cofounder and CEO, Make It Work, Inc.

Harvey W. Greisman, Senior Vice President and Group Executive–Worldwide Communications, MasterCard Worldwide

Margaret M. Gurowitz, Manager, Corporate Communication, Johnson & Johnson

Julie Hamp, Chief Communications Officer, PepsiCo

Steve Harris, Senior Executive, Corporate Communication, GM

Jeff Hunt, Principal and Cofounder, PulsePoint Group

Kim L. Hunter, President and Chief Executive Officer, Lagrant Communications

Raymond C. Jordan, Corporate Vice President, Public Affairs and Corporate Communication, Johnson & Johnson

Betsy Wood Knapp, CEO, BigPicture Investors, LLC; Cofounder, Knapp Foundation

Tom Kowalski, Vice President, Corporate Communications, BMW of North America

David Kramer, Director, Global Communications and Public Affairs, Google

Sydney S. Lindner, Associate Director, Corporate Affairs, Kraft Foods

Sally Maier, Senior Director, Employee & Online Communications, Corporate & Legal Affairs, Kraft Foods

Thomas R. Martin, Executive-in-Residence, The College of Charleston; former VP–Corporate Communications, FedEx Corporation; former head of corporate communication, ITT

Catherine Maxey, Public Affairs Director, Dow Chemical Company

Katharine McBridge, Corporate Communication, GM

Betsy McLaughlin, Chief Executive Officer, Hot Topic Inc.

Christine Miller, President, Christine Miller Consulting

Irv Miller, Group Vice President–Corporate Communications, Toyota Motor Sales, USA

Michael Mitchell, Senior Director–External Communications, Corporate & Legal Affairs, Kraft Foods

Erin Mulligan Nelson, Senior Vice President and Chief Marketing Officer, Dell Inc.

Bill Nielsen, Public Relations and Corporate Communications Counsel and formerly VP–Public Relations, Johnson & Johnson

Charles Perkins, Director, Public Relations for the Americas, Ernst & Young

Tom Pyden, Communications Consultant

Kevin J. Ramundo, Vice President–Communications, Network Centric Systems, Raytheon Company

Jim Reilly, former General Manager of Marketing Plans and Communications, IBM

Frank Shaw, Corporate Vice President for Communications, Microsoft

Gary Sheffer, Executive Director, Corporate Communications and Public Affairs, General Electric Company

Donna Sitkiewicz, Director, Employee Corporate Communication, Kraft Foods

Steve Streit, CEO, Green Dot Corporation

Simon Talcott, Head of Corporate Affairs, Kraft Australia/New Zealand

Alex Thibault, UCLA Anderson School of Management MBA alum, Class of 2011, and Vice President, Marketing and Business Development, Edilex International Ltd.

Becky Haglund Tousey, Associate Director, Archives & Information Resources, Kraft Foods

Melanie Villines, writer under contract with Kraft for *The Greatest Thing Since Sliced Cheese*, Kraft Foods

Karen Wickre, Senior Manager, Global Communications & Public Affairs, Google

Jane Wurwand, CEO of Dermalogica

Perry Yeatman, Senior Vice President, Corporate & Legal Affairs, Kraft Foods

FROM COMPANIES CHOSEN FOR EXTENDED CASES

Chevron

David A. Samson, General Manager of Public Affairs; Donald Campbell, Manager, External Communications; Helen Clark, Manager, Corporate Marketing; Mickey Driver, External Relations Advisor, Policy, Government & Policy Affairs; Jeff Glover, Editorial Manager; Joerden Legon, Editor of Chevron.com; Deborah McNaughton, Manager, Internal Communications; Robert Raines, Interactive Communications Manager, Corporate Marketing; Russ Yarrow, General Manager, California Corporate Affairs

FedEx

William G. Margaritis, Corporate Vice President, Global Communications
& Investor Relations; Matt Ceniceros, Senior Communications Specialist;
Howard Clabo, Manager, Media Relations; Cindy Dixon Conner, Manager,
Corporate Communications; Eric T. Epperson, Director, Workplace
Communications; Ryan Furby, Manager, Social Media Strategies; Sheila
Harrell, Vice President of Customer Service Operations; Joe Hopkins, Advisor,
Digital and Social Media Engagement; Renee Horne, Director, Digital Content
& Social Media Engagement; Mitch Jackson, Vice President of Environmental
Affairs and Sustainability; Dianna O'Neill, Manager, Digital Content &
Social Media Engagement; Pamela Roberson, Manager, Digital and Social
Media Engagement; Diane Terrell, Vice President, Strategic Communications;
Jennifer J. Thornton, Executive Assistant, Global Communications & Investor
Relations; Antoney Wilkinson, Staff Director, Global Communications;
Sharon Lloyd Young, Communications Advisor, Global Communications

Philips

Marike Westra, Vice President, Corporate Communications, Philips Lighting;
Marie-Helene Azar, Corporate Communications Officer; Ed Babrich, Head
of Business Transformation, Philips Lighting; Cameron Batten, Internal
Communications Manager, Philips Corporate Communications; Wander
Bruijel, Director Integrated Marketing Communications & PR, Philips
Consumer Lifestyle; Parik Chopra, Senior Director, Brand & Market
Strategy, Philips Lighting; Shai Dewan, Senior Press Officer, Corporate
Communications, Philips, Erin Farber, Communications Manager, Global
Marketing Management; Garrett Forde, General Manager and Executive
Vice President, Philips Lighting Europe, Middle East & Africa; Louis
Hakim, former Vice President Royal Philips Electronics & Chairman
Philips Electronics Middle East; Jeannet Harpe, Senior Director, Corporate
Communications, Consumer, Philips Lighting; Jennifer Hoover, Senior
Strategy Manager, Philips Lighting; Marjin Kamp, Content Production
Officer, Philips; Andre Manning, VP External Communications, Philips
Corporate Communication; Miriam Mobach, Senior Manager, Internal
Communications, Philips Lighting; Lindsey Mosby, Strategy Director, Philips;
Guido Mouws, Director, Customer Care Europe, Philips Lighting; Simon

Poulter, Communication Director, Philips Lighting; Eeva Raaijmakers, Senior Communications Officer, Corporate Communications, Philips; Robert Rooney, Senior Manager Global Pubic Relations, Integrated Marketing Communications, Philips Consumer Lifestyle; Jois van den Hurk, GM Cardiology Care Cycles; Geert Van Kuyck, Chief Marketing Office, Royal Philips Electronics N.V.; Frank Van der Vloed, General Manager Benelux, Philips Lighting

Schering-Plough

Fred Hassan, Chairman and CEO; Ken Banta, Head of Corporate Strategic Affairs; Rick Bowles, Senior Vice President, Global Quality Operations; Alex Kelly, Group Vice President, Global Communications and Investor Relations; Rob Lively, Vice President, Corporate Government Affairs; Vas Nair, Vice President and Chief Learning Officer; Tom Sabatino, Executive Vice President & General Counsel; Brent Saunders, Senior Vice President and President, Consumer Health Care; Peggy Schell, Assistant to Ken Banta; Helma van Leeuwe, Senior Director of Global Internal Communications; Susan Wolf, Corporate Secretary, Vice President–Governance

FROM CORPORATE COMMUNICATION PROFESSIONALS
STUDYING IN THE MASTERS PROGRAM
(MSCOM) AT THE UNIVERSITY OF LUGANO

Michele Bodmer, Senior Editor, External Communications, Credit Suisse; Suzy Chisholm, Country Marketing & Communications, Philips Healthcare; Simone C. Drill, Head of Events, Executive Director, Sponsorship & Events, UBS; Sukanti Ghosh, Head–Corporate Affairs, Barclays; Matthias Graf, Head Engineering Communication, Europe, Middle East, & Africa, Google; Stefan Hess, Senior Press Spokesman, Deutsche Post; Kirsty James, Head of Brand Strategy & Communication, Syngenta International AG; Lydia Kirchel, Corporate & Marketing Communications Manager Europe, Haworth; Kornelia Kneissl, Media Relations & Corporate Strategy, K2K; Amanda Martin, Senior Consultant, Dynamicsgroup; Erik Peters, Senior Communications Manager, Zurich Financial Services; Simone Rellstab-Drill, UBS; Thomas Scheuring, Project Leader, Branding & Advertising, Clariden Leu; Michele Tesoro-Tess, Managing Director, Reputation Institute Italy

INTERVIEWS WITH OR SURVEY
RESPONSES FROM COLLEAGUES

Paul Argenti, Amos Tuck (Dartmouth) School of Business

Patricia Bower, NYU Stern School of Business

Lee Cerling, USC Marshall School of Business

Sandra Collins, Mendoza College of Business, University of Notre Dame

Carter Daniel, Rutgers Business School

Bill Ellet, Harvard University School of Business

Nelson Gayton, Executive Director of the Center for Management of the
    Enterprise in Media, Entertainment, and Sports, UCLA Anderson School
    of Management

Mary C. Gentile, Director, "Giving Voice to Values," Babson College

Anne Grinols, Baylor University's Hankamer School of Business

Neal Hartman, MIT Sloan School of Business

Mary Lang, Comadrona Communications, Inc.

Roger Manix, Acting Chair, School of Cinema & Performing Arts, Tribeca
    Film Center

James McGaugh, Director of the Center for Neurobiology of Learning &
    Memory, University of California at Irvine

Mary Munter, Amos Tuck (Dartmouth) School of Business

Jim O'Rourke, Mendoza College of Business, University of Notre Dame

Lili Powell, University of Virginia, Darden School of Business

Lamar Reinsch, Georgetown University's McDonough School of Business

Pris Rogers, University of Michigan's Ross School of Business

James Rubin, University of Virginia, Darden School of Business

JD Schramm, Stanford Graduate School of Business

Jeff Sharlach, NYU Stern School of Business

Jim Suchan, Naval Postgraduate School

Gail Thomas, Naval Postgraduate School

Judy Tisdale, Kenan-Flagler Business School at the University of North
    Carolina

Yoram (Jerry) Wind, The Wharton School at the University of Pennsylvania

Rich Young, Tepper School of Business, Carnegie Mellon University

Jeffrey Younger, NYU Stern School of Business

FROM THE FILM INDUSTRY

Hal Ackerman, screenplay writer, novelist, and professor of screenplay writing at UCLA

Kim Aubry, ZAP Zoetrope Aubry Productions

Jay Boekelheide, filmmaker

Karen Everett, Documentary Story Consultant

Allyson Field, Assistant Professor, UCLA, Cinema and Media Studies

Neil Landau, Screenplay Writer and Visiting Assistant Professor, UCLA School of Theater, Film, and Television

Eddy Ring, sitcom writer

Fred Rubin, Emmy-nominated television writer and producer, UCLA professor

Richard Walter, Professor and Screenwriting Chair, UCLA School of Theater, Film, and Television

CHAPTER 1

1. Larry McMurtry, *Walter Benjamin at the Dairy Queen: Reflections at Sixty and Beyond* (New York: Simon & Schuster, 1999), 43.

2. Ibid., 27.

3. The early–twentieth-century European intellectual Walter Benjamin (whose essay McMurtry turns to periodically in his own autobiography, comparing and contrasting his experience and reflections with Benjamin's) linked the oral art of narrative to a period that predated mass media and his culture's preference for information. Unlike McMurtry, Benjamin concluded that storytelling lacked staying power. His essay is elegiac, acknowledging the irreparable loss to the culture caused by the decline of storytelling. See Walter Benjamin, "The Storyteller: Reflections on the Works of Nikolai Leskov," in *Illuminations*, ed. and with an introduction by Hannah Arendt and translated by Harry Zohn (New York: Schocken, 1968), 83–109. By contrast, McMurtry sees storytelling as a vibrant art. Though not the oral art of the rural storytellers he knew in his youth, storytelling lives on in fiction and film.

4. McMurtry, *Walter Benjamin at the Dairy Queen*, 43.

5. Ibid., 21–22.

6. Interview with Jim Reilly, April 22, 2009.

7. Mary Lang, response to the Management Communication Survey on the Uses of Storytelling in MBA Communication Courses, May 2009.

8. Interview with Bob Feldman, May 1, 2008. Emphasis mine.

9. Sven Birkerts, *The Gutenberg Elegies: The Fate of Reading in an Electronic Age* (Winchester, MA: Faber and Faber, 1994).

10. Interview with Irv Miller, June 11, 2008.

11. Interview with Betsy McLaughlin, February 19, 2010.

12. Interview with Tom Pyden, May 21, 2008.

13. Interview with Rob Lively, June 11, 2009.

14. Personal communication with Bill Margaritis, March 12, 2010.

15. There is a growing body of literature on cognitive psychology and narrative. For those with some understanding of psychology, see Nicole K. Speer et al., "Reading Stories Activates Neural Representations of Visual and Motor Experiences," *Psychological Science*, 20 (8), 2009, 989–99, which reports a study on how different parts of the brain track different aspects of story: "Some of these regions [of the brain] mirror those involved when people perform, imagine, or observe similar real-world activities. These results support the view that readers understand a story by simulating the events in the story world and updating their simulation when features of that world change" (1).

16. Jerome Bruner, *Making Stories: Law, Literature, Life* (New York: Farrar, Straus and Giroux, 2002), 32.

17. Jeremy Hsu, "The Secrets of Storytelling," *Scientific American Mind*, 19 (4), 2008, 50.

18. Interview with James McGaugh, January 30, 2012.

19. Robert Coles, *The Call of Stories: Teaching and the Moral Imagination* (Boston: Houghton Mifflin, 1989), 23.

20. http://www.ce.columbia.edu/masters/about.cfm?PID=38&Content=AboutProgram 4/13/2009, 1.

21. Rita Charon's *Narrative Medicine: Honoring the Stories of Illness* (Oxford: Oxford University Press, 2006) makes an eloquent personal and professional case for the importance of narrative medicine to training the new generation of physicians. Her edited volume (with Peter L. Rudnytsky), *Psychoanalysis and Medicine* (Albany: State University of New York Press, 2008), extends this case, and includes essays by distinguished literary scholars Sander L. Gilman and Geoffrey Hartman.

22. Rita Charon, "Where Does Narrative Medicine Come From?" in *Psychoanalysis and Narrative Medicine*, ed. Peter Rudnytsky and Rita Charon (Albany: State University of New York Press), 23. This is a case discussed earlier by Charon in ch. 9 of *Narrative Medicine*.

23. Peter Brooks and Paul Gewirtz, "Narrative and Rhetoric in the Law," in *Law's Stories: Narrative and Rhetoric in the Law,* ed. Peter Brooks and Paul Gewirtz (New Haven: Yale University Press, 1996), 2.

24. Ibid., 7.

25. D. N. McCloskey, *If You're So Smart: The Narrative of Economic Expertise* (Chicago: University of Chicago Press, 1990), 1.

26. Ibid., 15.

27. Closely akin to the work of McCloskey and Smart, Ed Leamer's *Macroeconomic Patterns and Stories: A Guide for MBAs* (Berlin: Springer-Verlag, 2009) makes a powerful case for studying macroeconomic data for the patterns that emerge through interpretation and for the resulting stories that can then be told about the data. He sees the study of economics as "literature" rather than "science": "The words 'theory and evidence' suggest an incessant march toward a level of scientific certitude that cannot be attained in the study of the complex self-organizing human system that we call the economy. The words 'patterns and stories' much more accurately convey our level of knowledge, now, and in the future as well. It is literature, not science" (3).

28. Richard Marius and Melvin E. Page, *A Short Guide to Writing About History, 6th edition* (New York: Pearson, 2007), 7.

29. According to historian and narrative scholar Hayden White, the historian's task must involve going beyond judging evidence and establishing the chronological ordering of events to creating a story. As cited by Debra Journet, "The Limits of Narrative in the Construction of Scientific Knowledge: George Gaylord Simpson's *The Dechronization of Sam Magruder*" in Jane M. Perkins and Nancy Blyler, *Narrative and Professional Communication* (Stamford, CT: Ablex, 1999), 95:

> The historian transforms chronicle [the ordering of events in time] into emplotted narrative through greater selection and exclusion, emphasis and subordination. Plots enable the historian to place a temporal boundary around the sequential events of the chronicle, so that there is a beginning, middle, and end, and to establish causal connections so that earlier events lead to later ones. The resulting narrative endows events with a meaning or significance they would not have as a mere sequence. (White, 1973, 1987)

See Hayden White, *Metahistory* (Baltimore: Johns Hopkins University Press, 1973); and Hayden White, *Tropics of Discourse* (Baltimore: Johns Hopkins University Press, 1987). There is also a long tradition of scholarship on historiography, or the writing of history. For a quite readable study that is ambitious in scope, see John Burrough, *History of Histories: Epics, Chronicles, Romances, and Inquiries from Herodotus and Thucydides to the Twentieth Century* (London: Penguin, 2007).

30. There is an enormous number of publications on narrative written by literary scholars. Highlighted here are just a few of the relevant works: Wayne C. Booth, *The Rhetoric of Fiction* (Chicago: University of Chicago Press, 1961); J. Porter Abbott, *The Cambridge Introduction to Narrative*, 2002); Wallace Martin, *Recent Theories of Narrative* (Ithaca: Cornell University Press, 1986); Mieke Bal, *Narratology: Introduction to the Theory of Narrative, 2nd edition* (Toronto: University of Toronto Press, 1994); and Gerald Prince, *A Dictionary of Narratology* (Lincoln: University of Nebraska Press, 1987). For specific attention to reader response theory, see especially Susan R. Sulieman and Inge Crosman, eds., *The Reader in the Text: Essays on Audience and Interpretation* (Princeton: Princeton University Press, 1980); Jane P. Tompkins, *Reader-Response Criticism: From Formalism to Post-Structuralism* (Baltimore: Johns Hopkins University Press, 1980); and Louise M. Rosenblatt, *The Reader the Text the Poem: The Transactional Theory of the Literary Work* (Carbondale and Edwardsville: Southern Illinois University Press, 1978). Some of this scholarly discussion is weighed down by jargon and only accessible to experts in literary theory. References to theory will appear across the chapters as they have practical application to storytelling in business.

31. According to screenwriter Robert McKee, a CEO can learn about leadership from screenwriters. McKee defines story from a screenwriter's perspective, identifies his views about the qualities of a good story, and talks about the importance of laying out the business challenges faced by an organization if one is in a leadership position, among other things. See "Storytelling That Moves People: A Conversation with a Screenwriting Coach," *Harvard Business Review*, June 2003, 51–55. Entertainment executive Peter Guber draws on his experience as a filmmaker, and that of a group of established professionals whom he brought together, to reflect on the importance of storytelling to business. See "The Four Truths of the Storyteller," *Harvard Business Review*, December 2007, 53–59. He develops his ideas further in *Tell to Win: Connect, Persuade, and Triumph with the Hidden Power of Story* (New York: Random House, 2011).

32. Mary C. Gentile, response to the Management Communication Survey on the Uses of Storytelling in MBA Communication Courses, May 15, 2009.

33. E-mail from James Rubin, June 2, 2009.

34. Personal communication with Lili Powell, May 26, 2009.

35. Patricia Bower, response to the Management Communication Survey on the Uses of Storytelling in MBA Communication Courses, May 2009.

36. Sandra Collins, response to the Management Communication Survey on the Uses of Storytelling in MBA Communication Courses, May 2009.

37. Lamar Reinsch, response to the Management Communication Survey on the Uses of Storytelling in MBA Communication Courses, May 2009.

38. J. D. Schramm, response to the Management Communication Survey on the Uses of Storytelling in MBA Communication Courses, May 2009.

39. Personal communication with Paul Argenti, June 2009.

40. Interview with Jerry Wind, December 10, 2009.

41. Interview with Jim Finn, May 23, 2008.

42. See James A. Berlin, *Rhetoric and Reality: Writing Instruction in American Colleges, 1900–1985* (Carbondale and Edwardsville: Southern Illinois University Press, 1987); David R. Russell, *Writing in the Academic Discipline, 1870–1990* (Carbondale: Southern Illinois University Press, 1991); and Nan Johnson, *Nineteenth-Century Rhetoric in North America* (Carbondale and Edwardsville: Southern Illinois University Press, 1991). These academic experts in the history of rhetoric provide scholarly studies on writing pedagogy and, more broadly, on communication in the United States. In ch. 3 of his book, Berlin analyzes three approaches to teaching writing in the early twentieth century that represent competing values: the skills focus, courses in responding to literature, and those in public discourse. In ch. 2 of *Writing in the Academic Disciplines*, Russell discusses the emphasis on public oratorical performance in nineteenth-century US higher education. See appendix A of Johnson's book for sample descriptions of humanities courses at a number of US universities during this period.

43. Interview with David A. Samson, April 10, 2008.

44. Although business communications (e.g., CEO speeches) that use stories can provide a way to understand our subject, these alone are quite insufficient. I had to go to the field, as it were, to interview experts and to observe the uses of storytelling at various sites. The reliance on expert knowers to understand a type of discourse is a well-established approach to conducting research in business communication, one that my coauthor Jone Rymer and I used in our study of the genre of the case write-up, an assignment used in business classes. See Janis Forman and Jone Rymer, "Defining the Genre of the Case Write-up," *Journal of Business Communication*, 36 (2), 1999, 103–33. The research method depended

upon earlier scholarly work. See John Swales, *Genre Analysis: English in Academic and Research Settings* (Cambridge, UK: Cambridge University Press, 1990).

45. By contrast, the typical Harvard case offers a story about an organization facing a crisis or set of challenges. Professional communication experts Jane Perkins and Nancy Blyler argue for the importance of creating narrative as a way to build knowledge about organizations. See Perkins and Blyler, *Narrative and Professional Communication*, ix–xvi ("Preface"). According to them, "narrative encourages researchers, teachers, and trainers, and practitioners to bring context and connection to the fore, to view human experience as essentially storied, and to consider knowledge-making as a narrative endeavor" (x).

46. Interview with Gary Sheffer, April 8, 2009.

47. Cheryl Forbes, a professor of writing and rhetoric, offers this consensus about story, in this instance for science writing: "good science writing . . . depends on the conventions of narrative—place, time, characters, dialogue, dramatic tension, humorous incongruity, suspense, mystery, intrigue, plot, and a believable, reliable narrator." See "Getting the Story, Telling the Story: The Science of Narrative, the Narrative of Science," in Perkins and Blyler, *Narrative and Professional Communication*, 79–92 (83). Similarly, narratologist Michelle Scalise Sugiyama summarizes the work of literary scholars in this way: "The literary consensus is that stories consist of character, setting, actions, and events—linked temporally and/or causally—and conflict and resolution." See "Reverse-Engineering Narrative: Evidence of Special Design," in *The Literary Animal: Evolution and the Nature of Narrative*, ed. Jonathan Gottschall and David Sloan Wilson (Evanston, IL: Northwestern University Press, 2005), 177–96 (180). These two articles are just a sample from an enormous body of literature on story that cuts across many disciplines, including literature and psychology, in what is known as the field of "narratology" (a discipline devoted to the study of narrative).

48. To look beyond these basics, you may want to turn to Chapter 2, on "craft," which focuses on the elements of a *compelling* story that gains and holds people's attention.

49. Interview with Andy Gilman, June 10, 2008.

50. Mary F. Merrill, in *Johnson & Johnson Reflections of Our Credo* (New Brunswick, NJ: Johnson & Johnson, 2009).

51. Interview with Valerie Di Maria, July 2, 2008.

52. Interview with Gary Grates, November 11, 2009.

53. Interview with Harvey W. Greisman, May 19, 2008.

CHAPTER 2

1. For instance, *technology* has a minor role in the Schering-Plough as well as in the Philips case, but has great importance to the Chevron and FedEx cases. Storytelling and *strategy* is central to the Schering-Plough and Philips cases but not to the FedEx case.

2. Arthur W. Page Society, "The Authentic Enterprise," 2007, 6.

3. "The Page Principles," 2011, http://www.awpagesociety.com/about/the-page-principles/(accessed October 8, 2011).

4. Ibid., 16.

5. By and large, I avoid the word *transparency*, which is often used to mean complete disclosure or honesty, because I find it to be problematic. In literal terms, "transparency" means that company insiders and outsiders alike are provided with a window to see every aspect of a business, but companies should not—and do not—reveal everything. Just consider the consequences to their competitive positioning were they to reveal their trade secrets or strategies and tactics for building market position.

6. Interview with Helen Clark, January 21, 2009.

7. Interview with Jeff Hunt, May 12, 2010.

8. Interview with Karen Everett, June 23, 2010.

9. See discussion on this topic in Janis Forman, "Leaders as Storytellers: Finding Waldo," *Business Communication Quarterly*, September 2007, 371.

10. In *Personality Not Included: Why Companies Lose Their Authenticity—And How Great Brands Get It Back* (New York: McGraw-Hill, 2008), Rohit Bhargava explains that "accidental spokespeople" are those stakeholders who are "not controlled by the brands they describe, but . . . influence the perception about those brands in a powerful way" (56).

11. In "Building Trust in Times of Crisis: Storytelling and Change Communication in an Airline Company," *Corporate Communications*, 11 (4), 2006, Roy Langer and Signe Thorup talk about the metaphor of the organization as an orchestra in their summary of research on organizational change:

> Organisational change communication can be seen as a polyphonic orchestration of an organisation's many voices. Rather than seeing an organisation as a single body with a single (management) voice telling the grand story, it should be regarded as an orchestra consisting of many different instruments and voices, each capable of performing in its own register and each with its own distinctive sound. All the different instruments and voices enable an organisation to play more than one tune. An orchestra consisting only of

drums may be able to produce a certain noise, as long as everyone can be persuaded to play in the same rhythm.

In a polyphonic perspective, communication management focuses on facilitating and coordinating all the voices of the orchestra with a view to creating polyphonic harmony, allowing space for the special qualities of each voice or instrument. This presupposes that there is enough space for each individual and for individual differences—including space for solo parts or local articulation. This presupposes that each voice is heard, making it possible to identify what it is capable of and what it wishes to contribute. The conductor of the orchestra (the management) does not use his baton to decide what should be played and how. (375)

12. Interview with David A. Samson, April 10, 2008.

13. Interview with Rob Lively, June 11, 2009.

14. Interview with Betsy McLaughlin, February 19, 2010.

15. David M. Kennedy, *Freedom from Fear: The American People in Depression and War, 1929 to 1945* (New York: Oxford University Press, 1999), 38.

16. See Brooke Harrington, "Introduction: Beyond True and False," in *Deception: From Ancient Empires to Internet Dating*, ed. Brooke Harrington (Stanford: Stanford University Press, 2009), 1–16. Harrington explains that "providing an excess of information can be an extremely effective tool of deception. The technique consists simply of disclosing far more information than is required or requested, making it difficult to find the essential data points among the extraneous ones. It might be compared to piling hay around a needle, or manure around a pony; at any rate, it exploits well-known limitations of human cognition when it comes to information search" (12–13).

17. The French thinker Jacques Derrida took up the concept of the "drugging" effect of writing in his essay "Plato's Pharmacy." He assessed Plato's view of writing as a "pharmakon," that is, "its ambiguous status as a remedy, a poison, and as remedy *and* a poison and, as such, as an opposing, ambiguous set of values" (71). See "Plato's Pharmacy," in *Dissemination*, translated, with an introduction and additional notes by Barbara Johnson (Chicago: University of Chicago Press, 1981), 61–171.

18. In *Mario und der Zauberer* (London: Grant & Cutler, 1990), the German scholar Ronald Speirs points out how the tyrannical stage hypnotist Cipolla is portrayed with the "theatricality of fascist politics" (17) of Mussolini's time; however, Speirs hastens to point out that "there are also important

differences between the two figures [Cipolla and Mussolini], some of which have to do with the fact that Mann's concerns in this story were not exclusively political, while others have to do with the fact that he did not consider fascism to be an exclusively Italian phenomenon" (19). In *Thomas Mann's Short Fiction: An Intellectual Biography*, ed. Mitzi Brunsdale (Cranbury, NJ: Associated University Presses, 1989), German literary scholar Esther H. Leser characterizes the diabolical storytelling capabilities of Cipolla in the following way:

> Cipolla's speech is . . . an enslaving instrument. His quick tongue first fascinates the crowd, and by blurring their judgment, it allows him to exert his hypnotic power on them. The narrator explains to his children that Cipolla is a conjuror, an "artist-magician" (*Zauberkünstler*), who uses language to manipulate his audience. . . . To him [Mann], the "Künstler" and the "Magician" comprise the storyteller's gift; the "Künstler" captivates the imagination through illusion, alluring, magnetic, irresistible in its deception. The Magician initiates listeners to mythical reality through the medium of the story. This duality identifies the storyteller as both a wretched swindler and the bearer of a divine theme. (194–95)

The figure of Mephistopheles in the Faustian legend appears in multiple classical works of Western literature, including the English Renaissance dramatist Christopher Marlowe's *Dr. Faustus*, Wolfgang Goethe's *Faust*, and Thomas Mann's *Dr. Faustus*.

19. Rousseau's influence on authenticity in personal storytelling will be discussed in Chapter 11.

20. Mary Lang, response to the Management Communication Survey on the Uses of Storytelling in MBA Communication Courses, May 2009.

21. Interview with Perry Yeatman, May 5, 2008.

22. Anne Grinols, response to the Management Communication Survey on the Uses of Storytelling in MBA Communication Courses, May 2009.

23. E-mail from Roger Manix, May 19, 2009.

24. For the craft of storytelling, see Stephen Denning, *The Leader's Guide to Storytelling: Mastering the Art and Discipline of Business Narrative* (San Francisco: Jossey-Bass, 2005); Peter Guber, *Tell to Win: Connect, Persuade, and Triumph with the Hidden Power of Story* (New York: Random House, 2011); and Jack Maguire, *The Power of Personal Storytelling: Spinning Tales to Connect with Others* (New York: Tarcher/Putnam, 1998).

25. Interview with Jim Finn, May 23, 2008.

26. Interview with Tom Martin, April 14, 2008.

27. Interview with Fred Rubin, October 5, 2010.

28. Interview with Neil Landau, July 30, 2010.

29. Interview with Jeff Hunt, March 12, 2010.

30. Nancy Duarte, *slide:ology: The Art and Science of Creating Great Presentations* (Sebastopol, CA: O'Reilly Books, 2008), 2.

31. Edward R. Tufte, *The Visual Display of Quantitative Information*, 2nd edition (Cheshire, CT: Graphics Press, 2001).

32. Interview with Jim Finn, May 23, 2008.

33. David Lodge, *The Art of Fiction* (New York: Penguin Books, 1992), 216.

34. Interview with Sharon Young, May 19, 2010.

35. E-mail from Angela A. Buonocore, December 2, 2010.

36. In his literary tour de force *Briar Rose* (New York: Grove Press, 1996), novelist Robert Coover presents variations of the "Sleeping Beauty" fairy tale, emphasizing through shifts in language, detail, and point of view different potential versions of the tale. Among others, these include a version on the sexual implications of the prince's struggle to climb the branches to reach the princess and, in another case, on his steadfast quest as a heroic act of endurance with his path to the princess littered with the bones of earlier contenders. Some versions are told from the prince's point of view, others from the princess's, and still others from that of the old crone (whose needle pricked the princess causing her to fall into a deep sleep).

37. In his study of a tale by the French writer Balzac, literary theorist Roland Barthes presents his idea of the "writerly" text (4) that applies here too. According to Barthes, the writerly text has a plurality of entrances—places where the reader "enters" the text (5)—and a plurality of meanings as constructed by the reader. His notion of the writerly text suggests that it would be useful for storytellers to consider where in a given story a reader (or listener) is likely to be engaged, why this is so, and whether they should change the story to take these "plurality of entrances" into account. In sum, should the listening storyteller assess the target reader's likely "entrances" into a story and adjust the story to take these into account? See *S/Z*, translated by Richard Miller and preface by Richard Howard (New York: Hill and Wang, 1974), original work published 1970.

38. Interview with Tena Clark, April 20, 2010.

39. In "Timesuck: The Battle for Our Leisure Time (and Money)," *MediaPost Publications*, July 15, 2010, media watcher Dave Morgan reports that "Facebook has hundreds of millions of members (many inactive, but enough active to constitute a massive audience) and, according to Nielsen, those in the U.S. spent an incredible 13.9 billion minutes per month on the site in the middle of last year [2009]." As further proof of the technology's growth, it is also reported in "You-Tube Scores 101 Online Videos Per Viewer in May," *Center for Media Research*, July 16, 2010, that "183 million U.S. Internet users watched online videos during the month of May [2010]." In "Lessons from the Top Brands on Facebook," *Online Media Daily*, August 16, 2010, Gavin O'Malley reports that of the 500 million users worldwide in 2010, 63 percent of adults online in the United States are now on Facebook.

40. From one vantage point, the conversations are online versions of those in the close-knit community of whittling cowboys trading stories at the west Texas general store described by novelist Larry McMurtry in *Walter Benjamin at the Dairy Queen: Reflections at Sixty and Beyond* (New York: Simon & Schuster, 1999)..

41. Page Society, "Authentic Enterprise," 12.

42. Ibid., 11.

43. In *Groundswell: Winning in a World Transformed by Social Technologies* (Boston: Harvard Business Press, 2008), social media experts Charlene Li and Josh Bernoff of Forrester Research studied the rise and growth of "social computing" and identified what they call the "groundswell": "A social trend in which people use technologies to get the things they need from each other, rather than from traditional institutions like corporations" (9). In effect, they look at the online social communities and the power of word of mouth among the likeminded in its influence on purchasing decisions. In *Digital Strategies for Powerful Corporate Communications* (New York: McGraw Hill, 2009), Paul Argenti and Courtney Barnes assess the impact of social media on companies' ability to influence important stakeholders (e.g., customers, investors, employees) and offer strategies to businesses for taking advantage of digital platforms and their capabilities. In *Digital Storytelling: A Creator's Guide to Interactive Entertainment, 2nd edition* (Amsterdam: Elsevier Focal Press, 2008), Carolyn Handler Miller is primarily concerned with providing historical context and practical techniques for the creation and assessment of digital games. She also devotes a chapter to their application to business goals.

44. Interview with Tom Martin, April 14, 2008.

45. Katie Delahaye Paine, "How Do Blogs Measure Up?" *Communication World*, 24 (5), September–October 2007, 30–33.

46. "Quantifiable Lift with the Addition of Social Media in Advertising," *Center for Media Research*, April 28, 2010.

47. Miller, *Digital Storytelling*, 29.

48. Richard Edelman, presentation at the annual meeting of ITT corporate communication professionals, "The Trust Barometer," New York City, November 17, 2010.

49. The 2011 Edelman Trust Barometer Survey

consisted of 30-minute telephone interviews conducted from October 11–November 28, 2010, with the exception of France and Germany, fielded January 3–13, 2011. The survey sampled 5,075 informed publics in two age groups (25–34 and 35–64) in 23 countries. All informed publics met the following criteria: college-educated; household income in the top quartile for their age in their country; read or watch business/news media at least several times a week; follow public policy issues in the news at least several times a week. (2011 Edelman Trust Barometer Executive Summary, 8)

The 2011 Edelman survey identified those factors along with "treats employees well" as most important in assessing corporate reputation (7).

50. 2011 Edelman Trust Barometer, January 18, 2011, 34.

51. The substantial academic literature on trust and its importance to economic activity is summarized by Karen S. Cook and Oliver Schilke, "The Role of Public Relational and Organizational Trust in Economic Affairs," *Corporate Reputation Review*, 13 (2), 2010, 98–109. See also Jared D. Harris and Andrew C. Wicks, "'Public Trust' in Particular Firm-Stakeholder Interactions," *Corporate Reputation Review*, 13 (2), 2010, 142–54. The authors assess how different stakeholders (e.g., employees, investors, customers) value different aspects of trust in judging a business. They also underscore the fundamental dilemma of trust in business:

Despite living in a society whose values largely undergird and enable modern capitalism, most people see business as an inherently amoral or immoral enterprise. In particular, the focus on profits and revenue generation that characterize business seems fundamentally at odds with a conception of morality built around concern for others and indifference to one's own interests. If our societal conception of business suggests that businesses are fundamentally cold-hearted and machine-like, completely absent of any consideration of ethics and focused solely on their own benefit, then trust in business may necessarily be generally low. (149)

The case I make for authentic storytelling assumes that profitable businesses can also be ethical ones.

52. Interview with Gary Sheffer, April 8, 2009.

53. Interview with Tom Martin, April 14, 2008.

54. Interview with Ron Culp, April 11, 2008.

55. Interview with Betsy McLaughlin, February 19, 2010.

56. See also Walter Benjamin's reflections on the storyteller's wisdom in "The Storyteller," in *Illuminations: Essays and Reflections*, edited and with an introduction by Hannah Arendt, translated by Harry Zohn (New York: Schocken, 1968). Benjamin notes: "the storyteller joins the ranks of the teachers and sages. He has counsel—not for a few situations, as the proverb does, but for many, like the sage. For it is granted to him to reach back to a whole lifetime (a life, incidentally, that comprises not only his own experience but no little of the experience of others); what the storyteller knows from hearsay is added to his own" (108).

57. Interview with Gary Sheffer, April 8, 2009.

58. Interview with Perry Yeatman, April 30, 2008.

59. Richard Rumelt, "Evaluating Business Strategy," in *Readings in the Strategy Process, 3rd edition*, ed. Henry Mintzberg and James Brian Quinn (Upper Saddle River, NJ: Prentice Hall, 1988), 56.

60. Equally relevant are definitions proposed by Kenneth R. Andrews and by Eric G. Flamholtz and Yvonne Randle. See Kenneth R. Andrews, "The Concept of Corporate Strategy," in Mintzberg and Quinn, *Readings in the Strategy Process*, 47–55. According to Andrews,

> corporate strategy is the pattern of decisions in a company that determines and reveals its objectives, purposes, or goals, produces the principal policies and plans for achieving those goals, and defines the range of business the company is to pursue, the kind of economic and human organization it is or intends to be, and the nature of the economic and noneconomic contribution it intends to make to its shareholders, employees, customers, and communities. (47)

For Flamholtz and Randle, *Growing Pains: Transitioning from an Entrepreneurship to a Professionally Managed Firm, 4th edition* (Hoboken, NJ: Wiley, 2007),

Strategy can be defined as "the different, yet integrated courses of actions that will be taken by a firm or business unit to compete effectively in its chosen markets in order to obtain desired results." Thus strategy implies both competition and intended achievement. Taking this definition a step further, strategy consists of (1) *where* (in what markets) a firm chooses to compete and (2) *how* the firm will compete in its chosen markets in order to achieve the best results. (148)

As with culture and branding there is a huge literature about corporate strategy, which is a core academic discipline in business schools and a fundamental set of activities in the life of an organization.

61. See Janis Forman, "Strategic Communications as Persuasive and Constitutive Storytelling," in *Narrative and Professional Communication*, ed. Jane Perkins and Nancy Blyler (Stamford, CT: Ablex, 1999), for a fuller discussion of strategy as a form of persuasive storytelling in plans and presentations.

62. Mary Lang, response to the Management Communication Survey on the Uses of Storytelling in MBA Communication Courses, May 2009.

63. In some tribal cultures even today, shamans—leaders believed to have special abilities to communicate with the spirits—perform tales drawn from nature and the supernatural. When invoked by shamans, these tales can tell the future, heal the psychically or physically sick, interpret myths, and celebrate the culture through retelling its history. Some Western and Eastern cultures, like those of ancient China and Greece, even employed professional storytellers to perform these tales.

64. Flamholtz and Randle, *Growing Pains*, 17.

65. Edgar H. Schein, *The Corporate Culture Survival Guide, new and revised edition* (San Francisco: Jossey-Bass, 2009), 217.

66. Ibid., 35.

67. Ibid., 35.

68. Ibid., 52.

69. Bill Ellet, response to the Management Communication Survey on the Uses of Storytelling in MBA Communication Courses, May 15, 2009.

70. Wally Olins, "How Brands Are Taking Over the Corporation," in *The Expressive Organization: Linking Identity, Reputation, and Corporate Brand*, ed. Majken Schultz, Mary Jo Hatch, and Mogens Holten Larsen (New York: Oxford University Press, 2000), 61.

71. Nicholas Ind, *Living the Brand: How to Transform Every Member of Your Organization into a Brand Champion, 2nd edition* (London: Kogan Page, 2004), 20.

72. There is a vast literature on corporate branding. See, in particular, Nicholas Ind's *Living the Brand*. See also the work of Mary Jo Hatch and Majken Schultz on corporate branding: *Taking Brand Initiative: How Companies Can Align Strategy, Culture, and Identity Through Corporate Branding* (San Francisco: Jossey-Bass, 2008); "Bringing the Corporation into Corporate Branding," *European Journal of Marketing*, 37 (7/8), December 2001, 1041–64; "Are the Strategic Stars Aligned for Your Corporate Brand?" *Harvard Business Review*, February 2001, 128–34; and of Majken Schultz and Mary Jo Hatch, "A Cultural Perspective on Corporate Branding: The Case of LEGO Group," in *Brand Culture* (London: Routledge, 2006), 15–33. They argue (across several publications) for the integral connection between corporate branding, on the one hand, and strategic vision, organizational culture, and the images of the corporation in the minds of multiple stakeholders, on the other. Unlike product branding, they contend, corporate branding has broad organizational implications beyond marketing and should represent efforts by top management, communications, and human resources as well as marketing (typically responsible for product branding).

In *Taking Brand Initiative*, they "developed a diagnostic model for assessing how well companies manage their corporate brands through alignment of their strategic visions, organizational cultures, and stakeholder images" (xvii). In other words, they argue that

> whenever you encounter a successful corporate brand, standing behind that brand you will find coherence between what the company's top managers want to accomplish in the future (their strategic *vision*), what has always been known or believed by company employees (lodged in its *culture*), and what its external stakeholders expect or desire from the company (their *images* of it). The basic principle of the Vision-Culture-Image (VCI) Alignment Model— that the greater the coherence of vision, culture, and images, the stronger the brand—is the central message of this book. (11)

See as well the work of David A. Aaker; in particular, *Brand Portfolio Strategy: Creating Relevance, Differentiation, Energy, Leverage and Clarity* (New York: Free Press, 2004); *Building Strong Brands* (New York: Free Press, 1996);

and *Managing Brand Equity: Capitalizing on the Value of a Brand Name* (New York: Free Press, 1991).

73. See Paul Argenti and Janis Forman, ch. 4, in *The Power of Corporate Communication: Crafting the Voice and Image of Your Business* (New York: McGraw-Hill, 2002), for further discussion of corporate branding as a key component of corporate communication.

74. This is especially true if a company's product or service is a commodity, such as gasoline. (This example is taken from Argenti and Forman, *Power of Corporate Communication*, 78.) What may then influence a consumer to decide between, let's say, two gas stations operated by two companies is likely to be the people associated with the brand, the people running and working for each company, what the company says it stands for, and whether it delivers on these promises.

75. In *World Class Brands* (Wokingham, UK: Addison-Wesley, 1991), marketing expert Chris Macrae describes this function as promoting empathy. According to him, the empathetic appeal of branding has to do with providing an affirmative answer to the question, "Does the brand promote an experience of belonging by reaching out to the most personal areas of human imagination with such confidence and familiarity that it feels like a kindred spirit?" (40).

76. According to Ind in *The Corporate Brand*,

the attitudes and behaviour of employees is fundamental to defining the corporate brand. To achieve the cohesion necessary to differentiate one brand from another requires the organisation to build a committed and loyal workforce. The problem that many companies face is the continued diminution of loyalty. Partly this is of their own making and partly it is a reflection of changes in society. To develop a stronger relationship companies need to work harder at ensuring their communications flow upwards, downwards and across—tailoring the messages to the audience whenever possible and making sure that there is a compatibility of interest. This approach suggests that companies should recognise the talents of the individuals that work for them and that their skills should be nurtured through empowerment and learning. (102)

77. In "A Cultural Perspective on Corporate Branding," Schultz and Hatch explain that corporate branding is focused on the organization as a whole: "As opposed to product branding, corporate branding highlights the important role

employees play in brand practice, making how employees engage with and enact the values and vision of the brand more profound and strategically important to corporate brands [than to product brands]" (15).

78. Olins, "How Brands Are Taking Over the Corporation," 61.

79. In *On Brand* (London: Thames & Hudson, 2003), Olins explains that reassurance has to do with the brand's coherence: "In a brand the entire experience from first contact to signing off must reinforce and underline trust. Everything must fit. Every tiny piece must reinforce everything else" (194).

80. Hatch and Schultz, "Bringing the Corporation into Corporate Branding," 1050–51.

81. Kevin Lane Keller, "Building and Managing Corporate Brand Equity," in Schultz, Hatch, Larsen, *Expressive Organization*, 115.

82. A case can increasingly be made that a solid brand raises stock price. See Olins, "How Brands Are Taking Over the Corporation," 51.

CHAPTER 3

1. Janis Forman, "When Stories Create an Organization's Future," *Strategy and Business*, 15 (Second Quarter 1999), 3.

2. In *Planning as Persuasive Storytelling: The Rhetorical Construction of Chicago's Electric Future* (Chicago: University of Chicago Press, 1996), James A. Throgmorton argues that city planning "can be thought of as a form of persuasive and constitutive storytelling" (xiv). This is a rhetorical approach to city planning in which planners are viewed as authors of the plans who compete for projects in contested arenas, such as city council meetings. He focuses much more than I do in this chapter on the interplay of opposing stories, a circumstance in which a single authority cannot command the creation and implementation of what we might call a master story.

3. In *Style: Ten Lessons in Clarity and Grace, 5th edition* (New York: Longman, 1997), linguist Joseph Williams looks at cohesiveness from a stylistic perspective: the features of writing that give the reader a sense of the "flow" in writing, the "connectedness" between one sentence and the next, and the stylistic features that contribute to this. I apply this idea to the larger unit of the story. In "Strategic Stories: How 3M Is Rewriting Business Planning," *Harvard Business Review*, May–June 1998, 41–50, Gordon Shaw, Robert Brown, and Philip Bromiley look at strategic business plans at 3M as stories rather than as a laundry list of action items in bullet-point form that appear in random order and without a

sense of the relationship among them. In particular, the authors underscore the importance of "narrative logic," with its focus on defining relationships among actions to be taken, the sequencing of events, cause and effect, and the relative importance of the actions. To them, the segments or "chapters" of the story are setting the stage, introducing the dramatic conflict or challenges facing the company, and reaching a resolution. I look at "narrative logic" as well—though I do not use the term—in two publications in 1999: in the article "When Stories Create an Organization's Future," and in a book chapter "Strategic Communication as Persuasive and Constitutive Storytelling," in *Narrative and Professional Communication*, ed. Jane M. Perkins and Nancy Blyler (Stamford, CT: Ablex, 1999), 121–33. The article focuses on the sequencing of events—or narrative logic—of stories and introduces the analysis tree as a tool to organize the "chapters" of the story. In the book chapter, I look at strategic stories as persuasive, as a form of argumentation about the next-stage development for a firm, using strategic business plans written by UCLA Anderson students as extended illustrations.

4. The Schering-Plough case is based upon extensive interviews, primarily at corporate headquarters, and e-mail communications as well as assessment of company documents and review of secondary research:

Interviews

Fred Hassan, chairman and CEO, on June 11, 2009

Ken Banta, head of corporate strategic affairs: interview A on May 13, 2008; B on June 11, 2009; C on June 12, 2009; and D on June 26, 2009; and by e-mail: A on July 2, 2009; B on July 27, 2009; and C on August 17, 2009

Rick Bowles, senior vice president, global quality operations, on June 12, 2009

Alex Kelly, group vice president, global communications and investor relations, on June 12, 2009

Rob Lively, vice president, corporate government affairs, on June 11, 2009

Vas Nair, vice president and chief learning officer, on June 12, 2009

Tom Sabatino, executive vice president and general counsel, on June 24, 2009

Brent Saunders, senior vice president and president of consumer healthcare, on June 16, 2009

Helma van Leeuwe, senior director, global internal communications, on August 24, 2009

Susan Wolf, corporate secretary, vice president–governance, on June 11, 2009, and June 12, 2009

Internal company documents referred to here include the following: Fred Hassan, "Introducing the New Schering-Plough," November 18, 2003, presentation to the board; "The Schering-Plough CORE Document," 2007; Fred Hassan, "WHY? This Combination," April 2, 2007, presentation; Fred Hassan, "In Tune and Executing with Excellence," Organon company presentation, 2007; Schering-Plough Evaluation, Leader Behavior Workshop, 2004; "The New Schering-Plough Leader Behaviors Toolkit," 2004; "The NEW Schering-Plough Development Planning Guide," no date; "Leader Behavior Launch Meeting"; "Q1 2004 Schering-Plough Earnings Conference Call"–Final, April 22, 2004, 9,061 words; © 2004 CCBN and FDCH e-Media; "A Message from Chairman and CEO Fred Hassan," 2009 Schering-Plough Corporation, http://www.schering-plough. com/company/message.aspx.

I also drew from publications in trade journals, the press, and online databases: Mergent Online, "Schering-Plough Corporation"; "Leading the News: FDA to Change How It Oversees Process of Manufacturing Drugs," *Wall Street Journal*, August 22, 2002, A3; "Schering-Plough Corporation: Recent Developments Announced by Schering-Plough Corporation," *Pharma Business Week*, October 1, 2007, 1,292 words, retrieved on July 14, 2009; and "Schering-Plough Reports Third Quarter Financial Results: Company Announces Beginning of Turnaround Phase," 4,713 words, PR Newswire.

5. This case was written before Schering-Plough's integration into Merck and takes that "preintegration" perspective.

6. Mergent Online, "Schering-Plough Corporation," 7.

7. Interviews with Ken Banta: May 13, 2008, and June 11, 2009.

8. E-mail from Ken Banta, July 2, 2009.

9. Interview with Ken Banta, May 13, 2008.

10. Fred Hassan, speech to investors, November 18, 2001.

11. E-mail from Ken Banta, August 19, 2007.

12. Hassan, "Introducing the New Schering-Plough."

13. "The Schering-Plough CORE Document," 27.

14. Hassan, "WHY? This Combination."

15. Interview with Ken Banta, May 13, 2008.

16. Interview with Tom Sabatino, June 24, 2009.

17. Interview with Ken Banta, May 13, 2008.

18. Hassan, "WHY? This Combination."

19. Quoted in "Schering-Plough Corporation: Recent Developments Announced by Schering-Plough Corporation."

20. Interview with Ken Banta, May 13, 2008.

21. Interview with Brent Saunders, June 16, 2009.

22. Hassan, "In Tune and Executing with Excellence."

23. Ibid.

24. Ibid.

25. Interview with Alex Kelly, June 12, 2009.

26. Interview with Brent Saunders, June 16, 2009.

27. Interview with Alex Kelly, June 12, 2009.

28. Interview with Helma van Leeuwe, August 24, 2009.

29. Ibid.

30. Interview with Helma van Leeuwe, August 24, 2009.

31. Interview with Brent Saunders, June 16, 2009.

32. Interview with Fred Hassan, June 11, 2009.

33. Interview with Alex Kelly, June 12, 2009.

34. Interview with Vas Nair, August 24, 2009.

35. E-mail from Ken Banta, July 27, 2009.

36. Interview with Tom Sabatino, June 24, 2009.

37. Schering-Plough Evaluation, Leader Behavior Workshop (emphasis mine).

38. Interview with Vas Nair, August 24, 2009.

39. Interview with Fred Hassan, June 11, 2009.

40. "New Schering-Plough Leader Behaviors Toolkit."

41. Ibid.

42. Interview with Vas Nair, August 24, 2009.

43. "NEW Schering-Plough Development Planning Guide."

44. "Leader Behavior Launch Meeting," slide 29, April 2004.

45. Interview with Tom Sabatino, June 24, 2009.

46. Interview with Susan Wolf, June 12, 2009.

47. Interview with Rick Bowles, June 12, 2009.

CHAPTER 4

1. Eric G. Flamholtz and Yvonne Randle have a body of work on cultural management programs—from diagnosis of the old, or current, culture to assessment of the new culture. They also present contrasting cases of companies that successfully and unsuccessfully manage culture and consider the financial consequences of having an effective culture. See, in particular, *Growing Pains: Transitioning from an Entrepreneurship to a Professionally Managed Firm, 4th edition* (San Francisco: Jossey-Bass, 2007); and *Leading Strategic Change: Bridging Theory and Practice* (Cambridge, UK: Cambridge University Press, 2008).

2. Interview with Tom Sabatino, June 24, 2009.

3. Interview with Ken Banta, May 13, 2008.

4. Interview with Ken Banta, June 11, 2009.

5. "Q1 2004 Schering-Plough Earnings Conference Call"–Final, April 22, 2004, 9,061 words; © 2004 CCBN and FDCH e-Media.

6. "Schering-Plough Reports Third Quarter Financial Results: Company Announces Beginning of Turnaround Phase," 4,713 words, PR Newswire.

7. Interview with Susan Wolf, June 12, 2009.

8. Interview with Ken Banta, May 13, 2008.

9. Interview with Tom Sabatino, June 24, 2009.

10. Interview with Ken Banta, May 13, 2008.

11. Interview with Vas Nair, August 24, 2009.

12. Jeffrey Skilling and Kenneth Lay, "Skilling and Lay's Last Letter to Shareholders of Enron," in Joel Amernic and Russell Craig, *CEO-Speak: The Language of Corporate Leadership* (Montreal: McGill-Queen's University, 2006), 152, lines 159–64.

13. Ibid., 147, lines 11–17.

14. Ibid., 148, lines 114–16.

15. Ibid., 152, lines 165–69.

16. See Donald Frame's translation of *Gargantua* in *The Complete Works of Francois Rabelais* (Berkeley: University of California Press, 1991). Ch. 33 tells the story of the "advice" offered to Picrochole by his counselors, but many of the chapters in the middle of this novel concern the differences in "strategic" leadership between the monomaniacal Picrochole and the thoughtful, conciliatory, and caring King Grandgousier (the giant Gargantua's father), who goes to war only when other realistic options have been foreclosed.

17. See Janis Forman, "Strategic Communications as Persuasive and Constitutive Storytelling," in *Narrative and Professional Communication*, ed. Jane Perkins and Nancy Blyler (Stamford, CT: Ablex, 1999), 131.

18. Interview with Ken Banta, June 11, 2009.

19. James O'Rourke IV, response to the Management Communication Survey on the Uses of Storytelling in MBA Communication Courses, May 2009.

20. See also Janis Forman, "Leaders as Storytellers: Finding Waldo," *Business Communication Quarterly*, September 2007, 369–73.

21. Interview with Michele Tesoro-Tess, August 2, 2008.

22. Forman, "Leaders as Storytellers."

23. Ibid., 370.

24. Interview with Ken Banta, June 12, 2009.

25. Interview with Rob Lively, June 11, 2009.

26. Interview with Tom Sabatino, June 24, 2009.

27. Ibid.

28. Ibid.

29. Ibid.

30. Ibid.

31. Interview with Brent Saunders, June 16, 2009.

32. Interview with Ken Banta, May 13, 2008.

33. Lea Peterson and Stella Voules, "Mastering M&A Communication: Helping Employees to Deal with the Deal," in *Reflections on M&A: The Human Capital Dimension* (New York: Mercer Human Resources Consulting, 2007).

34. Interview with Brent Saunders, June 16, 2009.

35. Interview with Alex Kelly, June 12, 2009.

36. Interview with Rob Lively, June 11, 2009.

37. Interview with Ken Banta, June 11, 2009.

38. Interview with Brent Saunders, June 16, 2009.

39. Much of the discussion that follows about using stories to support initiative is based on Janis Forman, "The Communication Advantage: Getting Buy-in for Your CHIP and Other Strategic Initiatives," *Johnson & Johnson Newsletter*, May 5, 2004.

40. Janis Forman, "When Stories Create an Organization's Future," *Strategy and Business*, 15, Second Quarter 1999, 3.

41. Ibid.

CHAPTER 5

1. Interview with Helen Clark, February 11, 2009.

2. Nicholas Ind, *Living the Brand: How to Transform Every Member of Your Organization Into a Brand Champion, 2nd edition* (London: Kogan Page, 2004), 20.

3. The Chevron case is based upon extensive interviews, primarily at corporate headquarters, and e-mail communications as well as assessment of company documents and review of secondary research:

Interviews

David A. Samson, general manager, public affairs: interview A on April 11, 2008; B on January 21, 2009; C on April 2, 2010

Donald Campbell, manager, external communications, on January 22, 2009

Helen Clark, manager, corporate marketing: interview A on January 21, 2009; B on February 11, 2009; C on April 13, 2010

Mickey Driver, external relations advisor, policy, government and public affairs, on April 2, 2010

Jeff Glover, editorial manager, on January 22, 2009

Joerden Legon, editor of Chevron.com, on February 11, 2009

Deborah McNaughton, manager, internal communications, on January 22, 2009

Robert Raines, interactive communications manager, corporate marketing, on April 13, 2010

Russ Yarrow, general manager, California corporate affairs: interview A on January 22, 2009; B on April 13, 2010

Internal company documents referred to here include the following: David J. O'Reilly, "Global Energy: The New Equation," CEO Leadership Series, June 23, 2004, http://www.chevron.com/news/Speeches;Release/?id=2004-06-23-doreilly, 6 pages, accessed February 17, 2009; David J. O'Reilly, "U.S. Energy Policy: A Declaration of Interdependence," keynote addressed to the Cambridge Energy Research Association (CERA), February 15, 2005, http://www.chevron.com/news/Speeches/Release?/id=2005-2-15-doreilly, 6 pages, accessed February 17, 2009; David J. O'Reilly, "Strengthening America's Energy Pillar: Recommendations for President-Elect Obama," November 2008; John S. Watson, "Remarks to the United States Chamber of Commerce," October 27, 2009, http://www.chevron.com/news/speeches/release/?id=2009-10-27-jwatson; Mickey Driver, "Offshore Media Trips," reports received on April 12, 2010, and dated May 22–23, 2006, May 20, 2008, and June 25–27, 2008; Julia Baggs, "Seismic Technology: How It Works"; Chevron Annual Report, 2007; "Inside Chevron," August 13, 2008; Chevron Annual Report, 2008; Chevron Annual Report, 2009; Chevron Corporate Social Responsibility Report, 2008; "The Chevron Way," 2009; Jeordon Legon, "Chevron Web Voice Brief," 2009; ad spots developed for Chevron by Young & Rubicam: "Untapped Energy External," "Rebranded Untapped Energy" (version 1), "Rebranded Untapped Energy Human Main," "Rebranded the Impossible Us" (version 1), "Rebranded the Impossible Us" (version 2), "Rebranded Renewable Energy," "Rebranded Renewable Energy Main," "Rebranded Renewable Energy Pbs," "Rebranded New Frontiers Us" (version 1), "Rebranded New Frontiers Us" (version 2), "Rebranded We Are Chevron Asia" (version 1), "Rebranded We Are Chevron Asia" (version 2), "Chevron Challenge Welcome Video," "I Will Conservation," "I Will Tomorrow," "California Glimpse Main Sd," "California Glimpse Main Pbs Sd (cc)"; Chevron poster, "Expressing the Power of Human

Energy Using Our Visual System to Tell the Chevron Story," 2010. Chevron online stories are accessible at http://www.chevron.com/stories/#/allstories/.

I also drew from publications in trade journals, the press, and online databases: Mergent Online, Chevron.com, April 25, 2010; Guy Chazan, "Chevron Pitch: Climate Is Its Concern, Too; New Campaign Aims to Portray Oil Major as Part of Solution," *Wall Street Journal*, October 18, 2007, B-7; Alice Z. Cuneo, "Women to Watch: Helen Clark," *Advertising Age*, 79 (22), June 2, 2008, S-16; Jean Halliday, "Chevron Says: Yes We Have Humanity," *Advertising Age*, 78 (39), 2007, 8.

4. Mergent Online, Chevron.com, April 25, 2010, 1.

5. O'Reilly, "Global Energy," 1.

6. Ibid. Emphasis mine.

7. O'Reilly, "U.S. Energy Policy," 2.

8. Ibid. Emphasis mine.

9. Ibid., 3.

10. Ibid.

11. Ibid., 3.

12. Interview with Russ Yarrow, January 22, 2009.

13. Ibid.

14. Interview with Helen Clark, February 11, 2009.

15. Interview with Helen Clark, January 21, 2009.

16. Ibid.

17. Interview with Helen Clark, April 13, 2010.

18. Interview with David A. Samson, April 2, 2010.

19. See Chazan, "Chevron Pitch"; and Halliday, "Chevron Says."

20. Chazan, "Chevron Pitch."

21. To see any of the Chevron online stories, go to http://www.chevron.com/stories/#/allstories/.

22. In *Narrative Discourse: An Essay on Method* (New York: Cornell University Press, 1980), the French critic and rhetorician Gerard Genette makes an important distinction in his discussion of point of view. He clarifies "a regrettable confusion between the question *who is the character whose point of view orients the narrative perspective?* and the very different question *who is the narrator?*—or more simply, the question *who sees?* and the question *who speaks?*" (186). In corporate storytelling, I would argue that when these two are one and the same—the one who speaks is also the main character in the story—there is greater credibility attributed to the story than if who sees and who speaks are not one and the same.

23. "Caring for South Africans with AIDS," http://www.chevron.com/stories/#/community/dunoon.

24. "Inside Chevron," August 13, 2008.

25. Interview with Deborah McNaughton, January 22, 2009.

26. See Roger Rogowski, "Best and Worst of Brand Building Web Sites, 2008," *Forrester*, October 10, 2008, updated October 27, 2008. The 2008 Forrester report evaluated the Web sites of twenty leading brands, judging Chevron.com to be the leader in terms of addressing user needs ("Brand Action") and communicating the "Brand Image" on the Web. Chevron came out on top of rival companies BP, Exxon, and Shell in this evaluation. The report singled out the "Will You Join Us" campaign for excellence in content, which "reinforces the company's brand attributes of partnership, integrity, and trust with function that invites ordinary citizens to participate in idea sharing about how to produce cleaner, more sustainable energy. High-quality images consistent with offline ads show people alongside green energy technologies such as solar panels and wind turbines."

27. Chevron poster, "Expressing the Power of Human Energy Using Our Visual System to Tell the Chevron Story," 2010.

28. Interview with Mickey Driver, April 2, 2010.

29. Mickey Driver, "Offshore Media Trips," May 20, 2008.

30. Mickey Driver, "Offshore Media Trips," May 22–23, 2006.

31. Mickey Driver, "Offshore Media Trips," June 25–27, 2008.

32. Legon, "Chevron Web Voice Brief," 2009.

33. Ibid., 3.

34. "The Chevron Way," 2009. Emphasis mine.

35. Interview with Russ Yarrow, April 13, 2010.

CHAPTER 6

1. Interview with Christine Miller, February 12, 2010.

2. See John S. Watson, "Remarks to the United States Chamber of Commerce," October 27, 2009, http://www.chevron.com/news/speeches/release/?id+2009-10-27-jwatson. The talk underscores and extends O'Reilly's assessment of these challenges.

3. Interview with Helen Clark, January 21, 2009.

4. Interview with Deborah McNaughton, January 22, 2009.

5. Interview with Russ Yarrow, January 22, 2009.

6. Ibid.

7. Interview with David A. Samson, April 11, 2008.

8. Kenneth Burke, "Terministic Screens," in *Language as Symbolic Action: Essays on Life, Literature, and Method* (Berkeley: University of California Press, 1966), 45–46.

9. Interview with Russ Yarrow, January 22, 2009.

10. Interview with David A. Samson, April 11, 2008.

11. Philips's "Sense and Simplicity" campaign is described in Chapter 9.

12. Interview with Gary Sheffer, April 8, 2009.

13. Jonah Bloom, "GE: The Marketing Giant Lights Up with Imagination," *Creativity*, 13 (10), October 2005, 22.

14. Interview with Catherine Maxey, June 9, 2009.

15. Ibid.

16. Liveris is quoted in Rick Mullin, "Dow's Emotional Pitch: Eschewing Facts and Figures, a New Ad Campaign That Shoots for the Heart," *Chemical and Engineering News: Business*, 84 (51), December 18, 2006, 37, http://pubs .acs.org/isubscribe/journals/cen/84/i51/html/8451bus2.html.

17. D. L. Ashlima, "Introduction," in *Aesop's Fables* (New York: Barnes & Noble Books, 2003), xxi.

18. Interview with Russ Yarrow, January 22, 2009.

19. Ibid.

20. George Lakoff, *Don't Think of an Elephant!: Know Your Values and Frame the Debate* (White River Junction, VT: Chelsea Green, 2004), xv.

21. Ibid.

22. Interview with Ray Jordan, April 23, 2009.

23. Burke, "Terministic Screens," 44. Emphasis in original.

24. Rita Charon, *Narrative Medicine: Honoring the Stories of Illness* (Oxford, UK: Oxford University Press, 2006), 118.

25. Interview with Helen Clark, January 21, 2009.

26. Interview with Jeff Glover, January 22, 2009.

27. Interview with Russ Yarrow, January 22, 2009.

28. Ibid.

CHAPTER 7

1. The FedEx case is based upon extensive interviews, primarily at corporate headquarters, and e-mail communications as well as assessment of company documents and secondary research:

Interviews

William G. Margaritis, corporate vice president, global communications and
investor relations: interview A on April 29, 2002; B on April 15, 2008; C
on March 2, 2009; D on April 30, 2010

Matt Ceniceros, senior communications specialist, on March 3, 2009

Howard Clabo, manager, media relations, on March 2, 2009

Cindy Dixon Conner, manager, corporate communications, on March 3, 2009

Eric T. Epperson, director, workplace communications, on March 2, 2009

Ryan Furby, manager, social media strategies, on May 19, 2010

Sheila Harrell, vice president, customer service operations, on June 30, 2010

Joe Hopkins, advisor, digital and social media engagement, on August 5, 2010

Renee Horne, director, digital and social media engagement, on August 5, 2010

Mitch Jackson, vice president, environmental affairs and sustainability, on
July 15, 2010

Dianna O'Neill, manager, digital content and social media engagement:
interview A on March 3, 2009; B on May 19, 2010; C on August 18, 2010

Pamela Roberson, manager, digital and social media engagement, on August
5, 2010

Diane Terrell, vice president, strategic communications: interview A on March
3, 2009; B on May 19, 2010; C on August 18, 2010; D on September 29
as e-mail response

Jennifer J. Thorton, executive assistant, global communications and investor
relations, on March 3, 2009

Antoney Wilkinson, staff director, global communications, on July 20, 2010

Sharon Lloyd Young, communications advisor, global communications, on
May 19, 2010

Blogs

Mitch Jackson, "Frugal Innovation in the Age of Access," July 6, 2010,
http://about.van.fedex.com/search/node/Mitch +Jackson+blog

Mitch Jackson, "Innovation: Knickers in a Twist," July 22, 2010, http://about.
van.fedex.com/search/node/Mitch +Jackson+blog

Internal company documents referred to here include the following: Frederick
W. Smith, "Our Human Side of Quality," *Quality Progress*, 23 (10), October
1990, 19–21; Diane Terrell, "The Reinvention of FXTV," April 11, 2006;
FY2007 Global Planning Meeting; Diane Terrell, "Telling Our Story," April
26, 2007; Diane Terrell, "FedEx One: Media Revolution—The Reinvention
of FXTV," A Strategic Management Council Update, August 24, 2007;

Diane Terrell, "FedEx: Ushering in a New Era in Communications," FedEx Worldwide Communications and Investor Relations FY09 Strategic Plan, May 19, 2008; "Social Media Guidelines for Employees" FedEx, June 1, 2010; "I am FedEx"; Computerworld Honors on FXTV, http://www.cwhonors.org/search/his 4a detail, asp?id=3244; FedEx intranet, "The Computerworld Honors Program," June 16, 2010, http://www.cwhonors.org/search/his 4a.asp?id+3244; Bruce Shutan, "Instant Delivery: FedEx Uses Social Media to Connect Workforce," Employee Benefit News, August 1, 2010, http://ebn.benefitnews.com/news/instant-delivery-fedex-uses-social-media-to-connect-work

FedEx online stories are accessible at http://www.mediacenter.fedex.designedcdt.com/:

"A Day in the Life of Joe Gautier," November 25, 2008

"Delivering the Titanic," November 20, 2008

"Dinstuhl's Fine Candy Company," February 12, 2010

"EarthSmart Outreach," August 16, 2010

"FedEx CIO Rob Carter Reflects on His 'Teach for America' Experience," February 6, 2009

"A Fleet of Food," September 4, 2009

"Handcrafted Lighting by Way of Cowboy Country," January 22, 2009

Eddy Chan, "A Humble Soul = An Open Mind," December 11, 2009

"I am FedEx: April Harding," May 5, 2010

"Indy Imaging," April 8, 2009

"In Person: John Mathias," February 4, 2009

"Malachy Bodhram," November 19, 2008

"Memphis Walks for the March of Dimes," May 1, 2009

"The Mission of Keyon Laws," November 27, 2008

"The 'FedEx Panda Express' 777 Freighter," February 4, 2010; "The 'FedEx Panda Express' Departs for China," February 4, 2010; "Tai Shan's Farewell from Washington, D.C.," February 5, 2010; "Flying the 'FedEx Panda Express,'" February 5, 2010; "Panda Wrap-up," March 23, 2010

"Return of the Penguins," November 21, 2008

"On the Road with Bill Bridges," February 24, 2009

"Rose Growers Ship by FedEx," January 19, 2009

Raj Subramaniam, "Inside India—Raj Subramanian's Perspective," March 2, 2009

I also drew from publications in trade journals, the press, and online databases: Gary Allen, "What's Hot in Corporate TV?" *Communication World*, October

1989, 16–19; Paul Cordasco, "Computerworld Honors," *PR Week US*, 5, August 2002, 18; "FedEx Express Honors Employees' Acts of Courage and Exemplary Dedication to Customer Service," *Business Wire*, October 28, 2003, 1836 words; FedEx Corp., *Mergent Online*, 1–12; "Tony Mosley Explains What Makes Federal Express So Good," *eCustomer Service World*, June 16, 2010, http://www. ecustomerserviceworld.com/earticlesstore articles.asp?type=article&id+343; Peter Pochna, Ted Cohen, and Will Bartlett, "Scholarship Work Pays Off for Walkers on Freeport Shore," *Portland Press Herald*, August 22, 1998, 1-B; Wayne Risher, "FedEx Honors 25 Who Cared—Awards Laud CPR Aid, Halting Dog Attack, Carrying Out Last Wish," *The Commercial Appeal*, November 13, 2009, C-1; Natasha Spring, "Delivering the Message One Person at a Time: EXCEL Award Winner Rajesh Subramaniam Talks About Communication's Impact on FedEx Canada Employees and Customers," *Communication World*, 23 (5), September 2006, 1781 words

2. FedEx Corp., *Mergent Online*, 5.

3. Smith, "Our Human Side of Quality," 19–21.

4. Ibid., 20.

5. "Tony Mosley Explains What Makes Federal Express So Good."

6. Allen, "What's Hot in Corporate TV?"

7. Pochna, Cohen, and Bartlett, "Scholarship Work Pays Off for Walkers on Freeport Shore."

8. Cordasco, "Computerworld Honors."

9. Ibid.

10. See Janis Forman and Paul Argenti, "How Corporate Communication Influences Strategy Implementation, Reputation and Corporate Brand: An Exploratory Qualitative Study," *Corporate Reputation Review*, 8 (3), Fall 2005, 245–64.

11. I conducted interviews with Bill Margaritis and his staff in the spring of 2002 for *The Power of Corporate Communication* (New York: McGraw-Hill, 2002),co-authored with Paul Argenti. This earlier work gave me a unique historical perspective from which to assess the progress in the work of the corporate communication group when I returned to interview staff in 2009 and 2010.

12. E-mail from Diane Terrell, September 29, 2010.

13. Ibid.

14. Interview with Ryan Furby, May 19, 2010.

15. E-mail from Diane Terrell, September 29, 2010.

16. Interview with Diane Terrell, August 18, 2010, and e-mail from Diane Terrell, September 29, 2010.

17. E-mail from Diane Terrell, September 29, 2010.

18. Interview with Diane Terrell, August 18, 2010.

19. Ibid.

20. Ibid.

21. Terrell, "Telling Our Story."

22. Terrell, "Reinvention of FedEx." Ultimately, this led to "a more unified culture by telling compelling stories of employees committed to excellence in customer service."

23. Ibid.

24. FedEx Worldwide Communications and Investor Relations FY09 Strategic Plan, May 19, 2008, 6.

25. Interview with Bill Margaritis, April 15, 2008.

26. Ibid.

27. Interview with Ryan Furby, May 19, 2010.

28. Interview with Eric T. Epperson, March 2, 2009.

29. Interview with Diane Terrell, August 18, 2010.

30. Interview with Bill Margaritis, April 15, 2008.

31. "FedEx Express Honors Employees' Acts of Courage and Exemplary Dedication to Customer Service."

32. "Delivering the Titanic."

33. Interview with Bill Margaritis, April 15, 2008.

34. Spring, "Delivering the Message One Person at a Time."

35. Risher, "FedEx Honors 25 Who Cared."

36. "FedEx Express Honors Employees' Acts of Courage and Exemplary Dedication to Customer Service."

37. Interview with Eric T.Epperson, March 2, 2010.

38. Interview with Dianna O'Neill, August 18, 2010.

39. "Day in the Life of Joe Gauthier."

40. E-mail from Diane Terrell, September 29, 2010.

41. "FedEx CIO Rob Carter Reflects on His 'Teach for America' Experience."

42. "EarthSmart Outreach."

43. "Fleet of Food."

44. "Memphis Walks for the March of Dimes."

45. Interview with Sheila Harrell, June 30, 2010.

46. Mitch Jackson blog, "Frugal Innovation in the Age of Access."

47. Mitch Jackson blog, "Innovation: Knickers in a Twist."

48. Interview with Sharon Young, May 19, 2010.

49. Interview with Dianna O'Neill, March 3, 2009.

50. Interview with Diane Terrell, May 19, 2010.

51. "EarthSmart Outreach."

52. Interview with Dianna O'Neill, May 19, 2010.

53. Ibid.

54. "I am FedEx: April Harding."

55. "In Person: John Mathias."

56. "Return of the Penguins," November 21, 2008.

57. "'FedEx Panda Express' 777 Freighter"; "'FedEx Panda Express Departs for China"; "Tai Shan's Farewell from Washington, D.C."; "Flying the 'FedEx Panda Express'"; "Panda Wrap-Up."

58. Chan, "A Humble Soul = An Open Mind"; Subramanian, "Inside India—Raj Subramaniam's Perspective."

CHAPTER 8

1. Interview with Dianna O'Neill, March 3, 2009.

2. "Meet the Millennials," Center for Media Research, March 3, 2010.

3. Interview with Eric T. Epperson, March 2, 2009.

4. Janis Forman, "An Interview with Alfred Kazin," Composition and Teaching, 1, November 1978, 27–28.

5. Ibid., 27.

6. Alain De Botton, "How to Express Your Emotions: An Excerpt from How Proust Can Change Your Life," in The Story About the Story: Great Writers Explore Great Literature, ed. J. C. Hallman (Portland, OR: TinHouse Books, 2009), 117.

7. "Dinstuhl's Fine Candy Company," February 12, 2010, http://www .mediacenter.fedex.designcdt.com/customer_spotlight (accessed October 12, 2011).

8. "Handcrafted Lighting by Way of Cowboy Country," January 22, 2009, http://www.mediacenter.fedex.designcdt.com/node/295 (accessed October 12, 2011).

9. "Malachy Bodhram," November 19, 2008, http://www.mediacenter.fedex. designcdt.com/customer_spotlight (accessed October 12, 201).

10. Interview with Sharon Young, May 19, 2010.

11. Guy De Maupassant, "Introduction," in *Pierre et Jean*, translated by Julie Mead (Oxford: Oxford University Press, 2001), 12.

12. Henry James, "Preface to *The Portrait of a Lady*," in *The Art of the Novel*, with an introduction by R. P. Blackmur (New York: Scribner's, 1962), 48.

13. Richard Blackmur, "Introduction," in James, *Art of the Novel*, xv.

14. Milan Kundera, *Immortality*, translated by Peter Kussi (New York: HarperCollins, 1999), 3.

15. Ibid., 7.

16. Avi Savar, "Think of Social Media as a Party," *MediaPostBlogs*, August 30, 2010.

17. Interview with Tom Kowalski, April 3, 2009.

18. Reported in Jessica Bruder, "Turning Business Owners into Stars of Their Own Stories," *New York Times*, October 14, 2010, B-8.

19. "Rose Growers Ship by FedEx," January 19, 2009, http://www.mediacenter .fedex.designcdt.com/customer_spotlight (accessed October 12, 2011).

20. "'Our Customer' Indy Imaging," April 8, 2009, http://www.mediacenter.fedex.designcdt.com/customer_spotlight.

21. Interview with Erin Mulligan Nelson, June 14, 2010.

22. Stuart Elliott, "JetBlue Asks Its Fliers to Keep Spreading the Word," *New York Times*, May 10, 2010, B-7.

23. "FedEx Express Honors Employees' Acts of Courage and Exemplary Dedication to Customer Service," *Business Wire*, October 28, 2003, 1836 words.

24. "Beluga Whales Make Their Way Home," August 13, 2009, http://www .mediacenter.fedex.designcdt.com/node/373 (accessed October 12, 2011).

25. "Tai Shan's Farewell from Washington D.C.," February 4, 2010, http://www.mediacenter.fedex.designcdt.com/tai_shans_farewell (accessed October 12, 2011); and "The FedEx Panda Express Departs for China," February 5, 2010, http://www.mediacenter.fedex.designcdt.com/ (accessed October 12, 2011).

26. In ch. 6 of *Working the Room: How to Move People to Action Through Audience-Centered Speaking* (Boston: Harvard Business School Press, 2003), communication consultant Nick Morgan describes the *quest* as one of four story types for making sense of human experience (based on the psychologist Carl G. Jung's archetypes): "The quest is probably the most fundamental way we have of shaping our experience and ways of relating to the world. In a Quest, a hero sets forth—often reluctantly—to achieve some difficult goal. Along the way she

encounters obstacles (dangers, enemies, roadblocks, and the like) that she has to overcome in order to reach her goal" (64).

27. Interview with Dianna O'Neill, March 3, 2009.

28. "The Mission of Keyon Laws," November 27, 2008, http://www.media center.fedex.designcdt.com/node/235 (accessed October 12, 2011).

29. Interview with Diane Terrell, March 3, 2009.

30. Interview with Dianna O'Neill, March 3, 2009.

31. "On the Road with Bill Bridges," February 24, 2009, http://www.media center.fedex.designcdt.com/video/our-people (accessed October 12, 2011).

32. Interview with Sharon Young, May 19, 2010.

33. Katie Delahaye Paine, "How Do Blogs Measure Up?" *Communication World*, 24 (5), September–October 2007, 32.

34. Charlene Li and Josh Bernoff, *Groundswell: Winning in a World Transformed by Social Technologies* (Boston: Harvard University Press, 2008), 9.

35. The fifth and, according to Li and Bernoff, the most difficult business goal for social media is "embracing." Here they recommend the following to businesses: "Integrate your customers into the way your business works, including using their help to design your products. This is the most challenging of the five goals, and it's best suited to companies that have succeeded with one of the other four goals already" (*Groundswell*, 69).

36. Interview with Ryan Furby, May 19, 2010.

37. Rich R. Karpinski, "Businesses Embrace Blogging," *Crain Communications*, 93 (8), 2 pages.

38. Interview with Jack Bergen, June 6, 2008.

39. Andrew Katz, presentation, "Case Study: Pepsi Refreshes the Brand," OMMA Conference, San Francisco, March 17, 2010.

40. Diane Terrell, "FedEx One: Media Revolution—The Reinvention of FXTV," Strategic Management Council Update, August 24, 2007.

41. E-mail from Diane Terrell, September 29, 2010.

42. Todd T. Wasserman, "Do You Need a Social Media Marketer?" *Brandweek*, 50 (14), April 6, 2009, 1.

43. Interview with Diane Terrell, May 19, 2010.

CHAPTER 9

1. Interview with Marike Westra, February 27, 2009.

2. The Philips case is based upon extensive interviews, primarily at corporate headquarters, and e-mail communications as well as assessment of company documents and secondary research:

Interviews

Marike Westra, vice president, corporate communications, Philips Lighting: interview A on February 27, 2009; B on July 6, 2009; C on July 8, 2009; D on October 11, 2010; E on January 13, 2011

Marie-Helene Azar, corporate communications officer, on July 8, 2009

Ed Babrich, head of business transformation, Philips Lighting, on January 18, 2011

Cameron Batten, internal communications manager, Philips corporate communications, on July 7, 2009

Wander Bruijel, director, integrated marketing communications & PR, Philips Consumer Lifestyle, on July 8, 2009

Suzy Chisolm, country marketing and communications, Philips Healthcare, on August 15, 2008

Parik Chopra, senior director, brand and marketing strategy, Philips Lighting, on January 19, 2011

Shai Dewan, senior press officer, corporate communications, on July 6, 2009

Erin Farben and Eeva Raaijmakers, leaders of brand campaign, on July 7, 2009

Garrett Forde, general manager and executive vice president, Lighting Europe, Middle East & Africa, on January 18, 2011

Louis Hakim, former vice president Royal Philips Electronics & Chairman Philips Electronics , Middle East, on July 8, 2009

Jeannet Harpe, senior director, corporate communications, Consumer, Lighting, on January 19, 2011

Jennifer Hoover, senior strategy manager, Philips Lighting, on January 19, 2011

Marjin Kamp, content production officer, Philips, on July 8, 2009

Andre Manning, vice president, external communications, Philips corporate communications, on July 8, 2009

Miriam Mobach, senior manager, internal communications, Philips Lighting, on January 18, 2011

Lindsey Mosby, Strategy Director, Philips: interview A on July 7, 2009; B on December 6, 2010; C on December 10, 2010

Guido Mouws, director, customer care, Europe, Philips Lighting, on January 19, 2011

Simon Poulter, communication director, Philips Lighting, on July 7, 2009

Robert Rooney, senior manager, global public relations, integrated marketing communications, Philips Consumer Lifestyle, on July 8, 2009

Jois van den Hurk, GM cardiology care cycles, Philips Healthcare, on July 6, 2009

Geert Van Kuyck, chief marketing officer, Royal Philips Electronics N.V., on July 8, 2009

Frank Van der Vloed, General Manager Benelux, Lighting, on January 18, 2011

Internal company documents referred to here include the following: On-line Company Profile, December 2, 2010, 1–2, http://www.usa.philips.com/about/company/index.pp; Simplicity Is . . . Global Marketing Management, March 2007, Koninklijke Philips Electronics N.V., Netherlands; Background Information Workshop Experts Healthcare Day, Global Corporate Communications Forum, February 13, 2008, 2 pages; "Smiling with MS," *Horizons in Healthcare*, February 14, 2008, 4; Philips Telling the Healthcare Story at GCMM: Overview of Preparations, July 17, 2008; "One Lighting 'North Star' Initiative: A Case Study," August 2009; Philips Advance Task GCMM: Corporate Communications Planning Team, July 17, 2008; Philips Day One Creative Task GCMM (Photo Exhibit), July 17, 2008; Philips Breakout Interactions with Medical "Frontliners" at GCMM CorpComm Planning Team, July 17, 2008; "One Lighting 'North Star' Initiative: A Case Study," August 2009; Philips Sense and Simplicity: Communications update, August 24, 2009; Philips Healthcare Communications Training, July 7, 2009; "Philips 'Sense and Simplicity': The Philips 'One Lighting Story' Training—'Simply Enhancing Life with Light,'" September 9, 2009; Healthcare Lighting, "Simply Enhancing Light with Light," 2010, 39 slides; Philips Start Stop Continue, 2009 and updated in 2010; "Philips Weighs in Against Obesity," 2010; One Lighting Survey, 2010; One Lighting Story Philips Facilitator's Guide, 2010; Simply Enhancing Life with Light . . . Automotive: Philips Lighting Communications Strategy, 2010; Simply Enhancing Life with Light . . . in Livable Cities: Philips Lighting Communications Strategy, 2010; Simply Enhancing Life with Light: Philips Communications Strategy—One Lighting Campaign Toolkits, 2010; Philips One Lighting Story—Questions & Answers, 2010; Philips Lighting, "Simply Enhancing Life with Light," 2010.

I also drew from publications in trade journals, the press, and online databases: *Creativity*, 15 (3), March 2007, 80; "Philips: Feeding Consumers a Line," *Marketing Week*, November 29, 2007, 1,115 words, http://global.factiva.com/hp/printasavews.aspx?ppstype=Article&pp=Print&hc=All Factiva, 1/7/2011; Michael E. Porter and Elizabeth Olmsted, *Redefining Health Care: Creating Value-based Competition on Results* (Boston: Harvard Business School Press, 2006); "Profile Geert Van Kuyck Q & A," *Marketing Week*, November 5, 2009, marketingweek.co.uk, 18; Michael Steen, "Reinventing the Philips Brand," *Financial Times*, March 24, 2008, 717 words.

3. On-line Company Profile.

4. Healthcare Lighting, "Simply Enhancing Light with Light," slide 4.

5. Interview with Geert Van Kuyck, July 8, 2009.

6. On-line Company Profile.

7. Here is the company's healthcare mission as stated in an undated internal document:

Giving people the best healthcare possible. It's your mission. It's our mission too.

We're dedicated to understanding the challenges you face—and helping you overcome those challenges. Every day.

We strive to improve the quality of people's lives and continue raising the bar on clinical excellence at lower cost.

Because healthcare simplified means improving healthcare for people, everywhere, every day.

People focused. Healthcare simplified.

8. Steen, "Reinventing the Philips Brand."

9. *Creativity*, 15 (3), March 2007, 80.

10. Interview with Erin Farben and Eeva Raaijmakers, July 7, 2009.

11. "Profile Geert Van Kuyck Q & A."

12. "Philips: Feeding Consumers a Line."

13. Interview with Andre Manning, July 8, 2009.

14. Philips Healthcare Communications Training, slide 4.

15. Interview with Robert Rooney and Wander Bruijel, July 8, 2009.

16. Interview with Andre Manning, July 8, 2009; interview with Marike Westra, February 27, 2009.

17. Interview with Wander Bruijel, July 8, 2009.

18. Philips Healthcare Communications Training.

19. Philips Day One Creative Task GCMM (Photo Exhibit).

20. Interview with Eeva Raaijmakers, July 7, 2009.

21. Ibid.

22. Ibid.

23. Interview with Marike Westra, July 6, 2009; interview with Robert Rooney and Wander Bruijel, July 8, 2009.

24. Interview with Wander Bruijel, July 8, 2009.

25. Interview with Marie-Helene Azar, July 8, 2009.

26. Ibid.

27. Interview with Robert Rooney, July 8, 2009.

28. Philips Breakout Interactions with Medical "Frontliners" at GCMM CorpComm Planning Team, slide 20.

29. Interview with Marie-Helene Azar, July 8, 2009; Philips Breakout Interactions with Medical "Frontliners" at GCMM CorpComm Planning Team, slide 20.

30. See Porter and Olmsted, *Redefining Health Care*. The authors explain the "care cycle" and its importance in this way: "Health care delivery today is centered on acute treatment. However, care-cycle thinking also exposes the crucial role of disease management, which involves closely managing a patient's illness over an extended period of time to improve compliance with medication and desirable life practices, detect impending problems early, and initiate timely remedies involving less costly interventions. Disease management is often most effective when it starts early, highlighting the value of early detection" (106). They go on to say: "At its most fundamental level, care-cycle thinking points to the importance of understanding those factors (lifestyle, environment, genetics, or otherwise) that increase the risks of contracting a medical condition, and of working with high-risk individuals to forestall or limit disease (with life-style modification or other steps) and detect it early, when it is most treatable" (106).

31. Interview with Louis Hakim, July 8, 2009.

32. Interview with Jois van den Hurk, July 6, 2009.

33. Interview with Lindsey Mosby, July 7, 2009.

34. Healthcare Lighting, "Simply Enhancing Light with Light."

35. Interview with Jeannet Harpe, January 19, 2011.

36. "One Lighting 'North Star' Initiative," slide 5.

37. Interview with Marike Westra, October 11, 2010.

38. Interview with Marike Westra, January 13, 2011.

39. Interview with Marike Westra, October 11, 2010.

40. "One Lighting 'North Star' Initiative," slide 11.

41. Ibid.

42. Ibid., slide 17.

43. Ibid., slide 15.

44. Ibid., slide 16.

45. Ibid., slide 17.

46. Philips One Lighting Story—Questions & Answers, 4.

47. Philips Lighting, "Simply Enhancing Life with Light," slide 23.

48. Ibid., slide 24.

49. Ibid., slide 25.

50. Interview with Garrett Forde, January 18, 2011.

51. Philips One Lighting Story—Questions & Answers.

52. Interview with Jeannet Harpe, January 19, 2011.

53. Philips Lighting Communications Strategy. Emphasis mine.

54. Ibid., 3.

CHAPTER 10

1. In "Shaping Conversations: Making Strategy, Managing Change," *California Management Review*, 39 (1), Fall 1996, Jeanne M. Liedkta and John W. Rosenblum discuss how some organizations use storytelling to create strategy rather than bring in storytelling activities after the strategy has been defined, as is the case for Schering-Plough and to a lesser extent for Philips. The strategic direction came first at Philips, but its refinement was an iterative process with the leadership. The authors argue for the importance of strategic conversation at all levels of an organization in the making of strategy, including the use of scenario planning, what I would call the testing of alternative strategic stories about the future, as part of this effort. Note that once the strategy and the stories communicating it are created, the stories are used to assist strategic decision making, to test whether a strategic decision contemplated should actually be taken, and to answer the question whether the decision is congruent with the strategy as articulated in the stories.

2. M. M. Bakhtin, *Speech Genres and Other Late Essays*, translated by V. W. McGree (Austin: University of Texas Press, 1986), 94 and discussed in Janis Forman, "Leaders as Storytellers: Finding Waldo," *Business Communication Quarterly*, September 2007, 369–73.

3. Interview with Marike Westra, October 11, 2010.

4. Interview with Frank Van der Vloed, January 18, 2011.

5. Interview with Jeff Hunt, March 12, 2010.

6. Interview with Becky Haglund Tousey, May 26, 2009.

7. Ibid.

8. Interview with Margaret M. Gurowitz, June 28, 2010.

9. Johnson & Johnson, *Reflections of Our Credo* (New Brunswick, NJ: Johnson & Johnson, 2009).

10. Interview with Paul Capelli, April 2, 2009.

11. Interview with Guido Mouws, January 19, 2011.

12. Interview with Jois van den Hurk, July 8, 2009.

13. Kenneth Burke, *Permanence and Change: An Anatomy of Purpose, 3rd edition* (Berkeley: University of California Press, 1984), 10.

14. Ibid.

15. Interview with Andre Manning, July 8, 2009.

16. Interview with Matthias Graf, August 11, 2008.

17. See, for example: Richard P. Feynman, *"Surely You're Joking, Mr. Feynman!" Adventures of a Curious Character* (New York: Norton, 1995); Stephen Jay Gould, *Bully for Brontosaurus: Reflections in Natural History* (New York: Norton, 1991); John McPhee, *Basin and Range* (New York: Farrar, Straus & Giroux, 1981); Oliver Sacks, *The Mind's Eye* (New York: Knopf, 2010); Oliver Sacks, *Musicophilia: Tales of Music and the Brain* (New York: Knopf, 2008); Richard Seltzer, *Letters to a Young Doctor* (New York: Simon, 1982); Lewis Thomas, *The Lives of a Cell: Notes of a Biology Watcher* (New York: Viking, 1974).

18. Sacks, "Persistence of Vision," in *Mind's Eye*, 158.

19. Feynman, "The Dignified Professor," in *"Surely You're Joking, Mr. Feynman!"* 173.

20. In the early 1990s, Stephen Jay Gould ("Prologue," in *Bully for Brontosaurus*) lamented that "vulgarisation" or the popularization of scientific writing was frowned upon in the United States as a kind of simplification; by contrast, he praised Europeans for their long and revered traditions in this regard, for instance Galileo's decision to write his two major treatises in the vernacular rather than in Latin and to frame them as a dialogue between student and teacher (11). Gould's assessment, even in the 1990s, seems to be extreme. Oliver Sacks, Richard Feynman, Lewis Thomas—to name just a few—were already publishing their "popular" work. Since then, the whole field of narrative medicine has been launched, with its attention to both medical storytellers and to the education of doctors to tell stories and listen for them.

21. Anne Bucher and Melanie Villines, *The Greatest Thing Since Sliced Cheese: Stories of Kraft Foods Inventors and Their Inventions* (Northfield, IL: Kraft Foods Holdings, 2005).

22. Interview with Melanie Villines, May 19, 2009.

23. James Cameron, presentation, CalTech, Pasadena, May 4, 2010.

24. Interview with Frank Van der Vloed, January 18, 2011.

CHAPTER 11

1. I don't mean to imply that the four cases selected for this study are the sole best-practice organizations. They were the ones I identified through my initial set

of interviews. There are likely to be other organizations that fit this description, and I welcome information about this from readers.

2. Interview with Nelson Gayton, May 6, 2009.

3. Interview with Tena Clark, April 20, 2010.

4. See Tim Milnes and Kerry Sinanan, "Introduction," in *Romanticism, Sincerity, and Authenticity*, ed. Tim Milnes and Kerry Sinanan (London: Palgrave Macmillan, 2010), 1–28. These literary scholars reflect on the centrality of authenticity to Romantic thought and writing and on the influence of this movement:

> Romanticism's preoccupation with authenticity and sincerity intensifies concerns and questions that had pervaded philosophy and literature throughout the eighteenth century. With the explosion of print, literary forms flourished and genres were transformed, reaching new networks of readers in the private and public spheres. The Romantic period saw a heightened awareness of this dissemination, a concern that focused on the authenticity of the selves who wrote such works as well as the sincerity of the feelings they expressed. Allied to this concern was a desire to discover a holistic self at the heart of writing, a hub at which the *meaning* of a word might be connected with the *truth* of an intention. (2)

5. Jean-Jacques Rousseau, *Oeuvres Complètes*, Vol. I. (Paris: Bibliothèque de la Pléiade, 1959), 278 (my translation).

6. Joan Didion, "On Keeping a Notebook," in *Slouching Towards Bethelehem* (New York: Farrar, Straus & Giroux, 1968), 134.

7. I am grateful to Barbara Shwom for reminding me of Didion's approach to "autobiographical truth."

8. See "On Keeping a Notebook." Didion goes on to say:

> I tell what some would call lies. "That's simply not true," the members of my family frequently tell me when they come up against my memory of a shared event. "The party was *not* for you, the spider was *not* a black widow, *it wasn't that way at all*." Very likely they are right, for not only have I always had trouble distinguishing between what happened and what merely might have happened, but I remain unconvinced that the distinction, for my purposes, matters. (134)

9. I make no attempt to discuss this topic with any depth. It is a subject taken up by scholars across multiple disciplines and may be familiar to you in the work of sociologist Erving Goffman, philosopher Martin Buber, and anthropologist Gregory Bateson. Perhaps most pertinent to my discussion and less familiar to business professionals is language scholar Karen Burke LeFebvre's *Invention as*

a Social Act (Carbondale: Southern Illinois University Press, 1987). There she argues that the communications we create are shaped by the social worlds we function in, that we compose texts with a sense of an inner "other self," an awareness of our imagined audience. She places her ideas in the context of scholarship from fields outside of her discipline: "If invention is indeed to be understood as a social act [and not just an act of self-expression], it is appropriate to explore it by considering the perspectives of major social theorists as well as rhetoricians and philosophers to see how they inform our study of how writers invent" (9).

Page numbers in *italics* refer to exhibits.

FXTV, 128–29; on personal priorities, 139; on social media strategy development at FedEx, 130–31; on stories as reward system element, 135; on value of employees telling stories, 155, 157
Thibault, Alex, 215, 216, 225
Thomas, Gail, 228
Thomas, Lewis, 200, 269n20
Thornton, Jennifer J., 226, 256–59n1
Thorup, Signe, 237–38n11
3M, 50, 247–48n3
Throgmorton, James A., 9, 247n2
Timing, 34, 38, 88
Tisdale, Judy, 228
Tousey, Becky Haglund, 193–94, 225
Toyota, 154
Trained incapacity, 197
Transparency, 24–25, 66, 68–69, 237n5
Tribal memory, 3
Trust: building, as general business objective, 44, 242–43n51; built by Schering-Plough's CEO, 57, 58, 59; Edelman Trust Barometer, 44, 242n49; stories as way to gain, 6, 126
Truth, storytelling distorting, 27–31, 238–39nn16–18
Tufte, Edward R., 37

UCLA Anderson Global Access Program (GAP), xiii
UCLA Anderson School of Management, x–xi
Unneland, Trond, 100

Values: conflict between personal and business, 11; as element of corporate culture, 49; expressed in "The Chevron Way," 109, 116; outlined in Schering-Plough's leadership behaviors, 65–70, 66–67, 72; reflected in Chevron stories, 98, 104, 112, 120; reinforced by FedEx's Purple Promise stories, 134, 135, 151, 155; stories to communicate, 50
Van den Hurk, Jois, 170, 196, 227, 264n2
Van Kuyck, Geert, 160–61, 227, 265n2
Van Leeuwe, Helma, 61, 64, 227, 248–49n4
Versions: as consideration when crafting stories, 38, 40–41, 240nn36–37; of "Nana Betty" story, x, 40, 217; of signature stories, 217–18, 270–71n9
Villines, Melanie, 200, 225
Viral, digital stories going, 43, 44, 78, 133, 157, 209
Vision: articulated in "The Chevron Way," 109, 116; brand as reinforcing, 51, 245n72; stories as way to communicate, 5, 50
Visuals: importance when crafting stories, 37; photos as, in Philips storytelling workshops, 162–65, 163; as "universal language," 202
Vloed, Frank Van der, 192, 195, 197, 201, 227, 265n2
Voice: authenticity of, in stories on Chevron.com, 106–8; Chevron's guidelines on, 107, 118, 123; importance in stories, 107–8; selecting, when crafting stories, 34–35; of significant others in authentic storytelling, 26–27, 237–38nn10–11
Voules, Stella, 82

Walter, Richard, 229
Walter Benjamin at the Dairy Queen (McMurtry), 2–3
Watson, John S., 112
Westra, Marike, 226, 264n2; on change in communication after storytelling workshops, 158; devised plan for storytelling in Philips Lighting sector, 174; facilitated